KNEE-DEEP IN SHAVINGS

Norm Blanchard at a Seattle Yacht Club juniors party on Lake Washington, en route to Medina, July, 1930. (BLANCHARD COLLECTION)

KNEE-DEEP IN SHAVINGS
MEMORIES OF EARLY YACHTING AND BOATBUILDING ON THE WEST COAST

Norman C. Blanchard with Stephen Wilen

Horsdal & Schubart

Horsdal & Schubart Publishers Ltd., Victoria, BC, Canada

Front cover photograph: The *Red Jacket,* by Rik Forschmiedt, courtesy of Vashon-Maury Island *Beachcomber*.

Back cover photograph: The *Mer-Na,* courtesy of Marty Loken.

This book is set in American Garamond Book Text.

We acknowledge the support of the Canada Council for the Arts for our publishing program.
We also acknowledge the assistance of the Province of British Columbia, through the British Columbia Arts Council.

Printed and bound in Canada by Transcontinental Printing, Sherbrooke, Quebec.

Canadian Cataloguing in Publication Data

Blanchard, Norman C. (Norman Carlisle), 1911-
Knee-deep in shavings

Includes index.
ISBN 0-920663-63-X

1. Boats and boating—Washington (State)—Puget Sound—History. 2. Boats and boating—British Columbia—Georgia, Strait of—History.
I. Wilen, Stephen, 1942- II. Title.
GV810.92.B52A3 1999   797.1'097977   C99-910276-1

Printed and bound in Canada

CONTENTS

The SIR TOM in the 1940s, near the end of her long career, Wheaton Blanchard at the tiller. (COURTESY OF MOHAI)

ACKNOWLEDGMENTS

PROJECTS SUCH AS recording the myriad stories that Norm Blanchard has carried in his head are often talked about, but seldom done. In that he himself suggested this to me, I have to first and foremost thank Norm for sharing so much of his life with me. The friendship we have developed over the past four years is a delight, and I am honored that Norm asked me to be his partner in working these wonderful stories into a format that all might enjoy.

Thanks are due to Norm's wife, Mary, for reading many of the first drafts and offering suggestions, but mostly for feeding me meals, cookies, pastries, candies and an infrequent libation while Norm and I toiled.

For help with locating photographs, thanks are due to the staff of the library at the Museum of History and Industry in Seattle, particularly Carolyn Marr, Howard Giske and Mary Montgomery; to Puget Sound Maritime Historical Society library volunteers Phyllis and Jim Kelly; to the Seattle Yacht Club and most especially Sally Laura; and to the Corinthian Yacht Club of Seattle and Karen Kast. I also wish to thank Sally Ayers, Cora Condon, Marty Loken and June Hellenthal Vynne for the use of personal photographs, and Ben Seaborn's daughter, Patricia, and Gosta Eriksen's daughters, Ingrid Holmdahl of Askim, Sweden, and Signe Franks of Göteborg, Sweden, for the use of personal photographs and for reading parts of the text and offering suggestions.

Finally, thanks are owed to my sister, Mary Wilen, and brother-in-law, Larry Love, for reading and re-reading these stories as they evolved and offering support, to marine historian Thomas G. Skahill and naval architect Bill Garden, for reading the stories and offering encouragement, to Terry Paine, owner of the schooner *Red Jacket*, for his assistance in tracking down photographs, and Hal Armstrong, Jr., for assistance in converting my Macintosh disks to PC.

Stephen Wilen
Seattle, Washington

INTRODUCTION

IN 1994 I RECEIVED a telephone call from master boat-builder Norman C. Blanchard. He explained that while recovering from surgery, he had been reflecting on his life, and had decided that he would like to record some of his many stories about the Seattle waterfront and prominent Northwest yachtsmen of years past. He made it clear that he was not thinking about writing a book — maybe something "magazine size" was the way he put it — and he asked me if I thought anyone would be interested in reading it. I was astounded, first that he had asked my opinion on a question for which the answer seemed so apparent to anyone other than Norm, and second because this was just the type of project I had thought for years someone should undertake. A sense of stewardship mandated my assisting Norm in realizing his wish and recording these stories.

Born in 1911, Norm Blanchard spent his boyhood on the Seattle waterfront, largely hanging around the various boat-yards operated by his father, N.J. Blanchard. In 1905, N.J., as he was known, established the company that bore his name and was, for over 60 years, one of the pre-eminent yards turning out wooden sailing and power craft on the west coast.

Norm Blanchard's reputation as a storyteller, and his remarkable memory for events and dates of more than half a century ago, are legendary. His knowledge of boats, boat-building techniques and yachting in and around Puget Sound spans the entire 20th century, from the earliest days of pleasure-boating to the demise of wooden boatbuilding and the acceptance of fiberglass. The wealth of information Norm has locked away in his memory is not limited to his own long life, but predates his birth, as he has managed to retain many stories he heard from his father and others. None of these stories had been recorded, so they were at some risk of being lost.

Over the course of four years as we worked, Norm's list of yachtsmen included more than 60 names. And what people these were — some famous, some unknown, but each having accomplished extraordinary things during adventure-filled lives. As the stories unfolded, how I envied Norm's being present for the launchings of the *Sueja II* and *Sueja III*, the *Katedna*, the *Samona*, the *Wanda*, and the *Navita*, but how privileged I felt to have had him share his memories with me. It also was becoming apparent that whatever might come of our project, it had transcended anything "magazine size."

Throughout the project I think Norm has continued to view it as an endeavor to record the lives of famous yachtsmen he knew. However, since he, and often his first wife, Eunice, played a role in the lives of these men, to my thinking the project has almost become Norm's own biography. The resulting collection of stories is not offered as a definitive history, but rather as the recollections of an extraordinary man.

Where questions arose concerning specific dates, names or events, every effort was made to substantiate the information. With this subject matter, however, much of which has not been recorded elsewhere, this could not always be done.

For clarification, it should be mentioned that Eunice Blanchard, Norm's wife of 50 years, died in 1985. He and Mary Barnard were married in 1991.

As we approach the millennium, we have left the era when a 115-foot, counter-stern motor yacht, with interiors of rosewood, could turn heads, and are in an epoch when 250-foot, electronically interfaced "mega yachts" with saloons that resemble hotel lobbies are the standing order. It is my wish that the stories recorded in these pages might transport the reader back to the glorious days of yachting, when greater consideration was given to good design, honest materials and a well-founded sense of seamanship and sportsmanship, than to how immense and turgid a creation one's money can build.

Stephen Wilen
Seattle, Washington

The Edwardian clipper-bow, 128-foot steam yacht AQUILO, *built in Boston in 1901 and brought to Seattle by John Eddy of Skinner & Eddy.* (COURTESY OF PSMHS)

REMINISCENCES OF MY FATHER, N. J. BLANCHARD, MY UNCLE CAL AND THE BLANCHARD BOAT COMPANY

WHEN HE WAS still a youngster my grandfather, Carlisle Patterson Blanchard, ran away from the boarding school in Prussia where his mother had enrolled him and went to sea. He spent five or six years as a deep-water man. Eventually he came ashore in San Francisco, and there he met and married my grandmother. They moved around a lot during the first years of their marriage — what I guess you would call an extended honeymoon — and eventually settled in New York. They had Aunt Meda first, then I believe Grandmother lost a baby, then my father was born four years later in 1885, and his brother, my Uncle Cal, two years after that.

My grandfather overheard talk at the clothing manufacturing company in New York City where he worked that the firm wanted to open a store in Seattle, and they chose him to open it. I know he came west before the rest of his family, probably directly to Seattle, so I presume he arrived in 1887. Grandmother was expecting Uncle Cal at the time, and, being a native San Franciscan, she headed west on the train to San Francisco, had the boy at her mother's home, and then, when he was a few months old, came up the coast on a steamer with her children. My father arrived in Seattle right around his third birthday in 1888. Grandfather managed the Seattle Clothing Company on Second Avenue, which was advertised during the Gold Rush as the largest Alaska outfitter on the Pacific Coast.

After the Seattle fire of June 6, 1889, he owned and operated Blanchard Outfitters on Front Street.

When they were children, both my father and my Uncle Cal liked toy boats and sailing, and of course my grandfather, having been a deep-water man, approved of their being interested in these activities. Grandmother used to tell us kids how she would take my dad and Uncle Cal, and of course Aunt Meda, when they were still small, with a picnic lunch over to the bluff in Belltown, where they could overlook the bay and watch the sailboat races. In those days people were far more interested in and involved with sailboat racing than they are now. There was also a lot of money won and lost because there were almost no other amusements in little old Seattle. You have to remember there were fewer than 10,000 people living here in those days.

Later, the family had a camp on Lake Washington on the west side of the point of land now called Laurelhurst; then, later still, they had a camp up the Hood Canal, where they had rowboats that my father built when he was still in his teens. What my grandfather sailed on I have no recollection, but he did have a clinker-built rowboat, and afterwards he had a 22-foot rowboat from New York that was really fitted out beautifully.

Other than their mutual interest in boats, my father and Uncle Cal were unlike each other in almost every other respect. My father apparently was always very quiet and very much of an introvert, and he remained that way all through his life, or at least as long as I lived with him. All through his business years with the Blanchard Boat Company he never liked to be a salesman. On occasion, when he had to be, he did quite well, but I'm sure his customers were the kind of people who came to us because of Dad's reputation. They were willing to do a lot of research and make their own decisions with only a little verbal help from Dad.

Uncle Cal was the socially minded of the two boys in the family. He was always out with the rest of the neighbors, and frequently, dinnertime would arrive and he would be missing, and my aunt and dad many years later both complained bitterly about how they had to go out yelling for Cal all over the neighborhood.

Uncle Cal was christened Carlisle Patterson Blanchard, Jr. He was known to us children as Uncle Colly, but his nickname with other people was always Cal. My grandfather, Uncle Cal and my father all joined the Elliott Bay Yacht Club at the same time, so they automatically became charter members of the Seattle Yacht Club when the two clubs merged.

My father had built a number of rowboats before he graduated from T. T. Minor Grade School, and he sold one of those,

Barge MEDA, *Lake Washington, September 24, 1895. Stroke: Meda Blanchard, age 15; midship oar: N. J. Blanchard, age 10; bow oar: Carlisle Blanchard, age 8; coach and owner: Carlisle Patterson Blanchard.*
(BLANCHARD COLLECTION)

a little launch that had a two-cycle gas engine in it, before he even left home. By the time he was 21 or maybe 22 years old, he had built a 36-foot sloop, which was launched in May of 1907, entirely in the so-called barn behind the family home at 905 21st Avenue near Immaculate Conception Church. It had been built as a carriage house at the same time as the house, but the family always referred to it as a barn. Uncle Cal had helped him with this project, but apparently there were lots of arguments and disagreements. According to my dad and especially Aunt Meda, other than his help in the construction, Uncle Cal never contributed anything in the way of materials or money to the building of the boat, so it was really my dad's boat. She was named the *Winona*, and my cousin Curley — Uncle Cal's only boy — had a photograph of her sitting in the alley behind the house on a big horse-drawn dray with three horses hitched to it. That's the way she got down to the salt chuck, where they slid her off the end of a pier into the bay at extreme high tide.

Of course my mother, Millicent Norton, was courted on the *Winona*, and after my parents' wedding in 1910 they honeymooned on her to Olympia and back. The *Winona* had no engine — she was strictly a sailboat. As soon as my mother was pregnant with me the boat had to go. She was sold to someone in Vancouver, B.C., and we never heard what happened to her after that.

After he was married, my father moved out of the family home, and he and my mother first had a flat on Yesler Way near where Garfield High School is now. It was only a short walk from my grandfather's house.

By that time Dad and the Johnson brothers, Dean and Lloyd, were partners in a boatyard on the Duwamish River, an arrangement that did not include my Uncle Cal. The flat on Yesler Way was not convenient to work, so Dad and my uncle, Val Vassar, built a house on South Fidalgo Street in Georgetown that was close to work. Val Vassar worked for Dad and the Johnsons, and he married my mother's oldest sister, so that's how he became my uncle.

Both Dad and Uncle Cal had mutual friends like the Johnson brothers, and they both knew Ted Geary, who was particularly my father's friend. My dad had sailed with Geary on both the

The WINONA. (Courtesy of MOHAI)

Spirit I and the *Spirit II*, which were campaigned actively against the Canadians and were in the forefront of racing as far as the Elliott Bay and Seattle yacht clubs were concerned.

The *Spirit II* was built in an abandoned firehouse up on Queen Anne Hill, but once the R Class became the predominant class in sailing competition, she was just another old raceboat that nobody wanted, so for the moorage against the

boat there was a raffle. I think that tickets were $20 each. Uncle Cal and a close friend each ventured $10, and the *Spirit II* became their boat. Then the friend suddenly got a job in Eastern Washington and wanted to sell the boat, so Uncle Cal sailed her to Vancouver, B.C., once again with no power, and, in this case no cabin, found a buyer after a few weeks and sold the boat.

If Uncle Cal owned anything else in the way of a sailboat right after that I didn't hear about it. Of course, World War I killed sailboat racing, but soon after Dad built the new shop on Fairview Avenue — I think it was late summer of 1924 — Uncle Cal took a vacation up Hood Canal and found a boat called the *Evelyn Mae* that had been designed by Leigh Coolidge for C. W. "Cully" Stimson. She was about 30 or 32 feet long, and she was lying in the cradle on the beach with the spars horizontal and shoved down in the cabin. I think he bought that boat for maybe $100 or less. The boat had been sitting there for several years, possibly as far back as World War I.

Uncle Cal brought her into Lake Union and tied her up at the shop and gradually got her back in shape with some help from my friend Ray Fletcher and me; I'm afraid I wasn't a lot

Cal Blanchard on the WINONA, San Juan Islands, 1911. (Blanchard Collection)

of help on this because I was only about 14. So he got her sailing on Lake Union, and she looked kind of shabby, needing paint, but he was generous with her and let Ray and me take her out to Sand Point on overnights, where we camped ashore. There was nothing in the way of accommodations inside the boat. She was very tender, and one of the things that Ray and I did — and Uncle Cal bought the necessary materials — was to mix sand and cement to hold iron punchings in the bilge, and that stiffened up the boat quite a bit. Later Uncle Cal sold her, and later still he got another old wreck of a sailboat.

She was yawl-rigged, and about the same size as the *Evelyn Mae*, but she did have an engine. My cousin Curley was six years my junior and starting high school about this time, so I think Uncle Cal probably bought that boat for Curley to use. It's interesting that while Uncle Cal liked to sail and did sail, he did very little sailing on any of the boats he bought. It is my belief that they mostly were business deals as far as he was concerned. And Uncle Cal had gone to work for my father in 1924 after Dad had the new yard, so of course there was also the advantage that he got free moorage at the boat company.

Uncle Cal was never a partner in the Blanchard Boat Company. He was always a worker, and he would look after the paint shop when Dad couldn't afford a painter. Dad and Uncle Cal had always been competitive since they were boys, and their problems continued through the years of their working arrangement. Finally, in 1942 or '43, my father and Uncle Cal separated, not amicably, and my Aunt Meda suffered considerably over their falling out. Uncle Cal became a wood-hull inspector for the army, and he stayed with the army for a number of years.

Shortly after my dad died in 1954, my wife Eunice and I went to a family potluck picnic at Uncle Cal's house over in Kirkland; I think he would have been in his mid-60s at the time. His wife had died by then, and his daughter and her husband were living with him. We were sitting around having a nice chat and because I needed a storekeeper — it was spring — I asked Uncle Cal, "How would you like to come back to the boat company?"

He laughed, because he had been unemployed for quite a long time, and asked, "What would I do now?"

I said, "Well, just exactly what you used to do when you and Dad were building the *Samona* — working in the storeroom and going to town whenever necessary, Ballard, for example, to pick up necessary materials."

And, by golly, he agreed. So he was with us at least three years when he decided — probably conditions decided for him — it was no longer worth the commute from Kirkland. There wasn't any I-520 floating bridge across that part of Lake Washington yet, so the commute was long and expensive.

Family relations with Uncle Cal remained good until he died, and I think he was 92 or so when he passed away. That pretty much covers my only uncle on my father's side of the family.

My father, Norman J. Blanchard, was born on March 22, 1885, in Brooklyn, New York. Dad began his schooling here in Seattle, and, although he was very quiet as a boy, he had little trouble in school until the ninth grade. That was the year the old Broadway High School opened, and his English teacher there was a lady. Both Aunt Meda and my grandmother felt that she literally drove my father from school. I suspect that the teacher was an older gal, and she was having the students try to do sentence diagramming and stuff like that, and Dad just couldn't understand it. Teaching methods at that time were considerably different than they are today.

A strange coincidence was that my future father-in-law, George Scholl, Eunice's father, was also teaching English at Broadway High that year, and I am convinced that if my dad had been in his class, George Scholl would not have permitted him to leave school, no matter what it took in the way of after-hours tutoring or anything. I'm sure my dad would have finished high school and gone for at least a year or two to the university, because George was a gifted teacher. He and I became friends very shortly after my first day in his class, and that was long before I knew my future wife.

So Dad talked his father into letting him leave Broadway High at mid-term of his freshman year and begin his apprenticeship with Mark Johnson — no relation to Dean and Lloyd Johnson, his first partners — riding the Yesler cable car out to the Leschi boat shop each day. Mark Johnson was the master there, and he probably ran no more than a three- or four-man shop. Of course, there were no unions then, and there was no formal arrangement in this country, such as there was in England, for apprenticeships, but that was still the way you learned to build boats. Mostly they built clinker rowboats for the boat livery houses.

In Seattle at that time there was a boat livery on Lake Washington wherever a cable or electric car line terminated, like at the foot of Madison Street, at Leschi, and down at Madrona Park. People would ride the cable car out to the lake for a picnic lunch, and then rent a boat from a livery. Real estate men also rented boats from these liveries to show clients pieces of vacant land.

In 1905 my father left his apprenticeship with Mark Johnson and teamed up with his friends, the Johnson brothers, Dean and Lloyd. They each chipped in $400 and that same year opened the Johnson Bros. & Blanchard yard on the old oxbow of the Duwamish River on South Fidalgo Street in Georgetown. One of the first boats that they built was the *Gwendolyn II*, which was actually my dad's project, because the Johnson boys were working at the Moran yard at the time, and this kept a project going at Johnson Bros. & Blanchard.

The crew of the newly formed Johnson Bros. & Blanchard yard, 1905. Left to right: Joe McKay, Dean Johnson, N. J. Blanchard and Lloyd Johnson. (COURTESY OF PSMHS)

Their friend, Ted Geary, began to bring them contracts for some larger boats, like the 100-foot, canoe-stern *Helori*, launched in 1911 for O. O. Denny. She was the largest motor yacht built on the west coast at the time, and was finished in 90 days at a cost of $10,000. There's an interesting photo of her being launched that shows her name painted on her stern, clearly misspelled as *Helora*. I don't recall whether the sign painter was at fault, or the photograph was doctored. And Dad, when people stopped by the yard to inquire about buying a boat, would reciprocate by sending them to Ted to have a yacht designed.

A couple of other sailboats were built at Johnson Bros. & Blanchard between the time my parents got married and when the United States entered World War I, one of them being a very nice Mower-designed 45-foot yawl called the *Ortona* for the architect John Graham. Another one, the *Nelsie*, was a schooner. The Johnson boys designed it on the loft floor, very much a commercial schooner-type design, and that boat had bad luck as a sailboat. She was off Commencement Bay when she caught fire, and they beached her below Dash Point. The insurance company declared her a total loss, but she was

Some of the Johnson Bros. & Blanchard crew, CA. 1912. Left to right: Val Vassar, Cal Blanchard, Henry Anderson, Cecil Foss, Joe McKay and Oddie Rohlfs. (COURTESY OF PSMHS)

above: Launching of the 100-foot HELORI *from Johnson Bros. &* *Blanchard, 1911. (Note the* *misspelled name at her stern. The* *name was created by combining the* *first names of the owners, Helen and* *Orion O. Denny.)* (COURTESY OF PSMHS)

right: The HELORI, *designed by Ted* *Geary and built by Johnson Bros. &* *Blanchard, was the largest motor* *yacht in the northwest when she was* *launched.* (COURTESY OF MOHAI)

refloated and rebuilt, and retained the name *Nelsie*, but from then on she became strictly a power boat.

After the *Sir Tom* was built in 1914 she was campaigned actively for years, always winning, and there were some rigging changes from year to year. One of the young fellows sailing on the *Sir Tom* was Fritz Hellenthal, he being the youngest member of the first crew. One time John Dreyer crewed also; he later became the yachting editor for *The Seattle*

The SIR TOM hauled at the Blanchard yard, foot of Wallingford Avenue, June 21, 1921. Norm Blanchard, one day shy of his 10th birthday, standing at keel. (COURTESY OF MOHAI)

Times, and was a very good reporter. The papers really gave the boats, even the yacht clubs, wonderful coverage in those days.

The *Kuskokwim River* of 1915 was the job that struck the death blow to Johnson Bros. & Blanchard, because they underbid the job. She was the first semi-diesel coastal freighter built on the west coast, 130 feet long, and had been designed by Ted Geary for John Graham to use in one of his business operations. Johnson Bros. & Blanchard were bidding on this job, and my dad argued and argued as best he could about the price, but he was a little bit handicapped because I think he was self-conscious about the fact that he had left high school in the middle of his first year. So he let the Johnson boys prevail in the bidding and they took that contract, but Dad was right — probably a little more than right because they had never built anything before quite as big or heavy as the *Kuskokwim River*, and they were in a brand-new yard.

The war in Europe had been going on for three years and shipbuilding of all kinds was taking place up in Vancouver, B.C., like gangbusters, so there was plenty of work up there. Finally, the bookkeeper showed Dad and the Johnsons that

The KUSKOKWIM RIVER ready for launching from the Johnson Bros. & Blanchard yard, 1915. The yawl ORTONA flies her dress flags for the occasion. Both vessels were owned by John Graham, Sr. (COURTESY OF PSMHS)

they were going to go in the hole on the *Kuskokwim River* job, so one Saturday the Johnsons just disappeared up to Vancouver. Of course, the company was into the bank, which was just a little local bank in Georgetown, and because the company went broke I think the bank went broke, too, although we were never sure about that. So, after the yard closed my father finished building the ship for the bonding company, and then went to work for Skinner & Eddy, the big shipyard where the Port of Embarkation was in World War II.

In 1918 I was in the first grade and my father was still working at Skinner & Eddy. When the general strike of 1919 began Dad had to leave Skinner & Eddy, and during that period he worked as foreman for Tregoning Boat Company out on Ballard Beach. When the strike was finally settled he went back to Skinner & Eddy, where he was foreman of all the deck equipment installation from midship aft for all the ships they were building at that time. Well, one morning between eight-thirty and nine o'clock a runner came looking for Dad, and when he found him he said, "You're wanted in the front office, Mr. Blanchard."

"Oh? When?" asked my dad.

"Right away, immediately," came the reply.

So Dad took off his coveralls, went up to the front office, and the secretary said, "Mr. Skinner wants to talk to you right away, Mr. Blanchard. You're to go right in and wait, he's on a long distance call right now."

When Mr. Skinner finally hung up the phone he said to my dad, "Norm, what are you doing working here?"

Dad said, "Well, Mr. Skinner, this company gave me employment when I needed it bad, and I figure this is where my loyalty lies."

"Oh, well, that's very good," said Mr. Skinner, "but Captain James Griffiths is a very close friend of this firm, and Ted Geary tells me that you're needed back at Tregoning's to finish that new yacht for the captain. Tregoning's has never built a yacht this big, and they don't know anything about yacht finishing. You'd better get out there and supervise the project."

My dad said, "OK, I'll pack up my tools and report there in the morning."

"Oh, no," Mr. Skinner said, "you need to go right now. Have you got a car?" I remember my dad telling this story at the dinner table, how he was sorry he couldn't tell Mr. Skinner he didn't have a car, so Mr. Skinner would have had him driven to Tregoning's in his personal limousine. Dad went and cleared out his locker, checked out of Skinner & Eddy and went back to Tregoning's to finish the 82-foot express cruiser that Ted Geary had designed for Captain Griffiths. Even though the boat was officially built by Tregoning Boat Company, Captain Griffiths never referred to her as having been built by anyone other than N. J. Blanchard.

Dad used his savings to establish the N. J. Blanchard Boat Company in 1919 on Lake Union at the foot of Wallingford Avenue. For the main building at the yard he rebuilt a 120-foot warehouse that had been part of the Naval Officers Candidate School on the University of Washington campus. He had bought it from the United States government after it had been declared surplus following World War I.

The first yacht my father built as the N. J. Blanchard Boat Company was a 62-foot schooner, the Geary-designed *Katedna*. She was a gorgeous yacht and a very good sailer, but the owner soon fell into financial difficulties. Geary was able to sell her for him in Southern California, where she became pretty well known. She changed hands a couple more times, and the

Launching of Captain Griffiths' second SUEJA *from the Tregoning yard, 1919.*
(Courtesy of PSMHS)

next thing we knew the yacht was on her way to Australia on a trip around the world as a honeymoon for a California couple. What kind of business the owner was in, and how he could afford a nice yacht, I don't know, but we do know that the marriage and the voyage ended in Australia, and the yacht was soon headed back to California with a hired Kanaka crew, Polynesian people. This was probably due to the fact that nobody would pay the duty, or maybe Australia wouldn't even permit the boat to be sold down there.

In any case, the *Katedna* was later sold to a gentleman by the name of George Webb, who lived on the east shore of Lake Washington, and who returned her to Seattle on a ship. He brought her into the yard, where my dad did a total rebuilding, refinishing and rerigging, and she got a new name, *Red Jacket*. George kept her moored in front of his place in Medina, a beautiful Tudor-style house just east of the old Medina ferry dock.

Late one foggy fall evening George got a telephone call from a neighbor, who said, "I think you ought to do some checking on the schooner. She looks to me like she's on fire from what I can see with my binoculars."

So they rushed out, and, hell yes, it was a fire. What they didn't know then, but figured out later, was that she had set off the automatic CO_2 system, and that had put out the fire, but it didn't put out the cause of the fire, so the CO_2 bottles hadn't done their duty, and she was burning again — her whole interior was engulfed in flames. They rushed back to the house and got some rifles, and eventually they were able to sink her by shooting holes in her below the waterline, and that put out the fire. She was refloated, brought to our place and rebuilt again, and the *Red Jacket* survives today down in Tacoma, still a beautiful yacht.

Dad's next sailing schooner was the *Aafje*, another Geary-designed schooner, a little heavier tonnage-wise than the *Katedna*, although shorter, at 58 feet. I don't have any recollection or knowledge of my father actually sailing on any of these boats, but I presume he did.

My father also built catboats at the foot of Wallingford — I believe there were ten in all. They were built from a John Winslow design, but Dad and Geary dreamed up a much better

above: The RED JACKET *ready for launching after reconditioning, Blanchard Boat Company, June 29, 1933. Cal Blanchard standing at the keel.* (BLANCHARD COLLECTION)

right: The schooner RED JACKET. (COURTESY OF SEATTLE YACHT CLUB)

cockpit arrangement so that if the boat capsized she would float on edge, rather than going completely upside down. I had good reason to remember that, because Dad and I were racing in one of them on Lake Washington and we capsized.

In 1922 the 90-foot steamship stern motor yacht *Wanda*, designed by Geary for the lumberman C. D. Stimson, was launched from the Wallingford yard. They always said she was 92 feet, but I have the original plans and the most I can make out of it is 88 feet and eight inches. But that sort of thing was quite common, to stretch the length of the boat. And she was quite a sensational boat. She was powered by Speedway gas engines, and triple screw.

Later that year Dad signed a contract to build the Geary-designed, 115-foot motor yacht *Samona* for Willits J. Hole, an oilman who lived in Balboa, California; however, just as work was about to begin on that yacht the yard burned to the ground, so the *Samona* got built out on Ballard Beach at the old Tregoning yard. Tregoning's had made a lot of money during World War I, and I guess they weren't doing much work in the early 1920s, so Dad could rent their old boat shop for the *Samona* project.

N. J. Blanchard, CA. 1924. (Asahel Curtis photo, Courtesy of Seattle Yacht Club)

Launching of the Geary-designed Hermina *from the Blanchard Boat Company in 1924. Norm Blanchard is flanked by the Seaborn twins, Ben and Jack.* (Courtesy of MOHAI)

The night of the fire Dad was interviewing a prospective bookkeeper at home for the *Samona* project, and we could hear all the firetrucks racing by. When he was finished Dad said, "C'mon, son, let's go to the fire," because that's what people did in those days. We had no idea where the fire was, and arrived at the plant just in time to see the roof collapse. Arson was always suspected, but it was never proven.

The next sailboat that I can recall was built at Dad's new yard at 3201 Fairview Avenue. This was the 42-foot schooner *Quascilla*, launched in 1924, and the only boat I can remember that was planked entirely with teak.

Dad was still sailing with Geary on the *Sir Tom* in 1924, although they had really split as working partners in 1923 over a financial disagreement. Ted was a real self-promoter, and when he insisted that my dad pay him a sales commission, it caused a split between them that really didn't get patched up until shortly before Dad died. So after Dad bought the lots on Fairview Avenue in 1923 for the new yard he worked alone, except for one power boat.

That was the 65-foot express cruiser *Hermina* that Geary designed for Bert Jilg in 1923, which was launched from the new yard in 1924. She was powered with twin 12-cylinder Van Blerck gasoline engines — "twelve buckets in a row" was the way Geary referred to them. That boat was fast! She could do around 28 knots. The *Hermina* eventually wound up down in the Bay Area and in the early 1950s she dragged her anchor and ended up being smashed to pieces on the beach northeast of Point Reyes.

After 1923 Geary started pushing all his jobs to Lake Union Dry Dock and Dad never had any partners again, although in 1926 Geary was forced to send the building of the 100-foot motor yacht *Malibu* to us. She was built for Mrs. May Rindge and her daughter, Mrs. Rhoda Adamson. Mrs. Rindge's son, Samuel, was married to Willits Hole's daughter, Agnes, and Mr. Hole had told Geary, "Nobody but N. J. Blanchard builds that boat," so Geary had to work with Dad on that job.

In 1925 I was 14, and that's the year I went south with my uncle on his ship, which was a 340-foot tanker. I called him my uncle, but he was really my dad's cousin, Oliver Lilly, and he was the captain. As we were having a snack in his cabin he asked me, "You want to go to California?"

I said, "I sure do," so he said, "Go home and get your clothes," and he called my mother because the ship was due to sail at six o'clock. I raced like hell and I made it.

The first morning out, on the twelve-to-four watch, which is always where they put the new hires, I polished all the brass on the bridge and then I took the wheel for the second two hours of the watch, and of course I was all over the damned ocean, and I knew I was doing a bum job. So immediately after going off watch I went aft and I studied how that lever arm on the steam valve ran the rudder engine.

The next day when I was on watch the first mate, whose name was Branchflower, unbeknownst to me, was standing behind me, and he asked, "What the hell goes on here?"

I looked at him, and he said, "Hell, yesterday you couldn't keep this ship on course, and today you're steering like a veteran."

So I told him what I'd done, and after that, Oliver Lilly was always kind of my champion. Both he and the first mate thought that was pretty sharp of me to have gone back and studied that lever arm, and it was a great learning experience at a time when I needed some confidence.

Soon after he was in business on Fairview, Dad incorporated and the family held stock. Besides my grandmother and Uncle Cal, there were other stockholders, like *Mrs.* Charles Seaborn, because her husband, Charlie, who was my dad's foreman at the time, was a real boozer and had big debts. Five shares went to the bookkeeper, Wallace Schoenman, in 1925, because he had been instrumental in helping Dad sell a 62-foot motor yacht to Mrs. A. K. Eskridge, a widow from Los Angeles.

Edwin Monk, Sr. was working for Dad at the time, and this boat was one of his earliest yacht designs, although he was not yet a naval architect. Mrs. Eskridge named the boat *Silver King* after the mine which was the source of her wealth. Schoenman and Uncle Cal had not only been helpful in getting Dad the job, but also in not letting him take that boat on a low contract price. They convinced him that he must figure his costs carefully before submitting a bid. As a consequence the company got $35,000, a profit of 15% or 18%, instead of my dad's usual 10%. Things were looking pretty good, but that summer of 1925, when she was launched, was the last big season for work on the large new boats. I think the main reason for this was that Geary was no longer giving Dad any work.

N. J. Blanchard delegated the design of the SILVER KING *to Edwin Monk in 1925, and this was Monk's first yacht design. Blanchard is on the dock at the Seattle Yacht Club, talking with the yacht's skipper.* (COURTESY OF MOHAI)

The MALIBU of 1926 was the last collaboration between N. J. Blanchard and Ted Geary. (COURTESY OF PEMCO WEBSTER & STEVENS COLLECTION, MOHAI)

top inset: Pilot house of the MALIBU. (COURTESY OF PEMCO WEBSTER & STEVENS COLLECTION, MOHAI)
bottom inset: The MALIBU framed, Blanchard Boat Company.
(BLANCHARD COLLECTION)

Often, after school was out for the day I would stop by the boatyard, and one afternoon I was sailing a model sailboat that I had built in Lake Union. Mrs. Eskridge was there — she was in town for a week to check on progress on the *Silver King*. She was very impressed with my model, so she asked me if I could build one like it for her nephew in Salt Lake City. I told her that I would be delighted to make her a model, but would have to speak with my father about the price. One thing we kids all knew was that in the Blanchard family, you didn't discuss money at the dinner table. So on the way home that evening I asked my dad if he thought ten dollars would be a fair price, and he acknowledged that he thought that would be fine, as long as I did a good job. That is the price I charged Mrs. Eskridge for the model, and she opened her purse and paid me in advance.

Some months later, in the spring, Mrs. Eskridge was again in town. She had an appointment at the Blanchard Boat Company one afternoon, and Mr. Schoenman informed me that she wished to speak to me. Well, she told me that the model sailboat was the best gift her nephew had ever received, and he just loved sailing it on the Great Salt Lake. She gave me a big hug, and that was a new experience for me. I can still remember the smell of her perfume. Then she removed a check from her purse for another ten dollars, and my mother took the check, added five dollars, and bought me a brand new knickerbocker suit.

In the mid-1920s Dad began to sense there was a change coming in yachting, and that the days of the large motor yachts might be drawing to an end. In 1924 he collaborated with the naval architect Leigh Coolidge and they came up with a standardized, raised-deck day cruiser — power boats with large foredecks and large cockpit pilot houses aft. Twenty-five of these boats were built between 1924 and 1930, and they ranged in size from 32 to 38 feet. The design became very popular and was copied by other yards on the Pacific Coast. Lake Union Dry Dock later came out with a larger version, which they called the Lake Union Dreamboat, and that name has come to be applied to all boats of this design, although, strictly speaking, the boats Dad built are not Lake Union Dreamboats. A number of the Blanchard raised-deck cruisers, the *Mer-Na*, *Faun*, *Resolute*, *Arlene* and others, are still actively cruising.

The Blanchard Boat Company crew at the new plant on Fairview Avenue, CA. 1924. The then-future naval architect Ed Monk, Sr., is leaning against the door at left. (COURTESY OF PSMHS)

There were always a few sailboats in the works at the N. J. Blanchard Boat Company. Some, like day sailers, were actually bigger than the popular Star boats that the kids sailed, plus sailing dinghies both smaller and larger than the 15½-foot catboats. In 1929 Dad launched a 48-foot cruiser called the *Gadget*, and the *Barbara Lee*, a 40-foot cruiser that was very similar to his other stock boats, although it was custom designed and built. I don't recall any other yachts from that year, but there may have been something in the line of commercial boat contracts. We did build small tugs and boats for the Fish and Wildlife Service and other government agencies.

Also, during the early and mid-1920s Dad built four rumrunners. I'm sure that he made good money on them. I remember the last one was just one enormous open runabout, and the boat was nearly finished when the payments stopped. It just sat in the shop for an extra year, but it was eventually finished and disappeared and I never saw it again — or at least if I did, I didn't recognize it.

It's funny, but I didn't find out until years later that Dad bootlegged all through Prohibition. All those places on the water were just naturals to get involved in bootlegging because you could always find a way to offload the booze at

Three Blanchard raised-deck cruisers at flank speed. Left to right: CUTTERHEAD, ELSINORE *and* DORLEON. (COURTESY OF MOHAI)

night. Every cabbie in town knew that for the right price, a customer could get a bottle of bootleg whiskey at the Seattle Yacht Club. I remember once that Dad took the family in the car out to a new housing development, which had a lot of little colored flags flying everywhere. Dad parked at the sales office and a dapper gentleman came out and greeted him like an old friend. Well, this dapper gentleman was none other than Roy Olmstead, the biggest bootlegger in the whole Pacific Northwest. Years later I asked my cousin, "Do you think my father was a bootlegger?"

"Hell, yes," she said. "What do you think kept the doors open at the Blanchard Boat Company during the Depression?"

In 1928 Ted Geary introduced the Flattie Class sailboat, which is now referred to as the Geary 18 Class. He made a

A Blanchard-built Flattie, or Geary 18, on Lake Washington. (COURTESY OF SEATTLE YACHT CLUB)

presentation at the Seattle Yacht Club and afterwards my dad got up and said he would build the first ten boats for $150 apiece to get something started, but he wouldn't start them until he had ten orders on the line. People actually wrote him the checks right then and there, because after those first ten boats were finished the price would immediately jump to $200. I also built a Flattie, and I actually started on mine two weeks before Dad started on the first ten, but I didn't finish it as soon as the stock boats were finished. For the next three years he kept Flatties in stock; he'd get orders for a couple and then build three or four more.

Around this time there was a terrible accident in a Star boat that involved three young couples. These kids were university students, freshmen, I think. It was October, shortly after the start of the school year, and the boy who was going to sail the boat had permission to take it from where it was moored at the Cascade Canoe House at Madison Park, next to Pioneer Hall on the property that is now the Parkshore retirement home. The boat was moored inside where it was quite well protected from the weather by the buildings that were on each side of it. The kids were going to go to a house party across the lake near Medina, but only the boy who was going to sail the boat had had any previous experience. Apparently he had not had much, because when they got out from the protection of the buildings, they suddenly realized that they had way too much sail.

Of course there were no floating bridges across Lake Washington to break the wind and seas back then, and the lake could get up waves that are much bigger than they are today. The kids had taken off the forward hatch cover and had placed an ice cream freezer down in the hatch, nice and snug. Under normal conditions, this was a good place to carry an ice cream freezer, but all the gear was stored forward under that hatch. They were probably running late and got in too much of a hurry, and the wind was carrying them north toward Sand Point, with waves coming over the stern. The boat had been equipped originally with watertight bulkheads at each end of the cockpit, and theoretically was unsinkable, but it was obvious that the boat was taking on too much water, and each time a wave came aboard it was getting a little heavier. So they jettisoned the ice cream freezer and got out the one life

Norm Blanchard and John Halberg in the BLUE BOOT, *Star boat #908, on Elliott Bay, 1928.* (BLANCHARD COLLECTION)

with the life jacket were the only two who survived this accident. All six kids were from very prominent Seattle families, and so sailboats and sailing were absolutely out as far as all the mothers of potential buyers were concerned. The Star boat that sank was raised by the insurance company and brought to our yard, and my dad reconditioned it; we had it there for sale, and on one occasion I got to sail it.

Then the Crash came in October 1929, and the following year I sold my Flattie at the 1930 Seattle Boat Show. It was held in the then-new Civic Auditorium Ice Arena, the first west coast pure boat show, although I didn't actually have my boat at the show. Dad had the *Mer-Na* at that show. She was the last one of the 36-foot standardized raised-deck cruisers he built.

I was handing out brochures about the Blanchard Boat Company when a mutual friend, J.L. "Joe" Patton, whose booth featuring just engines was right next to ours, called my name, asking, "Norm, where can my friend, Mr. Deming, get a boat like the one in the corner?"

My response was, "I'll sell him mine for $200."

Mr. Deming shouted, "Sold!" and so that's probably the easiest sale I ever made in my life.

A fast commuter, the 57-foot KENSINGTON *is shown at flank speed in Lake Washington on December 11, 1931, with her new Blanchard-designed and -built wheelhouse. The* KENSINGTON *has been owned since 1982 by Stephen Wilen.* (COURTESY OF PEMCO WEBSTER & STEVENS COLLECTION, MOHAI)

jacket and were looking for a bailer. They were close to what was later Sand Point Naval Air Station — the geographical marker was a place called Mud Lake just north of the only home on the Windermere bluff, which was the Denny mansion — when the boat sank.

One of the girls who couldn't swim had on the life jacket, but one of the other girls also couldn't swim. The three boys and the girl who could swim endeavored to keep her afloat, but the boys sank, and the girl who could swim and the girl

This was during the Depression, and by June 1931 when I graduated from Roosevelt High School, things were very tough and they just got worse. Dad lost the house we lived in on Naomi Place near Ravenna Park, and before that he had lost heavily on the house we moved out of when we moved to Naomi Place. He ended up signing it back to the contractor, who was a savvy old Swede. The old bugger kept coming down to the yard and telling me he had to have money. I know damned well he was far better off than Dad, and, finally, just to get him off his back, Dad signed the place back over to him. Just two weeks later Roosevelt declared a moratorium on all mortgage foreclosures.

Of course, we were a big family by then. My little brother, Wheaton, was school age, plus the four girls. Mother had been looking for a house for us out around Big Rock in the north Ravenna neighborhood, which was just beginning to be developed at that time, and I kept saying to her, "We should be moving down into an old place near the shop." I was thinking of the area that now is Campus Parkway, right north of the University Bridge. Finally, the real estate man was smart enough to realize that we had to move out of Naomi Place, and so he said, "I've got a brand new house over on the other side of the canal on the north side of Capitol Hill that I'd like to show you."

Norm Blanchard in a Hacker Craft owned by Ray Blanchard (no relation), 1930. (BLANCHARD COLLECTION)

About four or five years before this, Dad had bought two good-sized lots way out, not far from the old Interurban line, very close to where the Lakeside School is now. So he went to the bank, and, by God, they loaned him enough money for a down payment on this house to get us going. And, of course, I was awfully glad that there was a very small bedroom for me, and a very large bedroom you could put two sets of twin beds in for the four girls, and my parents had the intermediate size bedroom. So that really worked out for us. Wheaton, when he got too big to sleep in the parents' room, got a bed down in the basement, and after I had moved out he got my old bedroom. When I came back home on occasion, I slept down in the basement.

On moving day my oldest sister had to take care of all of the moving because Mother had had another one of her "nervous breakdowns," but, fortunately, the doctor she liked at the time was a female osteopath, and she had a house right across the street from ours. As soon as we got all moved in Mother recovered; she came over and was highly pleased with what my sisters had done. Anyway, those were tough times.

After I graduated from Roosevelt High School I immediately went to work for Dad. One of the first jobs that had to be done, something that had not been done since the building was built in 1923, was to retar the tarpaper roof, and Dad assigned that job to me.

Henry Anderson had been Dad's shop foreman, a splendid man who had been helpful to me in making my toy boats. Henry had left the boat company and become the boss at McNeil Island Federal Penitentiary, running the boat shop and carpentry shop down there. He stayed there until he retired, and he was instrumental in getting the chief of the guards to place an order with my dad for an Ingrid ketch, designed by William Atkin of Huntington, New York, and I imagine my dad gave Henry a small commission. Many of those double-ended Ingrid ketches were built because the design for them was featured in *Motor Boating* magazine, so for the price of a magazine, you could have yourself a set of plans.

The most experienced man employed at that time at the yard was Jim Chambers, and he had served his time, I believe, at the Fife yard on the Clyde in Scotland. He still spoke with a Scottish burr, and he was a real journeyman boatbuilder. It

Left to right: Norm, Meda and N. J. Blanchard, CA. 1930. (COURTESY OF MOHAI)

was under him that first winter, 1931, that I helped loft that ketch. I had helped on lofting before, but on this job it was just the two of us, and it was done very precisely, which was difficult because the table of offsets that the designer had provided was poor. In one case we had to make an adjustment of four inches, which was the most in my entire experience. There were a lot of little things that we did. For instance, the plans called for the fittings around the aperture for the propeller to be cast bronze around the rudder, and a cast bronze socket for the heel of the rudder, and all of the patterns for those castings were made by Jim Chambers, with some help from me. It was a very small crew that worked on that boat, and Dad helped.

Well, the chief of the guards retired and sailed the boat south, and I know neither Dad nor I ever got a chance to sail on it. Eventually it fell into the hands of Steve Newmark, who was a very successful boat broker in Wilmington, California. Steve was an enthusiastic sailor; he took that boat in the first Mazatlan race and won it boat for boat. He finished far enough in the lead that time allowances, which were used in mixed class races, weren't needed. As always in boat racing, it had a hell of a lot to do with the matter of whose hands were on the wheel. After he won the race he sent a copy of a magazine article about the boat to William Atkin, the designer, and he got a letter back from this man saying that — because of all the changes and corrections we had had to

make in her — he sure as hell didn't have anything to do with designing a monstrosity like that. Yet today that boat is very marketable, wherever she is.

Our friend and customer from Southern California, Dick Lerner, had an Ingrid after World War II that had been built by an amateur. The trouble was that most of the amateur boatbuilders didn't have a place to loft them properly, so they'd only lay out the sections, and then if a ribband or something wasn't fair, they couldn't see it until after the boat was planked. Dick's and, I think, six other Ingrids were racing as a class down there. The Wilmington Boat Works had a marine railway and turntable, so they made arrangements to haul all those boats one weekend. Dick later told me, "Hell, all you had to do was walk around those boats and you could easily see why Steve's boat was the fastest."

In 1933 a group of people out for a Sunday walk came by the boat company and peeked in the door to look at the Star boats, which were priced at $750. They thought they were nice little boats, but said for that price they would really want a cabin. After they left, Dad thought for a few minutes, and then said, "Dammit, let's build a cheap sailboat with a cabin on it," and that's what led to the development of the Senior Knockabout, which was one of our all-time best sellers. We built a total of 97 Senior Knockabouts between 1933 and 1947, and some 70 of them are still around. The Senior Knockabouts ranged from 22 feet, six inches to 26 feet, six inches, and there was a Junior version that was 20 feet.

The next boat that comes to mind, one that we built as the country started to come out of the Depression, is the *Sea Rest*, 66 feet long, designed by Edwin Monk, who was by then a licensed naval architect, for O. D. Fisher of Fisher Flouring Mills. She was originally designed for, and bid plans called for, 65 feet, and then Ed Monk and Mr. Fisher decided that she'd look a lot better if she had one more foot of hull aft, and we did get, if I remember correctly, $600 extra for adding that one foot to the hull of the boat. We got the contract around November 1, 1936, and she was launched and finished in 1937.

The *Sea Rest* was a godsend that produced a lot of activity and interest, because the Depression had really ground down to its low ebb by then, although it was just barely beginning

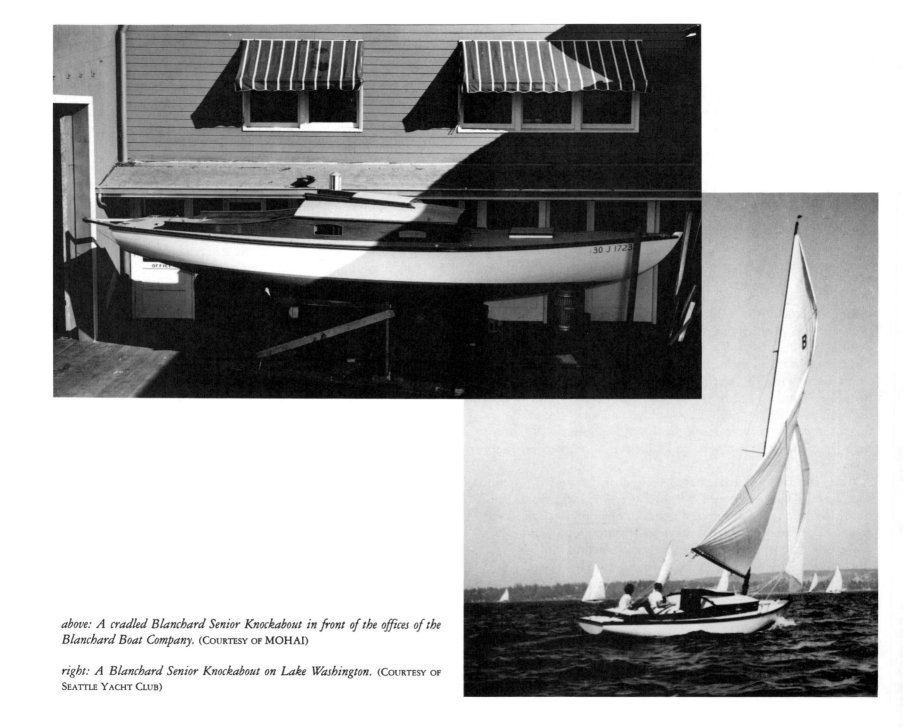

above: A cradled Blanchard Senior Knockabout in front of the offices of the Blanchard Boat Company. (COURTESY OF MOHAI)

right: A Blanchard Senior Knockabout on Lake Washington. (COURTESY OF SEATTLE YACHT CLUB)

above: O. D. Fisher's SEA REST ready for launching, Blanchard Boat Company, 1937. (BLANCHARD COLLECTION)

right: The SEA REST at launching, Blanchard Boat Company, 1937. (BLANCHARD COLLECTION)

to get over as far as we were concerned. After that job was finished my dad met with Mr. Fisher one Sunday evening at the office and he showed him the books and how we actually had gone in the hole $3,500 or $3,600 above and beyond the cost of labor and materials.

Mr. Fisher asked my dad, "Norman, why are you showing me all this?"

Dad said, "Because I expect you to do something about it."

"Norman," Mr. Fisher said, "I can't be a Santa Claus."

So Dad asked him, "Don't you realize that these unpaid bills constitute a lien against your vessel?"

"Oh, no." He never knew anything like that about marine law. So that evening ended with Mr. Fisher taking the bills with him. He paid them with a personal check, and my dad signed a note that we would work off $3,500 worth of mainte-nance, spring haulout, and bottom painting, things like that, and I think it was three years before that note was worked off.

I was pretty disenchanted with this guy Fisher, even though he and my dad seemed to take a liking to one another. He asked Dad if he would like to go fishing with him out at Sekiu, at that bight that's just inside Neah Bay. Dad went out there fishing with him two or three times. Of course, Mr. Fisher had a cook and a skipper aboard who were pretty much year-round employees, and Dad and Mr. Fisher would sit back in the cockpit with their fishing poles, and the cook would keep their drinks refreshed. I think that probably Dad's attrac-tion to Mr. Fisher was because he was certainly a successful businessman, and my dad figured the more he associated with him the more he'd learn from him. However, I doubt that Dad actually thought of it that way consciously.

The TOLA, *left, and a Blanchard "33" framed, Blanchard Boat Company, 1937.*
(BLANCHARD COLLECTION)

After the *Sea Rest* the next job of considerable note was the *Navita* for Clare Egtvedt, president of the Boeing Company. We built the *Navita* for $85,000, and you couldn't duplicate it today because you can't get the kind of material we had then. She's still here in Seattle, down at Lockhaven Marina, and I'm afraid that the new owner isn't going to be much better than the previous one, who really didn't use the boat at all. He'd just go down to the moorage and sit aboard it each day.

The following year, 1938, we built a nice Bill Garden sloop, about 45 feet long, called the *Arguella*. It was for a California client, whom we only saw twice, once when he signed the contract and again when he came up for the launching.

That same year we had another contract to build a large, single-screw power cruiser for a client in Tacoma. He furnished a great big, surplus Packard V-12 engine for the boat. He had gone to William Atkin, a guy I considered to be a cheap naval architect, to get the design for the boat, and we had several problems with it, so that was not a happy contract at all. This owner never could come to a decision about whether he really wanted to own a yacht or not, and every time I saw the boat down in Tacoma after we completed it she looked rather shabby.

During those years we built five boats for Keith Fisken, the president of the Seattle Cedar Lumber Company. He was one of the finest men we ever built a boat for. We started with a little 20-foot Junior Knockabout which he bought for about $300. After he'd had one season in the Junior Knockabout he apparently sold it to a friend over on Bainbridge Island, and, probably at my suggestion, had Ben Seaborn design a 25-foot sloop which we built with auxiliary power and two berths, a very handsome little craft. The following year we built a 31-foot boat for Keith that had the same power, a Kermath "Sea Cub."

Then before the war we built him another one, this time 35 feet, and after the war we built him a 40-footer, which he called *Nootka*. If I recall correctly, he later sold that boat to Dr. Carl Jensen, who renamed it *Kate II*. Previously, Dr. Jensen had owned the *We're Here*, which he had renamed *Kate*. Later, the *Kate II* was owned by Ned Skinner. Of all the boats we built, I think that would be my choice if I could have one just like it. It's certainly as big a boat as I would want, ideal for

cruising with two couples. All the boats we built for Keith Fisken were planked with western red cedar, which, of course, was easy for him to obtain, so the quality of the planking on those boats was as good as you could get any time, any place.

Keith Fisken's sloop the Nootka, *later owned by Ned Skinner, who renamed her the* Kate II, *the name she still carries.* (Courtesy of MOHAI)

Between Christmas and New Year's, 1940, our very good friend, Joe Patton, who owned and operated the Seattle Marine Equipment Company which sold Sterling and Kermath engines, paid us a visit. We had built a boat for Joe during the Depression. Whenever Joe came around the yard he would arrive around 4:30; this time it was about 5:30 or 5:45. I think he particularly wanted to come when he was reasonably sure that only Dad and I would be there.

So he sat down in the office and said, "Well, gentlemen, I thought I'd rather have you two be the first to know that as of the new year there's not going to be any Seattle Marine Equipment Company. All my suppliers" — he represented several pump and other auxiliary-type machinery builders, as well as prime mover engines — "have informed me by mail or by telegram that as of January 1st there will be no further production for civilian use. So if you think of something..." meaning could we come up with anything in the line of work for him to do.

Dad and I said something to the effect, "Why, we can think of a project right now, and that is this great big roll of plans here."

The plans had arrived recently from the navy, for air-sea rescue boats. We had opened them, of course, and had read about the first two pages of the specifications, which were mostly about financial responsibility, and realized that the Blanchard Boat Company at that time was unable to qualify for a navy contract of any size. The navy would have disqualified us because there was no way we could have shown that we had the financial resources to complete a contract. After about an hour of discussion Joe asked if he could take the plans and specifications home. He had been an aeronautical machinist's mate during World War I, so he was familiar with naval procedure as of that time.

I was married by then and in those days Eunice and I lived in an apartment farther south on Broadway from my parents' house, so I rode home with Dad each evening. As we drove home that night I said to him, "If we can make any kind of tie-up with Joe Patton, he'd be the best person in the world."

Dad asked, "Why do you say that?"

"Because we both know he's 100% honest," I replied.

Eunice Scholl on the BLUE BOOT, *Star boat #908, CA. 1932.* (BLANCHARD COLLECTION)

And Dad said, "Yes, I think so, too."

The result of the joint venture we had with Joe Patton was that he acted as purchasing agent, and in 1943 the Blanchard Boat Company disincorporated. Of course, the company shares had been worthless anyway, and over the course of World War II Dad got to the point where he was able to buy them back for face value. Except for the *Silver King*, and maybe one or two other contracts, the company had been so unprofitable in the pre-war years that we could barely justify our existence. If

Dad had had any business sense at all he would have given up years earlier, but building boats was all he ever wanted to do.

By disincorporating the company, in the long run we could realize a much better profit than we could have as a corporation, paying the corporate income tax. But when my dad disincorporated my Uncle Cal left, because he already had a job lined up as a hull inspector for the army. The army had a lot of wooden vessels in Alaska during World War II. Joe did not invest any money in the Blanchard Boat Company. From the beginning he said, and this was of first importance to him, "At the end of hostilities, if we come to any arrangement, I'm out," and I think he was thinking of me when he made that announcement. The arrangement we had with Joe was that for the first contract, he and the Blanchard Boat Company would split any profit or loss 50-50, the next contract would be split 55-45, with Joe stepping down five percent with each new contract. That's the way Joe was perfectly willing to have it, and it was a hell of a deal for Dad because he was able to increase his profits due to his increased purchasing capacity.

That's how we came to bid on our first navy contract, which was for three air-sea rescue boats that were only 45 feet long. Soon after that the navy standardized the design for 63-foot air-sea rescue boats which were a lot faster and fit their requirements much better. The other companies that got contracts for these boats were the Wilmington Boat Works in Wilmington, California, a little outfit in New Jersey, Wheeler Boat Company in New York, and Hacker Craft in Algonac, Michigan. Wheeler and Hacker Craft had contracts for ten boats, and Wilmington Boat Works had fifteen.

It was at this time that Dad decided he had to have a better car. He could see that the war eventually would bring a halt to new automobile production, but you could still buy a car then, so he and Mother flew to Detroit. I think that that was the first commercial airline flight either one of them had made, and he called us from his hotel after he'd gone out to Algonac to check on Hacker Craft.

He asked, "Do you want to know how Hacker Craft is coming on their contract?"

We said, "We sure do."

"Well, they have not yet received their first panel of plywood," and he asked me, "How are you doing?"

I told him, "Well, we launched the first boat today, right before lunch, and we moved the second boat back into position after lunch, and laid the keel for the third boat."

"That sounds pretty good," he said, and that was that.

Time went on, and we were being held up by the navy. On those contracts we had to buy all the lumber, but the navy shipped the big items: engines, radio phones and other equipment. So I finally called Rusty Fellows at Fellows & Stewart, Inc., a boatbuilder down in Wilmington — he had grown up in the business like I had, a little older than I was, but we had many things in common — and I asked him, "Have you got engines down there?"

He said, "Engines? We've got them stacked three high and they're taking up all the damned room in the yard. We've got 30 of them."

I said, "That's all I need to know."

The next day I called the officer at the Supervisor of Shipbuilding and I said, "If you don't get us a truckload of those engines up here by Monday you're very apt to have a lawsuit on your hands," or something to that effect. Sure enough, on Monday a carload of engines arrived from the east. So we got our boats delivered and accepted by the navy in September.

The main thing about that job that sticks in my memory was when we had the first boat's frames all up on the keel and the engine beds in. The beds were all connected to the frames by bronze angles. There was a lot of strength there; the engine beds themselves were two- and one-half-inch spruce, with a plywood face inboard and outboard on each engine bed, so they were very rigid. They were all glued and screwed together so that the engines rested on three- by four-inch steel angles bolted to the inboard sides, or the inboard side of the outboard bed and the outboard side of the inboard bed.

The deck framing was in place, and I was walking along the top of what would eventually be the deck, and I mistakenly put my toe on a cross-spawl that was nailed up from below. It came loose, and I wound up flat on my back on the two starboard engine beds. Very fortunately for me, Martin Monson, who was not a terribly big man, about the same frame as

center: Three Knockabouts nearing completion at the Blanchard Boat Company, 1937. The bow of the TOLA is visible at the right. (COURTESY OF MOHAI). insets clockwise from top left: Oskar Carlsson, long-time paint shop foreman, applying varnish to the hull of a 28-foot Gar Wood runabout, hauled at the Blanchard Boat Company for maintenance. (BLANCHARD COLLECTION); a speedy little day cruiser, designed by Norm Blanchard, that never went into production due to the outbreak of World War II. (BLANCHARD COLLECTION); a celebration at the Blanchard Boat Company after signing a contract with the U. S. Navy Bureau of Ships for ten picket boats during World War II. The three seats closest to the camera are occupied, left to right, by Norm Blanchard, Lorraine Slingsby, bookkeeper, and N. J. Blanchard. The accordionist was a popular Seattle entertainer of the time named Zak. (BLANCHARD COLLECTION)

myself, but very well built and very strong, had heard me coming. He was standing on the floor straddling frames, but he was able to grab my right arm just before I landed, and consequently all I broke were two of the transverse processes on the left side of my spine. But it knocked all the wind out of me, and I really thought I was dying. By the time my breath came back — I have no idea how many minutes it was — practically every man in the shop within a radius of 50 feet or more was standing there gawking.

Cecil Foss was a fourth-year apprentice who, five or six years later, became a competitor, but he saw what happened and rushed into the office and said, "N. J., Joe, I think Norm stove in a couple of frames," meaning my ribs.

The three of them came rushing out, and just about that time I could say something so I told them, "Find a hunk of plywood big enough to slide under me." They did this, and several hands pushed up from below without moving me too much, and, as my shock began to wear off, I decided that my spine was not broken. So, slowly and cautiously — it just so happened I had had a very good First Aid refresher course at the University of Washington — I got up and climbed out of the boat, which Cecil Foss later told me was the worst thing I could have done. We didn't even have an invalid's litter at the boat company, but, needless to say, we got one soon after that. I went into the office and sat down in the wicker chair in the public area of the office.

Joe was getting ready to go downtown to do his pickups, because he was our purchasing agent, so I said, "Joe, could you drop me off at the Cobb Building? I think I ought to see my doctor."

And Joe said, "I think that's a hell of a good idea."

Joe had recently purchased a single-seat Studebaker, a very classy car, and we got down to the Cobb Building — of course Fourth Avenue was still a two-way street — and he stopped right in front of the door, and, wow, getting out of the car was a lot harder than getting in, but I did manage.

He asked me, "Are you sure you're going to be all right?"

I answered, "I think so," and walked across the sidewalk, which seemed kind of wide, and then up three steps to the level of the foyer, and through the doors.

The Cobb Building still had elevator operators and a starter/supervisor, with nice uniforms; a young woman was facing the elevator, and I asked her, "Is there someplace I can sit down?"

She turned and looked at me, and said, "*Just a minute!*" She got a wheelchair that they kept right there, got me into it, and wheeled me up to Dr. Robert Freeman's office. By then I was really hurting. Dr. Freeman was an old-style physician and surgeon. He would not have a nurse or any other sort of assistant in the office when he was there. Everything between him and his patients, and I imagine especially money, was strictly and 100% private. If you wanted to see Dr. Freeman you simply went and sat in his waiting room until he had time to see you, and you took your turn without even having numbers. He lived at the University Club when Clare Egtvedt still lived there, so he was pretty well acquainted with the Blanchard Boat Company, far more so than he would have been otherwise. He would come by with Clare once in a while when we were building the *Navita*, so he knew a little bit about me.

The young lady who had wheeled me up there rapped on his door, and he cracked it, so she explained the situation to him. He said, "Well, we can't do anything without an X-ray. Could you take him over to the lab in the Stimson Building?"

She said, "I'd be glad to." The Stimson Building was torn down more than 20 years ago, but it was right across the street south of the Cobb Building, so we went back down in the elevator to the basement and through the tunnel under University Street. Apparently Dr. Freeman had called the lab and told them we were coming, because when we got up there they put me in ahead of anybody who was waiting.

After the technician had taken his pictures he asked me, "Can you stay there? Are you anywhere near comfortable?"

I answered yes, I thought I could.

"Well," he went on, "I just want to soak these X-rays about ten minutes to be sure they're OK." So after about five or six minutes he lifted one of them up to the light.

I said to him, "I really should get back to the plant."

And he said, "I'm afraid, young man, you're not going anywhere for a while."

They got me back to the Cobb Building, in which they used to have an eight- or nine-bed clinic, where Dr. Freeman had removed my tonsils a year or so before. After he had reviewed the X-rays Dr. Freeman came down to the clinic and told me he was going to have to put me in a plaster cast, but he had to get back to his office, so he would come back and do it before he went home for dinner. He put me in the cast that evening, and it was a damned uncomfortable night because the cast was cold.

My dad came down to see me that evening, and he said, "Now don't worry, son, we're going to take care of this." Well, Washington State Industrial Insurance paid all the bills, so that's how it was taken care of.

One day in October we got a call from Captain Bjarne Qvale of American Ship & Supply, which was a marine supply house. Captain Qvale was a Scandinavian and always had certain things that he could sell us. "You ever build any clinker boats?" he asked me.

I said, "Sure. If you go back through our records far enough you'll find that we've probably built hundreds." Dad was absent for some reason or another, so I had to do the talking with Captain Qvale.

He said, "Got to have two in ten days."

I asked him, "Will you bring me the plans or do I come and get them?"

He answered, "There aren't any plans."

I said, "Look, I know I'm not supposed to ask, but I'm going to ask anyway. Are these for lifeboats for some vessel in port?"

He answered, "That's right."

"Well," I replied, "could we have one of her present boats to copy?"

"It'll be there before you can get back from lunch," he replied.

It was just an ordinary, single-axle truck that brought it out to the shop, and I'm not just talking about safety. I'm talking about at least 52% of that boat hanging over the end of the truck bed. If it had been peacetime they never would have gotten away with that. Well, it turned out that these boats were for the fruit express ships that had been coming in to Seattle. We frequently called them "banana boats" and they were beautiful ships.

Before we got very far along with the first pair of lifeboats we got an order for a second pair, because one of the sister ships had come in. We had the first two boats about 75% done and the second two started, and the boat we were copying was sitting out in the rain when Captain Qvale came by with a companion one day, a man I figure was about my dad's age.

Captain Qvale said, "Sorry you can't converse with this gentleman," and he introduced us, "but he doesn't speak any English at all."

The gentleman walked right over to the boat that we were copying, and then he went in the shop door, which was wide open even though it was raining a little bit, and, much to my amazement, he practically jumped up onto the staging, which was table height on 30-inch sawhorses, and then he turned around and beckoned.

The captain said, "You'd better come with me," and they yakked it up in Norwegian, and finally he turned to me and said, "He paid you a pretty nice compliment."

I said, "Well, that's nice, but what did he say?"

"He said you're doing a better job than the boat you're copying. From him that really means something because for the last 25 years or more he's been the chief of the Norwegian government's Lifeboat Safety Department."

Another interesting thing happened on that job. The lifeboats had to have shaft logs so they could have engines, if engines could ever be found for them. Sure enough, one boat in each contract got an engine, and they were furnished. At that time we had a young journeyman boat-builder on the job who had never been with us before. He was about my height, five foot nine, but he probably weighed 25 or 30 pounds more than I did because he was very muscular. So when two engines arrived on the captain's truck, I knocked the crates off and said to this chap, "I'll go get the four-part purchase." I went and got it, and, much to my amazement, when I got back to the truck, the crate was empty and the engine was on its bed. This chap had just picked it up in his arms and carried it up the stepladder — not an ordinary ladder, but a very steady, moveable one that we'd built a long time ago — and set it down right where it belonged in the boat.

While that job was still in progress, December 7th — Pearl Harbor — came, so we thought it would only be a matter of a week or two and we'd have a call from the Navy Bureau of Ships to go ahead and build some more air-sea rescue boats, but nothing happened. January came and went, and then in early February, a really nice, early spring day, a pair of army officers walked in. I think one was a captain and the other may have been a colonel, and they had a civilian with them, and were carrying a roll of plans.

I conducted them into the office, and they said, "Well, we just thought maybe you people could build some of these boats that we need for Alaska," and they unrolled a set of plans by Ralph Winslow. He had an excellent reputation, and produced very fine plans. The only thing we suggested to them was that the east coast design, with a little short mast and cargo boom, wouldn't reach any dock in Alaska.

They said, "Undoubtedly you're correct, but there's nothing we can do about it from here, and the only thing we're authorized to do is get some of these built."

"Well," I said, "we've already got a bid in to the navy. Our bid was dispatched a week ago, and we haven't heard anything yet, but we've built three of their boats already in the preparedness program."

The civilian spoke for the first time and said, "Gentlemen, I only left Washington the day before yesterday, and there's absolutely nothing we can do on the telephone. We'd be lucky to even get into the Bureau of Ships at all. This being Thursday evening, let's send a night letter explaining the situation. We'll give them until Tuesday for an answer."

Dad and Joe were right there, and I was sort of in and out.

The civilian called up on Tuesday at about two in the afternoon and asked, "Have you heard anything?"

And we said, "No, not a word."

"Well," the fellow said, "let's give them till about ten tomorrow morning, and I'll be out to see you." Of course, he didn't arrive until about ten minutes till eleven. I think it was just before he arrived, or immediately after, that a telegram arrived from the navy via Western Union: *No award contemplated.* So we signed up with the army for four of these 65-foot, heavy construction, freight and passenger boats.

Not more than three business days after that we got a telephone call from the Bureau of Ships, Commander somebody or other. He wanted to negotiate a contract, so we had to tell him what had happened. We could tell that this poor man, just by his voice, was damned near on the point of exhaustion, and he said, "Can you please give me the name of whoever signed that telegram?"

We said, "Of course," and read it to him. He thanked us, and we proceeded with the army contract. We built four boats on the first contract, and then three more. The Lester & Franck Company also bid on them, and they built four, and then three.

These boats were supposed to have Enterprise diesels, modern, relatively high speed engines with a reduction gear, but the navy already had their dibs on all that, so we had Kahlenberg semi-diesels that weighed at least twice, if not two and a half times, as much as the Enterprise. So, unless the ship was loaded with heavy cargo forward, she was very definitely down by the stern.

Fortunately for us, the Kahlenberg heavy duty people sent out a representative to make sure that the Blanchard Boat Company could properly install their engines. They were beautifully built, but big and heavy, and just barely went into the space allowed. The representative was a fine mechanic and he knew marine engines and boats. He was staying at the New Washington Hotel on Second Avenue, and one day he didn't show up for work, and when we finally made some inquiries, we found that he was in the hospital with a ruptured appendix. We had several engines installed by the time he could get back on the job, and the army took those boats away as fast as we could finish them.

The equipment throughout those boats was kind of old-fashioned and definitely east coast type. The anchors had all chain, and one of the things I wanted to do was take two anchors just exactly alike and move one length of chain all in one piece between them. That way, if you had 300 feet of chain and you wanted to set both anchors you'd have 150 feet for each of the anchors, but if you were in deeper water you could pay out all 300 feet and set one anchor.

Later, I talked to some of the boys who actually went north with those boats, and one fellow said to me, "We certainly stayed up all night one night and froze our teeth off worrying about the length of the anchor line. We were anchored with the engine dead off one of the Aleutian Islands — to be perfectly honest, we didn't know exactly which one it was — with an onshore wind and both anchors out, blacker than pitch, but we could still see the surf, and it wasn't more than 50 or 60 yards under our stern. Fortunately, we were able to get the damned engine going again."

We'd had several more inquiries from the Bureau of Ships while we were working on the army contracts. They had by then changed the name from air-sea rescue boats to picket boats. They had the same hull, but they had big, six-cylinder gas engines now. In fact, the first ones had V-12s. Otherwise the basic structure was exactly the same, but the purpose was entirely different — they were now used for coastal patrol. These boats had twin 50-caliber machine guns mounted in a tub right aft of the wheelhouse, and two depth charges on each port and starboard rail, and a gadget on the back end where they could burn smoke pots to lay a smoke screen. I never heard how many there were at any one place, but generally speaking, there were around a half dozen or more at a port, so that they could practise a first line of defense if attacked.

A Blanchard-built navy picket boat of 1943. (COURTESY OF PSMHS)

World War II navy launching, Blanchard Boat Company. Norm Blanchard, left; N. J. Blanchard, back row center. (BLANCHARD COLLECTION)

We built ten of those, then ten more, then five more, and finally an order for ten more, but on that last ten we had a cancellation order part way through the contract because the war was over. So by the end of the war we had built 35 of those boats for the navy. The Shain Manufacturing Company on Westlake Avenue got four contracts for ten boats each, but the Washington Boat Works was so slow, and apparently there had been some dissatisfaction at the local Supervisor of Shipbuilding's office down on Harbor Island, that they only got three contracts for ten boats each.

Just before VJ Day came we'd caught up on our navy work — and I hadn't had any time off — to the point where I was able to take a short vacation — one week plus two weekends. Before the war we had built a 40-foot ketch for an airline pilot by the name of Grover Tyler. During the war he was working back in Cleveland, and he had asked me to look after his boat, the *Cavu*, while he was gone, in exchange for being able to use it. So Eunice and I and our friends, John Amsbury and his wife, had a nice cruise in the *Cavu*. We were just about on the international border, within a hundred yards one way or the other, coming from Victoria back to Port Townsend, when the announcement came over the radio that the Japanese surrender had been signed.

Very soon after the war was over Dad got a call from the broker at the Washington Boat Center, who said, "I've got one of your boats over here. People are mostly picking up anything they think can make do." He went on, "It's an estate situation and the owner wants her sold. Come over and take a look at her."

Dad said, "Sure," and he did, and it was a standardized, raised-deck cruiser we'd built for a man named Art Webb. His business was the American Tar Company, also at the foot of Wallingford Avenue, and the boat was called the *Susie*, still carrying her original name.

Finally, after he'd looked it all over, Dad asked, "Does the engine run?"

"Oh, yeah, sure," the man said, so Dad asked, "Well, what are you asking for her?"

The broker said, "$2,500."

Dad said, "I'll buy her for that."

N. J. and Millicent Blanchard's 36-foot raised-deck cruiser Susie *and Norm and Eunice Blanchard's "33"* Aira, *renamed* Aura, CA. 1951. (BLANCHARD COLLECTION)

He had the boat hauled and in the process of cleaning it the bilge got filled with water. Dad drilled a hole in one of the garboards to drain the bilge, but he forgot to plug it before he put the boat back in the water, so she went down by the bow up to the fo'c's'le lockers. My father was not a person to make mistakes like that.

Well, he and Mother had that boat until he died in 1954, and it was a wonderful thing because for the first time in his business and married life, he was able to leave and be gone for a week or ten days, maybe even three weeks. He rarely did, of course, but he and Mother enjoyed that boat a long while, and always kept her in good shape.

The day after Thanksgiving, in 1945, Eunice and I took off early in the morning, drove to Spokane, and came back the next day with a four-month-old baby boy, our adopted son, Norm.

Ben Seaborn had been at the Boeing Company when the war started, but he got hired away by Henry Kaiser Company Shipbuilding in Richmond, California, right across the bay just a little north of Oakland. It was a big shipyard where they were building Liberty ships like mad. Ben was married by then and he and his wife, Tink, had a baby girl. After the war Ben

Blanchard family portrait, June 22, 1946, Norm Blanchard's 35th birthday. Back row left to right: Norm, Elsie, Pauline, Gigi and Wheaton. Front row left to right: Meda, N. J., Millicent. (BLANCHARD COLLECTION)

left: N. J. and Millicent Blanchard on the TOLA, 1937. (BLANCHARD COLLECTION)
right: Norm and Eunice Blanchard on the sun deck of the Seattle Yacht Club, CA. 1943. (BLANCHARD COLLECTION)

came back up here ahead of his wife and baby on a preliminary visit, and they joined him later. They couldn't find a place to live, so they moved into an apartment that he fixed up in his mother's basement, which was only a block from our house. He set up his drafting table in the basement there and it wasn't long before Keith Fisken contacted him about a new boat, and very soon Keith had a set of plans, so we were off and running before January 1, 1946.

In 1947 we signed a contract for a 50-foot, tri-cabin cruiser, designed by Edwin Monk for Lyman Thomas, the Packard motor-car dealer in Seattle. The boat was named *Miss Blondee*, and she was a very straightforward, good-looking boat, good quality specifications in all respects, but somewhat affected by automobile design, especially in that we had to have round corners in the windshield. We made a three-dimensional template of the windshield and it was formed out of plexiglass, but because we were afraid the window seals might leak, or there might be other problems with it, we did not throw out the template.

For power, the owner furnished two Packard motor-car engines with marine transmissions, installed as V-drives. One day this fellow, the Packard dealer, said to me, "It's utterly ridiculous that you don't have fuel gauges on your tanks."

I said, "Well, I'd be glad to put them in if there were any that I thought were any good."

He had me put in automotive fuel gauges — Packard, naturally — and I had the satisfaction of showing him they wouldn't even last one season. The neophyte yachtsman never stops to think of the fact that even when it's dead flat calm there's enough disturbance in the water that the boat never ceases to move.

Sometime after the winter of 1947-'48 we began one of the happiest customer relations we ever had with a gentleman named Winslow "Casey" Jones of the Jones-Orth Cutterhead Company. Everybody knew him as Casey; nobody ever called him anything else. He and his wife were both little people. Casey was at least three or four inches shorter than I was, and Mrs. Jones could almost pass for a little girl. Their daughter was actually Mrs. Jones' sister's child, and she was a head and shoulders taller than either one of them.

Casey had bought the *Miss Blondee* from the Packard dealer, who hadn't kept her for very long, and he always brought her to us for drydocking. One day he said, "Fellows, I really think

The MISS BLONDEE, designed by Edwin Monk, Sr., and built by the Blanchard Boat Company, photographed in 1947. (COURTESY OF SEATTLE YACHT CLUB)

Left to right: the schooner RED JACKET, the sloop SYMRA and the sloop SPIRIT II, all old racers, CA. 1950. (COURTESY OF PSMHS)

I'd like to build a new boat, but I don't know anything about naval architects. What would your advice be?"

I said, "Well, they've both worked in the yard with the tools, and we wouldn't recommend one over the other, but we know both Bill Garden and Edwin Monk well, we're good friends with both of them, and we're very anxious to keep it that way. We would be very disappointed if you didn't choose one or the other."

A day or so later Casey said, "You've only made it harder for me."

I said, "I've been thinking about it, too. What I suggest is that you go to Ed Monk, you tell him that you've got the *Miss Blondee* and what you want to change about it" — and of course she was powered with V-drive gas engines, and he wanted diesels — "and what you want him to do is give you a preliminary plan, and fully expect to pay for it, and then without showing him Ed's plan you go and give the same speech to Bill Garden."

That way he could choose on the basis of the preliminary plans. Well, Bill Garden came up with a unique, walk-around bridge in front of the wheelhouse, and so he got the nod, and we built the first *Blue Heron*.

Mrs. Jones believed that nobody should have a boat more than 60 feet; 60 feet should be absolutely enough boat for anybody. Bill's plan called for 62½ feet, and Casey said to Bill, "I don't know how you're gonna do it, but we've got to get it under 60 feet."

Bill said, "Around here, practically everybody talks about feet on deck, but the standard on the nationwide basis is waterline length." So this boat was officially 58 feet long, and that's the way it came out.

Casey wanted a contract with us that gave him permission to come in on the weekends with a friend who was retired, but who had been employed by him for years, and they wanted to do the piping and plumbing. They were more than happy to have us approve, and make suggestions, but he wanted to do the work because he wanted to know how everything functioned on the boat. So that was the beginning of a wonderful relationship.

Three or four years later we were building the second *Blue Heron* for Casey when, on a Sunday in February after it had

The first BLUE HERON, *designed by Bill Garden for Casey Jones. Casey Jones, left, and Norm Blanchard.* (COURTESY OF PSMHS)

been very cold, I'd gone over to the boat company to turn off the bleeder valves on the hydrants because the weather forecast was for moderating temperatures. I had just got back into the office when the door opened and in came Mr. and Mrs. Jones. The new *Blue Heron* had already been launched and was in the covered mooring, and on the heating plant there was one of those whirly-gig vents for a furnace smoke outlet. It was blowing pretty good, a northwest wind, and as soon as we got aboard the boat Casey noticed the vent was whirling and making a racket, so he grabbed his oil can and up he went.

As soon as the pilot house door closed behind him Mrs. Jones said, "We've just come from seeing Mr. Fisher's boat that he had built in Holland," and of course it was a steel boat — these people had made each others' acquaintance through

Casey Jones' second yacht to bear the name BLUE HERON. (COURTESY OF PSMHS)

the fact that they had boats — and she said, "Oh, it has beautiful varnish work, but it's hard to see under the shipping cover," because they were not going to unload it until they got it down to Portland. And she threw her arms around my neck and she whispered in my ear, "Casey said he wouldn't trade him for $100,000 to boot!"

I have a nice photo of Casey and me, just the two of us, standing on the bow of the second *Blue Heron* a year or two before it was bought by the actress Julie Andrews, who almost lost it in a fire, but that's another story.

Eventually there were a *Blue Heron III*, and *IV*, and then Casey died, and his wife didn't last very long after that, but, oh, what happy memories I have of Mr. and Mrs. Winslow Jones.

Dad died of a heart attack in March of 1954, just shy of his 69th birthday. He and Mother had gone to Long Beach to visit my sister, Pauline Pfeiffer, for Christmas, 1953. She lived near Ted Geary and his wife, and it was while they were down there that Dad had his heart attack. Mother called Ted and asked him the name of his doctor, and Ted not only got his doctor on the job, but he came over and he and my father were able to have a reunion and briefly become good friends again. It had been a little over 30 years

since their split. Of course, Dad didn't really fully recover from that heart attack, and died the following March.

I was the executor of the estate, and was now president of the Blanchard Boat Company, and I think it was either late June or July that year when this very unprepossessing lady, a mature lady in just an ordinary housedress, not particularly sharp looking, happened to see me. She said, "I understand that Mr. Blanchard has passed away, and that his boat is for sale."

I said, "That's correct. I'm his son."

So she asked, "Could I see it?"

I said, "Of course. That's it right there."

Her eyes opened up, and she said, "Really?"

I took the key out of my pocket, opened the doors, showed her the boat, and she said, "Oh, dear, I can't do anything, but I know my husband will buy it."

So I said, "Well, at the moment I don't have anybody I consider a real prospect. We've shown it half a dozen or more times, but I don't think there's anything in the way of an offer."

Blanchard Boat Company in the snow, 1949. (BLANCHARD COLLECTION)

She said, "Oh, my husband can get down here, but I don't think it will be until after six o'clock."

I said to her, "Why don't you go into the office and call him, and if he says he'll come directly from work, I'll wait for him, even if it's seven o'clock." So she did that, and he came — he was a chubby lawyer — and they bought the boat and took it away.

I did see the *Susie* once soon after that, going down the lake. Besides the regular dinghy that my dad had, which was a clinker, there were two more dinghies on top of the boat, and they weren't really stowed, they were just sitting there, and I kind of thought to myself, I wonder what's going to happen to the poor *Susie*. Well, late that summer, I think it was actually after Labor Day, they called and he said, "I understand you can drydock the boat on Friday night and we can paint the bottom ourselves."

I said, "That's correct."

And he said, "I'll come in on Friday," and I said, "Fine."

N. J. and Millicent Blanchard in California, Christmas, 1953. This was probably the last photograph taken of N. J. Blanchard. (BLANCHARD COLLECTION)

When he brought the boat in she already looked like she had been in their hands for five years, and this was still the same year they bought it. He said, "We had a little scare. We were going over to Sucia Island from Orcas Island and we got on that reef out there" — a well-marked reef — "so I'm a little concerned about the keel, but we got off without any great difficulty."

I put the boat on the drydock and, my God, he'd ground enough slivers off the bottom of the keel that it was almost round. So I told the watchman that they'd be out to paint the bottom of the boat, and Sunday evening I got a call: "Got the bottom painted and she's ready to go back in the water."

I asked, "What about the damage on the keel?"

"Oh," he said, "we took care of that." I soon found out that the way this fellow had taken care of the damaged keel was that he had trimmed all the splinters off with a hatchet!

At the end of World War II Dad was in a position to do some investing, and he'd had no previous experience other than with the Blanchard Boat Company. Eunice and I had purchased the company from him at the end of the war for $30,000 worth of debentures, ten percent, and had incorporated again with Dad as the president, so he almost had two salaries. I can't remember too much about his cars, but he and Mother had some nice trips; they went to Alaska one year on a coastal steamship — I think it was the old *Aleutian* — and spent the holidays each year in California because two of my sisters were living down there.

Part of Dad's estate included the Ravenna Cleaners on University Way. He had bought the cleaners partly on the advice of my mother's younger brother, my Uncle Ted, and it was making money for him. The majority of the business came through a call office on University Way, and the cleaning plant was over on Roosevelt Way; it was an old petroleum operation of the type that were rapidly passing out of business because they were about to be outlawed by the city. And Dad put my brother, Wheaton, in there full time to run it. The first thing Wheaton had to do was get rid of Uncle Ted because Uncle Ted would lean over the clean laundry and perspire on it. Dad had had a premonition about Uncle Ted, and he had the money to buy him out.

Wheaton could soon see that the driver who brought the clothes from the call office was making all the dough. He was being paid union wages whether the truck was full or just half full. Next door to the call office there was a greasy spoon restaurant that had had a fire. Uncle Ted arranged a lease on the property, so Dad was able to get rid of the old petroleum operation and set up the new plant as non-flammable.

Wheaton and his wife, Marion, were practising Catholics, and she was pregnant for the third time, so Wheaton figured he needed a raise. He had done well by Dad, having gotten rid of the old petroleum operation, but Dad had done quite a bit of work himself on the new building to get it ready, and he told Wheaton that he couldn't have a raise. So Wheaton took a job in Fairbanks, Alaska, sight unseen, and moved the family up there. It wasn't long before their two boys were picking up swear words, so Marion put her foot down and said, "We've got to go back to Seattle, to civilized country."

By then Dad had died, so Wheaton took over the management of the Ravenna Cleaners for Mother, who really had no business sense. After consultation with a lawyer he got her to agree to buy another plant, and Mother ended up with a second cleaning plant at 85th and what was then called Bothell Way, and is now Lake City Way.

Dad's estate had left each of the girls and Wheaton one-fifth of his $15,000 investment in the Blanchard Boat Company, and, of course, there was a little accrued value due, too. Wheaton had called me from Fairbanks after the funeral and asked me, "Is there any way I can get some money out of my interest in the boat company?"

I said, "Well, gee, it puts me in an awfully awkward position. I have to do the right thing by the girls, too. About the best thing I can offer is to buy back your stock for the same price that we sold it to Dad a year ago."

"Well, how much would that amount to?" he asked.

"Oh, about $2,500, something like that," I replied.

"That would be great," he said. He needed it for his new business. So that had taken care of his one-fifth. Later that fall I wrote checks for each of the four girls.

My sister, Pauline, had come up on a visit. I'm almost nine years older than she is, and undoubtedly I was feeling low, over-worked and depressed at the time because of these matters, and when I handed her her check I said, "Now you know, Pauline, I feel it's my duty, as your older brother, to tell you that this money is coming to you from your father, and it's yours, and you should put it in a special bank account of your own."

But she said, "Why, I couldn't do anything like that." In those days it just wasn't considered proper for a wife to maintain a bank account separate from what she shared with her husband.

From my father's death in March, 1954, until June, 1955, my mother was a widow. She expected that I would take Dad's place in her life, and be at her beck and call, and it wasn't easy, but eventually she did meet and marry George McVey, a man I subsequently came to love.

George had been a railway telegrapher, I think back in Kansas, and because he already knew both International and Morse code he was also a ham radio enthusiast. He had friends he talked to in lots of different places, including a resident on Queen Anne Hill by the name of Beebe, who owned Beebe Hoists, which manufactured hand-operated winches, a nice business. Mr. Beebe was a friend of ours — my folks had played cards with the Beebes — and he had just lost his wife, so Mother went over to commiserate with him one Sunday. Well, George McVey happened to be visiting Mr. Beebe, and very quickly Mr. Beebe said, "George, why don't you take this lady to church this morning?"

So they went to St. Mark's Cathedral, where Mother had been going ever since Dad died, although she had converted to Catholicism so she could marry Dad in a Catholic church. Well, one thing led to another, and George moved to Seattle. He had a son who had been transferred by Boeing from their Kansas plant to Seattle, and who was an acquaintance of mine. So within a year or so Mother and George were married, and she was late to her own wedding because she was driving around with the car full of her old lady friends. But that got her off my back.

George and I became friendly enough that when I needed a storekeeper I hired him. When we were busy we'd have a hell of a time keeping the material up for the job if we didn't have a store-keeper; I couldn't be storekeeper all the time. So that worked out pretty well until I began to realize that George's driving was so poor that he might have an accident, so when I had a good excuse we agreed that he wouldn't work for me anymore.

Of course, George was there when Mother had her stroke. Whatever brought it on I have no idea. So for not quite a year — and I was quite amazed by this — George's daughter, Dorothy, left her husband in Bengazi, North Africa, and, with her little girl, who was about ten years old, came to Seattle, where she'd never been, took Mother out of the nursing home and cared for her at our home. Later, somebody told me that George had written to her and told her that she had to do this for him.

At any rate, Dorothy came and took care of Mother just as though she were her own mother, and finally Mother died and, of course, Dorothy couldn't get out of that house fast enough. That was in 1964, so Mother outlived my dad by ten years.

Also, in 1964 we had a second fire at the plant, but we rebuilt and continued to operate until I sold the company and retired in 1969. The people who bought it didn't know a thing about operating a boatyard and drove it into the ground

Norm and Mary Blanchard with the EMILY G, Norm's last boat, at Hardy Island, August, 1991. (BLANCHARD COLLECTION)

within a very few years. I was fortunate to be able to retire at a relatively young age, but with all the changes that had occurred in the boatbuilding business it was time to get out.

Looking back on my years with the Blanchard Boat Company, I feel much satisfaction in the knowledge that in over 60 years of operation, Dad and I were able to build almost 2,000 fine boats, commercial and pleasure, power and sail, many of which are still being used by owners who maintain them in fine condition.

Eunice, young Norm and Norm Blanchard on the AURA, CA. 1957.
(BLANCHARD COLLECTION)

QUENT WILLIAMS
THE PERENNIAL SEATTLE YACHT CLUB
COMMITTEE MAN

QUENT WILLIAMS WAS a real character around the Seattle Yacht Club and local waterfront scene for decades. He was a journeyman shipwright from Michigan, who had served his apprenticeship at Gar Wood Boats in Algonac. Quent and his new bride, Elsie, came out to Seattle on their honeymoon, which must have been around 1906, and he was so taken with everything he saw, the mountains, the sound, that I don't think he ever did go back to Michigan. He soon circulated down to the Seattle Yacht Club, then located on Elliott Bay, where he made the acquaintance of the Rohlfs, Oddie and his younger brother, Adolph, who owned a yawl named the *Aquilla*. The *Aquilla* was built from the same lines as the *Gazeka*, which had been built up in Vancouver, B.C. and was later owned by George Wiley.

The Rohlfs brothers invited Quent to go out sailing with them, and of course this was on a Sunday because in those days everybody worked a full day on Saturday. So Quent was out sailing on Elliott Bay with Oddie and Adolph Rohlfs, and all of a sudden, without any previous discussion, Oddie turned to Quent and said to him, "Here, hang onto this, will ya'?" and he handed Quent a hand-trolling line that he had been fishing with for some time. After a few moments Quent realized it was a fishing line that he had just been handed, and all of a sudden he had a fish on the line. Well, they landed the fish, and it was at least a 25-pound salmon. Quent was so

proud and pleased with that catch that he walked with that salmon all the way up to the hotel, which later became Columbus Hospital, where he and his wife were staying at the time; he let his arm hang straight down limp so that the tail of the salmon dragged on the sidewalk all the way up the hill.

Oddie and Adolph Rohlfs, along with their father, operated a boat shop and cabinet works down on the Elliott Bay waterfront. Being the older brother, Oddie worked right along with his father, but Adolph got the breaks and managed to get a degree in geology from the University of Washington. Later, Oddie Rohlfs worked for my father for years, and was always in charge of the joiner work on any of the finer yachts that my father built. He was very much like a dear and much-loved uncle to me. Adolph, the geologist, had one son, Otto, who was a contemporary of mine, and attended Lincoln High School when I was attending Roosevelt. Oddie and Adolph had gone up to Vancouver and bought themselves a little raised-deck sloop, not nearly as pretty as Harold Yetterdahl's *Codger*, but Otto was never much involved in small-boat racing.

Oddie Rohlfs always preferred to work for my dad, but he did work for other yards occasionally when work at the Blanchard Boat Company was slack, especially during the Depression. He was still in charge of the joiner work by the time we were completing the army and navy contract work during World War II. I always considered him to be one of the most interesting of my many "uncles" among the crew of the Blanchard Boat Company, because he took a special kind of interest in me, especially as I was growing up.

To return to Quent Williams, whether it was that fishing experience or not I don't know, but Quent was hooked on Seattle. In fact, as soon as he had set himself up in an office, he framed the return half of his train ticket back to Detroit and hung it on the wall. Quent had been a member of the Detroit Yacht Club, and he immediately applied to, and in 1907 was admitted to, the Seattle Yacht Club.

Quent called his business the Washington KD Boat Company; the KD stood for knock-down. He built himself a boat that he figured, I'm sure, would be a speculation boat, very much in the style of a trolling boat, with, as I recall, a two-cylinder inboard engine, and very nice accommodations. He named her the *Kay Dee*. I was down below in her a couple of times, but I was pretty young and don't remember much about her. For many years the *Kay Dee* was a very active committee boat for the Seattle Yacht Club races.

Although Quent would most properly be called a power boat man who was very interested in sailing, in his early years in Seattle he owned a sloop named the *Spray*, which he raced against the *Sir Tom* shortly after she was launched in 1914. Ted Geary, Colin Radford, my dad and some of the other *Sir Tom* crew used to like to tease Quent, but he was always just as decent a fellow as could be. I remember that about the time the Lipton Cup arrived, Quent designed and built the *Myth*. My dad always referred to her as a "skimming dish" because of her hull design. She was very poor competition for, and hopelessly outclassed by, the *Sir Tom*.

Shortly after my dad moved his shop to the foot of Wallingford Avenue during the winter of 1919-'20, Quent started his own yard on the Lake Washington Ship Canal just east of the first and earlier jack-knife railroad bridge. About the time I became a junior member of the Seattle Yacht Club, Quent sold the *Kay Dee* and immediately started to build the *Kay Dee II*, and she was as different from the *Kay Dee* as night is from day. She really looked like a Gar Wood design, with her big runabout hull, a forward cockpit, and a trunk cabin fore and aft with a small pilot house amidships. I don't know what

her power was, but she was all mahogany, 36 feet long. She was a great boat for Quent because he was the perennial committee person for the Seattle Yacht Club. When the *Kay Dee II* wasn't the committee boat he would patrol the race course in her, trying to keep the commercial traffic from interfering with the sailing contestants. *Kay Dee II* is still afloat in Canadian waters.

Quent was never a very savvy businessman. Even before the Crash of 1929 he was having a tough enough time of it in his boat shop that he went into the manufacture of fly screens, screen doors and made-to-order window screens. While he did manage to hang onto his business until the latter part of the Depression, he suddenly discovered that his property had been sold for taxes, which was quite a blow. However, within a short time Quent had found employment as an inspector for the army shipbuilding operations. Later, he worked as a merchant of surplus World War II marine equipment. When he finally did retire from business, he brought me a souvenir, which was a yard-long aluminum straightedge that was meant to be used with a drafting machine; it is a nice keepsake.

Quent Williams, CA. 1938. (COURTESY OF SEATTLE YACHT CLUB)

Quent Williams, by the way, was responsible for my winning my first race when I skippered my Flattie No. 8, that Ray Fletcher had helped me build at the boat company after school. Burt Davis and Chet Dawson had gone partners in one of the first Flatties built by the Blanchard Boat Company, and that boat very easily seemed to win most of the impromptu races being held on Portage Bay prior to Opening Day that year. Quent found me someplace, I can't remember where we were, and he said to me, "Norm, I want to tell you something. You know, this early in the year we frequently have a nice spring day coming with light southerly winds in the forenoon and sometime in the afternoon the northwest wind comes up, and that is something for you to remember."

So, on Opening Day, 1928, that's exactly what happened. I was remembering what Quent had told me and was keeping to the westward of Burt Davis as he was leading me at the last of the southerly wind, and Ray Fletcher and I saw the northwesterly wind coming and caught it several minutes before Burt did. That put me in the lead, which I was able to keep for the rest of the race. That was the only race I won from Burt Davis, and neither one of us missed a single race that season. So this win was quite a thing in my young life; I had just turned 17.

Quent and his wife, Elsie, had a daughter who was just about my age. It was obvious that his wife did not like the Seattle Yacht Club. My own mother never hesitated to go to a yacht

Quent Williams, CA. 1959. (WILEN COLLECTION)

club party if my father wanted to go, and especially if there was drinking at the club — and now I'm talking about when I was younger, still a grade schooler, and Prohibition was on. Quent's wife probably felt that the club was a social clique, and she wouldn't fit in. It was always hearsay, of course, but the word around the club was that Quent would have loved to be commodore of the Seattle Yacht Club, and he would have been a good commodore, but Elsie always ruled him out as a possibility.

Although he and Elsie were eventually divorced, Quent never did become commodore; however, he always held some kind of committee job at the club, and he was the club historian. As historian he collected all sorts of newspaper articles, things like that, but he had all this information stuffed into boxes, instead of really organized; after Quent's death, rather than sending those boxes to the Seattle Yacht Club, his second wife just sent them to the dump.

For all his life Quent was an avid yachtsman and a real stalwart of the Seattle Yacht Club.

Seattle Yacht Club ladies tea honoring guest Queen Marie of Romania, 1926. (COURTESY OF SEATTLE YACHT CLUB)

A SAILOR'S STEW OF ELLIS PROVINE,
"TEAKWOOD KID," GARRETT AND MORLEY HORDER,
JOHN WINSLOW, AND THE *LITTLE GWEN*

THE FIRST *GWENDOLYN*, which was often referred to as the *Little Gwen*, was built in a vacated or surplus fire department building on Queen Anne Hill in 1903 and '04. The Johnson brothers built her, and Ted Geary was involved, too, because he grew up and was still living on Queen Anne Hill. The *Gwen* had a very low trunk cabin and slim accommodations. Originally the Johnson boys owned the boat. Soon after she was launched, my father and Dean Johnson and two other guys sailed her to Juneau, Alaska, but as soon as they got there and discovered that bread was one dollar a loaf, they got out of town as quickly as they could. I guess the prices on goods up there were still being inflated by the Gold Rush. Those guys made that trip in record time, standing two men to the watch, and they sailed night and day, Seattle to Juneau and back to Bellingham in 42 total days.

After the *Gwendolyn II* was built by my father, the *Little Gwen* wound up in Vancouver, B.C., and it was Ellis Provine who bought her and brought her back. When Ellis got her she needed much overdue maintenance, so he brought her into our yard and had a new, higher trunk cabin put on for much improved headroom, and had quite a bit of work done to get her into sailing condition. Over the years he continued to be a steady customer.

Ellis owned the Blossom-Provine Lumber Company on 85th Street at Phinney Avenue. Now my dad had been buying much of his lumber from Erlich-Harrison, which was a very fine lumber company down in the industrial area on South Hanford Street, so when Ellis continued to be a good customer of the Blanchard Boat Company, Dad started buying lumber from him, too. After all, Ellis had a certain reasonable quantity of ordinary dimension stock, necessary for staging, especially if my dad was building a big boat. Ellis also knew the suppliers and frequently stocked red cedar.

And that reminds me of another wonderful character. My father bought teak directly from "Teakwood Kid" for as little as 30¢ to 35¢ a board foot during the Depression. Teakwood Kid was always dressed to the nines, all four feet, ten inches of him, and had connections directly with Siam (now Thailand). He kept stocks in San Francisco, maybe Portland, but his base was Los Angeles. He would call on Dad each fall at least once in person. Dad and Teakwood Kid seemed to like each other, and they always had a great time together.

A couple of other wonderful friends of mine were Garrett and Morley Horder. Gary was just a trifle older, I think 14, maybe 18, months, than me, and his brother, Morley, was about four years younger than Gary. Their uncle was Ellis Provine, and that's how I made the acquaintance of the Horder brothers, on a sail with Ellis up to English Bay, to the Royal Vancouver Yacht Club in 1927. John Winslow, the naval architect, was really the sailing master of the *Gwen*. He was an

American, and had been trying to develop a practice up in Vancouver, but had given up on ever being able to make a go of it, so he came back to Seattle.

In fact, John Winslow was sailing the *Gwen* in the Seattle Yacht Club race on Lake Washington in April of 1929 when he suddenly said, "Ellis, take the tiller, I don't feel quite right." He slid on forward down into the corner of the cockpit, leaned back against the cabinet bulkhead, and died of a heart attack right then and there. A wonderful gentleman. I really remember everything about the 1927 trip with great pleasure because of his being along. And Ellis was equally nice; he just wasn't quite the sailor that Winslow was.

Gary Horder and I became good friends, and he crewed for me in my Flattie in 1928, at least for some of the races. We were both invited by Charlie Frisbie to go to the 1929 PIYA Regatta at the Royal Vancouver Yacht Club on the *Norn*, along with Charlie, his wife, Cappie, and her sister. There were just three bunks on the little *Norn*, which had been built for Bill Hedley, the violinist, but we had a great trip with Charlie, and remained good friends right through the years. Of course, it helped that Gary and I had done better in my Flattie in that regatta than the Canadians, because we had better sail material than they had. I still have a scrapbook of snapshots of that trip, given to me by Charlie.

Later, Gary started sailing with Charlie Ross on Charlie's Star boat, and eventually he sailed with him at the Star Class World Championships in Long Beach, California in 1933 or '34. Shortly after that Gary moved to New York to work for the home office of one of the very big insurance companies there. Eunice and I were married in 1935, and once, when we were in New York, I went looking for Gary in his office, but he was out to lunch, and when I got back to the car there was Gary *kissing my wife*.

Gary was a man of great warmth who sailed with many outstanding east coasters. Upon his return to Seattle, he had a Robb ketch built in England, a Rosinante yawl built in Hong Kong, plus a sloop, a ketch, and three day sailers designed by Bill Garden.

Our paths seemed to separate after Gary came back west, although he continued to sail with a lot of different people on the bigger boats. Gary married Jocelyn Clise, who still lives near Poulsbo. He died in 1986 but his brother, Morley, survives him. And that pretty much finishes this little story.

AN EARLY-DAY FATHER AND SON
TEAM OF YACHTSMEN
C. W. WILEY AND GEORGE WILEY

FOLLOWING THE LOSS of its lease on the Brighton Boathouse near the foot of Battery Street in 1904, the Elliott Bay Yacht Club had begun to lose its spark, and one of the members who helped revitalize the club, and was also very active in organizing the drive for a new clubhouse over in West Seattle, was C. W. Wiley. He served as commodore of the Elliott Bay Yacht Club in 1907 and '08, with Ted Geary as his vice-commodore. Wiley was president of the local Todd Dry Docks and he owned a fine schooner named the *Henrietta* prior to World War I.

My first acquaintance with C. W. Wiley came about in the mid-1920s when he commissioned Malcolm McNaught to design a 34-foot sloop for him. McNaught was working at the time at the Blanchard Boat Company. He always wanted to become a naval architect, but he eventually moved back east to Rhode Island, where he established himself as a marine surveyor. McNaught designed this sloop, which Wiley called the *Lady Alice* because his wife's name was Alice. She was built at Todd Dry Docks and he kept her on a mooring buoy off his property in Port Madison. He only used the *Lady Alice* for a day sailer, because he already had a large diesel cruiser, also designed by Malcolm McNaught, named the *Alician*.

The *Alician* had been built at Todd Dry Docks in 1924, and originally came out with a plumb stem, but later Mr. Wiley saw the plans for Captain James Griffiths' *Sueja III* and he didn't much like the fact that she would be a little longer than the *Alician*. He had the *Alician* pulled up in Todd Dry Docks and had the original bow torn off and a clipper bow put on her to make her a little longer than Captain Griffiths' boat, which was 116 feet long.

C. W. Wiley. (COURTESY OF SEATTLE YACHT CLUB)

clockwise from top left: C. W. Wiley's ALICIAN being readied for launching from Todd Dry Docks, Inc., 1924. (COURTESY OF PEMCO WEBSTER & STEVENS COLLECTION, MOHAI); *The joinery in the ALICIAN's main saloon was as elaborate as could be found in a yacht.* (COURTESY OF PEMCO WEBSTER & STEVENS COLLECTION, MOHAI); *The ALICIAN after the addition of her clipper bow to make her longer than her rival, the SUEJA III. Note the added height to her stack to effect the profile of a steam yacht.* (COURTESY OF PEMCO WEBSTER & STEVENS COLLECTION, MOHAI)

A few years before the Crash of 1929 Wiley had purchased some property on a point on the northwest side of the interior of Port Madison, a very attractive location for the home he built, which is still there. He had a boathouse built of the same kind of concrete block construction as the home. The boathouse and a garage, with quarters above, were finished before the big house was really much more than well started. The boathouse had a big marine winch in it, and complete marine railway equipment for hauling the *Lady Alice*. Eventually the house was finished, and before the Wileys moved in Eunice and I had a nice tour of it. The main thing I remember about that tour was that Mr. and Mrs. Wiley had a big square bedroom with separate "his" and "hers" bathrooms in opposite corners, which I thought at the time was rather strange, but I was still pretty young then.

Eventually Wiley sold the *Lady Alice* to my old friend, John Soderberg, the 1955 commodore of the Seattle Yacht Club, and the next boat in his fleet, and I believe it was his last, was a motor sailer that was designed by Walter Lynch. She was 58 feet long, and he had her built at Todd Dry Docks, too, and she also lay on a mooring buoy in Port Madison. I don't recall for certain the name, but again he worked his wife's name into it; I think it was just *Alice*.

It must have been sometime in the late 1930s that Wiley went east for the annual meeting of the Todd Dry Docks Company, and he died back there. According to the newspapers it was a heart attack, but the gossip in the shipyard was that he had committed suicide, although I don't know if this was anything more than just gossip. Whatever the situation, the fact was that Wiley had had all of his boats built and worked on at Todd Dry Docks, probably at company expense, and the word was that he had gotten into some kind of difficulty over this back east and had put a bullet through himself. For a long time, however, he was a very active yachtsman, both in Puget Sound and British Columbia waters. The Wileys didn't live in that big house more than three or four years, and it was sold after his death.

C. W. and Alice Wiley had two adopted sons. The boys' natural parents had been good friends of the Wileys, and had been killed. George Wiley was the only one of the brothers I really got to know. The other brother contracted tuberculosis as a young man and was living in a sanitarium in California when he committed suicide.

As a young married man, George bought a 32-foot cruiser from my dad. About 1925 or '26 he came into the boat company, and I just vaguely remember him talking to my dad, kind of apologizing for the fact that he had ordered a Lake Union Dreamboat. Otis Cutting of Lake Union Dry Dock, being very friendly with C. W. Wiley, had given George a very attractive price on one of their new Dreamboats. The Lake Union Dreamboats were 42 feet long, and had been brought out in direct competition with the Blanchard Boat Company's standardized cruisers.

Eventually George Wiley became my neighbor. After Eunice and I moved into our first house on Boyer Avenue East, number 2703, during World War II, he lived at 2713 Eleventh Avenue East, just one block up the hill. George was a member of the Queen City Yacht Club, where he kept his boat, and we frequently had pleasant conversations when he was on his way down to the clubhouse. Until his death George cruised rather extensively on the *Marian II*, which was the name of his Dreamboat, although I can't ever recall his being gone for more than two or three weeks at a time. His only child, a daughter, married a man who had grown up in Port Madison, and she continues to live in Port Madison as a widow.

Prior to World War I George had a sloop, the *Bat,* and in the 1940s, he had a motor-sailer kayak built to Bill Garden's design. Later, he had a mini-tug of Ken Smith's which he had when he died.

We always had an excellent friendship with him, both as neighbors and as a customer, when we would drydock and paint the bottom of the *Marian II*, and perform other small jobs for him. It was from George Wiley's estate that the *Marian II* became the property of my good friend and the first commodore of the Pacific Northwest Fleet of the Classic Yacht Association, Herb Cleaver. Herb and his wife, Virginia, owned that boat until Herb died in 1998, so she's only had two owners.

THE ARCHITECT YACHTSMEN
JOHN GRAHAM, SR., AND HIS SON, JACK

THERE ARE A lot of stories about John Graham, Sr. He was a very successful architect who designed the old Seattle Yacht Club that was built in 1909 on pilings over at Duwamish Head in West Seattle, and the present clubhouse that opened on Portage Bay in 1920. He was also an early commodore of the Seattle Yacht Club and served two terms, in 1913 and again in 1929. He designed and built a home for his family at Port Madison on Bainbridge Island, and I think the Graham family always lived on the island.

Mr. Graham had Ted Geary design him a beautiful yawl. It must have been in 1911 or '12 because I know she was competing by 1913, and, of course, my information about her is from the stories I heard many times. One morning Dad came into the kitchen when we were still living in Georgetown to be close to the Johnson Bros. & Blanchard yard. Dad always shaved before he went into the kitchen, and this morning he already had his tie on, no jacket yet, and I remember my mother just looking at him puzzled, so he volunteered, "Well, I'm going to town this morning and if I can sign up this architect fellow for this yawl that Ted's designed for him I'll be home for lunch. Otherwise I'll take the South Park car."

Well, my dad got the job and they built the boat, which was called the *Ortona*. She was a good-looking yawl, about 45 feet. One thing that Mr. Graham insisted on was that she was going to be light down below. He didn't want all those gingerbready

Cover art for the Sunday magazine section of THE SEATTLE TIMES, *August 22, 1920, in recognition of the opening of the Seattle Yacht Club's new clubhouse.* (WILEN COLLECTION)

panelled bulkheads that were built at that time. He wanted smooth bulkheads enameled white, so somewhere my dad found a source that had some edge-grained fir, six-quarter surfaced — which would really be one-inch surfaced — that was really dry, and six inches wide. They ripped it right down the middle and there was nothing but white lead in the joints. They edge nailed these pieces all together and then hand-surfaced it crossways, so it was about one inch thick, and that's how they made the bulkheads. Of course, it was very, very strong.

A few years later, the *Kuskokwim River* was launched also on the Duwamish River at the new plant location, about a mile down river from the old location. Just before she slid into the river there was a photo taken of her, with signal flags flying, and the *Ortona* is lying in the foreground in that photo.

In the early years the *Ortona*'s crew consisted of Mr. Graham, Ted Geary, my dad, Lloyd Johnson and Fritz Hellenthal. She won the Seattle Yacht Club's Potlatch contest in 1913, but lost the 804-mile Seattle to San Francisco race in 1915. Later that year, though, both she and the *Sir Tom*, which Geary was skippering by that time, brought back trophies from the races at the San Francisco Exposition.

John Graham, Sr.'s SOVEREIGN, built in Bellingham as a power boat and converted by Graham with dubious success to a schooner. (COURTESY OF SEATTLE YACHT CLUB)

My first recollection of John Graham was when he owned a 40-foot auxiliary schooner called the *Sovereign*, which had actually been built as a power boat in Bellingham. She had a pointed stern, or canoe stern, if you prefer. Originally the boat had had a canopy over the cockpit, but he had removed that and tried to make a motor sailer out of her, but that was a failure.

In the fall of 1920 Mr. Graham was acting as race committee chairman for the Seattle Yacht Club when we were having catboat races. I was nine years old, and the youngest crew member. Ted Geary was teaching the Mills girls to sail; I'm sure his ulterior motive was to sell a big boat to Papa Mills. These girls were about 15 years old, close together, and very *propah* young ladies.

The big rivalry in the catboat fleet was between Ted Geary, Mr. Graham's son, John Graham, Jr., who was always called Jack, and my dad. My dad just loved to beat Geary. This was an October race, and the *Sovereign* was anchored a little north of the old ferry dock at Madison Park on Lake Washington. I was crewing for my dad. The race course headed south down to Leschi, around a buoy we had there, and then diagonally across the lake to Medina. It was a pretty long race for those little

Crew of John Graham, Sr.'s ORTONA, CA. 1913. Left to right: Ted Geary, unidentified, N. J. Blanchard, John Graham, Sr., Lloyd Johnson, Fritz Hellenthal. (COURTESY OF SEATTLE YACHT CLUB)

boats. There was a lot of wind that day, and it was cold and overcast, but I don't remember any rain — typical fall weather.

The wind was very, very gusty, and as we were coming on a broad reach halfway back from Medina to Madison Park, each time a gust of wind hit, the sail would belly out, lift the boom up and the boat would heel to port, and then the gust would pass and the boom would drag in the water. This cycle had happened maybe a dozen times, and previously, on rounding the mark, my dad had told me to raise the centerboard because we were in second position. Geary was anywhere from 35 to 100 yards ahead of us, and we were about that much ahead of anybody else in the race. We were right smack in the middle of Lake Washington, south of where the Evergreen Point Bridge is today.

Dad had been sitting on the windward side, and I on the other, and the boat would almost dip its deck as we did this rocking business. What happened next was that when we were probably four-fifths of the distance back to Madison Park, we actually capsized to windward. I don't remember if I was holding on and lost my grip or whether it just threw me into the water between the sail and the cockpit, but I only had to dogpaddle two or three strokes to grab hold of the boom, and Dad, in the meantime, had got hold of the rudder. The boat could not swamp; it was floating high on its edge.

In the meantime, Mr. Graham, who was a savvy sailor, had his binoculars on the fleet of catboats and kept counting them, anticipating just this sort of thing. As soon as he couldn't get the right count — I think there were eight of us — he started handwinding in the chain on his anchor windlass, but he ran out of breath. After all, he was a middle-aged man by then. So he stopped and picked up his binoculars again, and could count eight boats — the right number — so he paid out chain on the anchor line and went below and put some Turkish towels in the oven of his coal stove.

Dad and I passed one of the boats that had passed us when we were capsized, finished the race and rounded right up to the *Sovereign*. Mr. Graham took our line, I must have thrown it to him, and I dropped the sail and climbed into the *Sovereign's* cockpit. Mr. Graham held the headstay on the catboat while my dad got aboard. My teeth were chattering like castanets, so

Mr. Graham told my dad, "You take the lines on these other boats while I take care of the boy."

He took me into the galley and stripped me and opened the oven door and dried me off with those hot towels, and then wrapped me in a World War I army blanket. On the cabin bulkhead he had a fiddle shelf that had been made for a bottle of White Horse whisky and two tumblers. Mr. Graham poured about one-quarter inch of whisky in the bottom of the glass, took it over to the galley pump, two jerks on the pump, then handed it to me and said very forcefully, "You drink that right down!"

Holy cats, I thought, that was the most awful stuff in the world. What was I going to tell my mother? But of course, it was only a matter of ten minutes or so, and I *do* remember that awful-tasting stuff felt pretty good in my stomach, and then I was asleep. I think they even got my clothes pretty well dried out before I woke up. And when I did tell my mother about the whisky Mr. Graham had made me drink, she just said, "But dear, that was medicinal."

As far as I can recall, the *Sovereign* was Mr. Graham's last sailboat for a while. In 1923 the *Mary* was launched for J. S. Ives, who was then vice president and general manager of the Stimson Mill Company. She was a 65-foot motor yacht with a steamship counter stern, designed by Geary and built at Lake Washington Shipyard. She had a raised pilot house and a long, canvas-topped boat deck aft. Within about two years Mr. Ives had commissioned a larger yacht, and he sold the *Mary* to Mr. Graham, who renamed her the *Blue Peter*. His next yacht was also a Geary design, built by Lake Union Dry Dock in 1928, and this is the 96-foot *Blue Peter*. He lost her during the Depression, in 1933, when he sold her to a man in Los Angeles and she didn't return to the Pacific Northwest until she was purchased by Horace McCurdy in 1949. She's been in the McCurdy family now for decades, beautifully maintained to this day, and still one of the finest yachts in these parts.

In the years leading up to the Depression Mr. Graham and C. B. Blethen, publisher of *The Seattle Times*, had become pretty good friends. They were both heavily engaged in the stock market when the Crash came in October, 1929, but by the spring of 1930 or '31 these two

John Graham, Sr.'s first BLUE PETER, *designed by Ted Geary and built as the* MARY
in 1923. (COURTESY OF PSMHS)

The BLUE PETER *as she appeared during John Graham, Sr.'s ownership.* (COURTESY OF PEMCO WEBSTER & STEVENS COLLECTION, MOHAI)

guys went back into the market thinking it had already really hit bottom, and Mr. Graham actually wound up having to go through bankruptcy.

As soon as he got his local affairs cleaned up reasonably well Mr. Graham left for Shanghai, China, to recoup his losses. The Japanese had bombed the town practically flat, and there was plenty of work for him to do there. His daughter, who was older than Jack, went with him, but Jack stayed here and continued with his education the best he could, but those years were really tough. Apparently Papa Graham was able to hold onto the family home at Port Madison. The Bon Marché department store building, which he had designed, was new at that time, and through that connection Jack had a job, and eventually he became a floorwalker at The Bon Marché.

Around 1939 Mr. Graham had made enough money working in Shanghai that he could come back to Seattle, and the first day after he arrived back he went around to anybody who was still alive to whom he owed money, and they all got paid back, but without any interest.

After Jack Graham graduated with a degree in architecture, which would have been shortly before World War II, he and his father formed a partnership, but that didn't last a year. I

John Graham, Jr., "Jack," CA. 1924. (ASAHEL CURTIS PHOTO, COURTESY OF SEATTLE YACHT CLUB)

think that within eight or ten months they were in court to settle some kind of disagreement, or maybe it was the dissolution of their partnership.

Eventually Mr. Graham was able to have Phil Rhodes design him a nice little sloop, about 32 feet, with four bunks, and a reasonably normal beam, although much narrower than what is built now. He had this boat built by Jenson's up in Friday Harbor, but he was never very happy with it, especially since his last boat had been the big fantail yacht, *Blue Peter*. So he became acquainted with Anchor Jensen of Seattle and, along with Harold Lee, they designed a 62-foot diesel-powered motor yacht with an old-fashioned round stern, which Graham named the *Pelagic*, and I think she was in his estate when he died, probably in the late 1950s.

John Graham, Sr. had purchased a Star boat for Jack, which my father had built, when Jack was still in high school. Jack was born about 1908 and began sailing as a youngster. By the age of 12 he was the champion catboater for the Seattle Yacht Club races. Later he was an active crew member on the *Sir Tom*. In my opinion, he was always a hothead, and he had a pretty stormy relationship with the Blanchard Boat Company through the years.

John Graham, Sr., CA. 1924. (ASAHEL CURTIS PHOTO, COURTESY OF SEATTLE YACHT CLUB)

Seattle Yacht Club juniors party in the locks, 1920s. (COURTESY OF SEATTLE YACHT CLUB)

C. W. "Cully" Stimson had brought the *Live Yankee* out to Seattle from the east coast. She had been designed by L. Francis Herreshoff and built by Britt Brothers in Massachusetts. She was certainly the largest R Class boat ever built.

After Cully lost interest in the *Live Yankee* when the Six Metre Class took over the challenge for the Lipton Cup, he left the boat at our dock. We pulled her out, pulled the mast, and moved her onto the north side of our pier. One day Dad got a call from Cully, who said, "I want you to bill me as of this date for anything I owe you on the *Live Yankee* because I've just sold her to Jack Graham, and any future work will be at his expense."

The following Saturday morning, without one word, Jack showed up at the boat company with three or four friends, and they proceeded to strip the paint off the sides of the boat; over the next three or four weekends they completely refinished the exterior of the boat from the deck all the way down to the bottom of the keel. They just helped themselves to our sawhorses, which were about 30 inches high, and our staging planks, 2 by 12 inches by 20 feet, and Dad was considerably annoyed. When those guys had the boat ready, Jack called my dad and said he wanted the *Live Yankee* put in the water and the mast dropped in the hole —

nothing more. The mast was up in the rafters, some 22 feet above the floor, and I did that work for him.

The total bill was something like $90, but when Jack saw it he started haranguing Dad, telling him, "You'll have to reduce this ridiculous bill."

My dad said something to him, and I can only imagine his exact words: "Now you listen to me. I've known you since you were in diapers. That bill is precisely and exactly honest, and you're going to pay it, and pay every nickel of it without one cent less, and you're going to do it right away quick, within the next three days," or something to that effect. Dad was in desperate financial shape at that time. Jack had some kind of a sassy answer, and turned on his heels and walked out.

Apparently somebody talked some sense into him, though, because the next day he called the office — my sister Meda answered the phone — and asked if he came out right away would my father settle the bill for the amount specified. My sister came out into the shop and found Dad and asked him, "Mr. Graham wants to know if you'd still settle the bill for the same figure you said yesterday."

My dad told her, "You go back to the phone and you tell him if he's here by 12 o'clock with a certified check I'll accept it." So when Jack came by my father took the check and said to him, "Now, Jack, don't come back here again," and he never did, until after my dad was dead.

Soon after this the short-lived partnership with his father failed, and Jack went back east. He was married by then and had several small children. I think that for a while his main residence was in or near Washington, D.C. Apparently he was doing well enough in his architectural practice that he bought the *Maruffa* in Chicago during World War II. She was a 67-foot yawl, designed by Phil Rhodes and built by Pendleton Shipyards in Maine in 1935. She had been in storage in Chicago, and he took her out through the Erie Canal with her masts on deck, down to the Chesapeake, where he had her rigged. She was a gorgeous thing, even as she was designed originally, before her rigging was redesigned.

No later than 1946 or '47 Jack brought the *Maruffa* through the Panama Canal to Seattle. He put her in Grandy's yard and had Ben Seaborn completely redesign the deckhouse.

They also moved the galley from way forward to way aft, and right there in the stern he built a kind of table that you could slide around on a circular seat.

One year in the early 1960s, the first part of September, after I had the new railway at the north side of the plant, which I got from Frank Prothero, I got a call from Jack Graham. "Norm, can you drydock the *Maruffa*?"

I replied, "Yes, I can."

"Well, now," he continued, "you know she draws 14 feet and she weighs..."

Jack Graham's Phil Rhodes-designed yawl MARUFFA. (COURTESY OF PSMHS)

I interrupted him. "Jack, that drydock was only completely installed here less than two years ago, and I've had a cannery tender on there that I know would go more than double the weight of the *Maruffa*."

Oh, well, he didn't know that. He continued to explain. "Two years ago we wooded her from the rail down to the bottom of the keel. The people who painted the Space Needle have compounded a new bottom paint of their own formula, and it has to be sprayed, and I won't have anybody but them do it. The boat will have to be tarped in, lights inside the tarp, and a heater, so that from the time they start spraying for the next 20 hours or so, overnight, that heater has got to be kept going and the temperature can't drop below 60 degrees."

So I replied, "Well, I've got enough tarps, I think. If I haven't, I know where I can rent some. I also have a regular contractor's space heater, and if one isn't adequate we can get another one."

As it turned out, we had pretty good luck on the weather. Jack had this same fellow working for him for years; he was a crackerjack as long as he was sober, and he took great pride in the *Maruffa*. Well, he had accumulated a list of things to be done, and, of course, Jack had a list of his own, and they had typed up all this stuff, a page and a half, single-spaced, so the boat was there in our yard at least a week, maybe eight or nine days. We finished the work and got all our invoices together, made up the bill for Jack, and Bill Sheffield, our purchasing agent, put it on my desk. The final amount was something over $2,000. I had warned everybody in our crew — there were only about seven or eight of us working at that time — and especially Louise Sheffield, our bookkeeper, "There's going to be a fight over this one." And I said to Bill Sheffield, "It's an honest bill, it's got to go out just the way it is, but this guy's going to be roaring."

About ten days later Jack called me up and asked, "Are you going to be in this afternoon?"

"Yes, I'll be here all afternoon," I told him.

So he came over, found me, and said, "Norm, I just wanted to come and tell you, we're delighted with the work on the *Maruffa*, and I wanted to come by and hand you this check myself for full payment."

God, I was never so surprised in my life. I didn't know it at the time, but he was planning to take the *Maruffa* back east and go in the New York Yacht Club cruise. After Jack designed Northgate Mall, which opened in the early 1950s, the very first suburban shopping center of any consequence anywhere, as far as I know, his architectural practice had really boomed. He had opened an office in New York, as well as the one he kept in Seattle. Eventually he also had offices in Stockholm and London, so he was really in the bucks for a while.

So Jack took the *Maruffa* back through the Panama Canal and up to New York. Bob Watt went along as a crew member. Somewhere up there on the east coast, they took her into one of the big yards because the *Maruffa* needed some kind of mechanical repair. This yard was perfectly capable of doing the needed work, but they couldn't drop their other customers to accommodate Jack. Bob Watt went looking for the manager or owner, and said to him, "Look, I served four years apprenticeship as a machinist, I've got a degree from the University of Washington in mechanical engineering, and Mr. Graham is willing to guarantee that if there is any problem after we're done he will make it right. Would you be willing to let me use your equipment to do this job?" So they agreed, and it worked out just fine.

One of the other yachts that was in the yard at the time had a young captain who was smarter than most, as young captains tend to be, and it ended up that Jack took him along to New York and they went in the New York Yacht Club cruise and the Fastnet race in England. Jack still had this smart-alecky young captain, and somewhere over there in Europe the kid got drunk, and Jack eventually got fed up with it, paid him off and bought him a ticket back to the United States.

While Jack owned her the *Maruffa* sailed or raced successfully all over the world, from Hawaii to Greece, but eventually he sold her, and her end came when she was lost in a storm off New Zealand. Jack next had a steel-hull power boat built in Holland, and he called her the *Tartar*. She was about 85, maybe 90 feet, and had a nice, big deckhouse, all varnished teak, and a low wheelhouse forward, the way the *Malibu* was

as Geary designed her. But he soon had to go back to sail, and his next boat was a high-powered fiberglass yawl. I think she was powered by a pair of 4-71s, because she could do 9½ or 10 knots if he really pushed her. Several of his friends said he really enjoyed that boat more than any he'd ever had, and he should have stayed with her, but five or six years later he sold her and commissioned another boat.

This next boat was, I think, Jack's final boat, and she was really like a great big enormous Star boat, hard chined and all, so you might say he had come full circle. There's a half model of her on the wall in the bar at the Seattle Yacht Club, although I don't know why, certainly not because anybody thought much of her design. Her hull was welded aluminum and he had her built by some yard up in the Alpine hills of southeastern France. They'd never built a boat that big before, and he incurred a lot of expense in getting her down to the sea and launching her. I remember that at the time it sounded to me like he'd stumbled onto a bunch of young fellows who were just learning the boatbuilding business. We heard that there were all kinds of lawsuits involving that boat.

Once, after he had her in Seattle, a former neighbor of ours, living on Boyer Avenue East, saw the boat just sitting there with a crew of five men onboard, and one of the people who was at the house and who knew Jack pretty well wired him, "How about a one-day charter?"

"Sure," came the reply, "$1,500." So they didn't do it.

Jack once had a collision with that boat. I believe he was under sail in Puget Sound and collided with a ferry. The ferry was found responsible, but the collision really crushed in the whole front end of Jack's boat and her nose was collapsed back about ten feet. So they simply cut off the damaged portion and built a whole new nose and welded it on.

By this time Jack had been divorced by his first wife, and soon he was living with his secretary in his waterfront home on the southwest side of Bainbridge Island. I was not close enough to the situation to know if he ever married his secretary, but Jack passed away in 1991. And that pretty much concludes the story of Papa Graham and his son, Jack.

THE REMARKABLE PEIER BROTHERS

TWO OF MY most unforgettable friends and mentors were the Peier brothers, Rudie and Anton. I can only guess when they were born, but I would think Anton was born about 1895 and Rudie a little later. They were younger than my father, but not quite a full generation removed from my own age. The Peier family was of solid German stock. The boys' grandfather had emigrated from Germany and he lived with them and undoubtedly talked to them at length about the old country. Their father, Anton, Sr., was a brewmaster, and he died around 1928, so I never knew him. Ma Peier — that's what we all called her, although her name was Minnie — survived her husband by some 30 years, and she was a major influence on her boys.

Rudie and Anton were both born in Tacoma, but the family moved to Seattle when the boys were small. The parents bought a house that still stands at 3505 Densmore Avenue North in Wallingford, and Rudie and Anton were raised in that house. It was no surprise that these brothers grew up to become the finest yachtsmen I had the honor of knowing and sailing with, because they had a great fascination with boats from their earliest childhood. Growing up a few blocks north of Lake Union, they started sailing on the lake when they were just kids and the lake was still in its natural state. This was well before the locks connecting Lake Union with Puget Sound were built.

I think they were building boats from the time Anton was about 12. They always had something to sail, starting out with rowboats and ordinary flat-bottom skiffs and other little sailboats, and by the time they were in their mid-teens they had built a half dozen or so boats. I'm sure that as kids they even sewed their own sails. They were constantly scraping together pennies, nickels and dimes to buy materials to build boats.

Rudie and Anton did the most amazing things to earn money. When summer blackberry season began, Ma Peier would fix sandwiches for the boys each Saturday, and, with their sandwiches, each of them carrying two five-pound lard pails, they would set out on foot from their house, walking north to where Washelli Cemetery is today on Aurora Avenue North. That was out in the country in those days, and Rudie and Anton had a native wild blackberry patch, the genuine, little blackberries, where they would fill their lard pails. Then they would walk back around the north and east sides of Green Lake, and down Ravenna Boulevard to the old Latona Bridge, which was right where the I-5 bridge crosses Lake Union now. The Latona Bridge was a hand-operated swing bridge, and the bridge tender would go out and put the wrench on the pinion gear and push it around and around to swing the bridge out if a boat wanted to pass through.

Rudie and Anton would cross this bridge and head right up the streetcar tracks to that big frame colonial mansion with the beautiful pillars that still stands on Harvard Avenue at East Edgar Street. There was a Chinese cook who worked in that house, and he would pay them one dollar for a full pail of wild blackberries, because the owner of the house, Mr. Parsons, who was vice president of the Dexter Horton Bank, was just crazy about wild blackberry pie. So they'd have two dollars apiece most Saturdays all through blackberry season, and they'd get on the Broadway streetcar that ran by the house and ride downtown and go to a barber school and get their hair cut for a nickel. By the end of blackberry season they would generally have saved $20 or so.

Rudie and Anton had made a coaster from a piece of 2- by 12-inch plank and some buggy wheels. One time when they needed lumber for boatbuilding, they started out from their house with this coaster, walking west through downtown Fremont and out Leary Way Northwest, which was an unpaved road in those days. Where First or Second Avenue Northwest intersects Leary Way there was a large area that was tide flats, because this was still before the locks had been built, and it took both of them pulling that coaster without any load on it to cross that open area to the Seattle Cedar Lumber Company mill office. They walked into the office, and there was a tall, gangly old bookkeeper standing at his desk. He peered over his glasses at the boys and asked them, "What do you kids want?"

"We want to buy some cedar boards," came the reply.

The bookkeeper dressed them up and down with his eyes. "G'wan, get the hell outa here, you haven't got any money," he told them, or words to that effect.

Now, the door to the president's office was open, and he came out of his office just as Rudie and Anton were about to leave and said to them, "Just a minute, boys." They stopped, and he continued, "What do you want to buy cedar lumber for?"

The boys replied, "We want to build a boat."

"Oh," said the president. He looked at the bookkeeper and said, "Jackson, these boys' money is just as good as any other customer's. One thing that you've got to remember is that boys who build boats don't get into trouble."

After graduating from Lincoln High School, Anton went to Detroit and served a three-year apprenticeship at the Winton

Rudie, left, and Anton Peier, on tiller, receiving a free tow, CA. 1910.
(BLANCHARD COLLECTION)

Motor Car Company. Rudie went to work in the Fisher Flouring Mills office.

As the war clouds were gathering over Europe, both Rudie and Anton were the right age for the service. Rudie was drafted into the army during World War I, but Anton had already volunteered earlier for the navy.

At one point the subchaser Anton was assigned to was hauled out at City Island, New York, at the Robert Jacobs yard. This was during the spring of 1917, and there were a lot of boats laid up in the yard with their winter covers still on. Being an avid sailor, Anton wandered around the yard until he spied a nice little 32-foot cruising sailboat all covered up, and for sale at a price he thought he could manage.

He got to thinking about this little boat, took some measurements, calculated the weight of the lead keel, and then went to some of his best friends on the crew of the subchaser and said, "Hey, fellas, if we each put up a couple of hundred bucks we can buy this boat. It's got its winter cover on it and we can take off the lead keel and sell it, and have our money back." So that's what they did. They bought that little boat, and every time they went into that particular yard they had a nice little clubhouse where they could do a little drinking, or just sleeping undisturbed.

Because the brothers' father was a brewmaster, there was always alcohol around the Peier home. Before the Volstead Act was passed and Prohibition was on the horizon, Rudie wrote to his brother in New York, "This damned fool state of ours has gone dry, and it looks to me like the whole damned nation is going to go dry, too, so take this hundred bucks and put whatever you can with it and buy us a stock of booze."

Anton knew that the father of one of the crew members was in the wholesale liquor business in downtown Manhattan, so they went over and saw this boy's father, and, yes, he'd be glad to sell them any amount. So Anton put a little over a hundred of his own dollars with the hundred dollars Rudie had sent him, and began to line up bottles on the counter. All of a sudden he looked at the gentleman who was selling him the liquor and said, "I've got to figure out where I'm going to stow this. Can I leave it here with you?"

"Oh, sure," the man replied. "We'll just put it back in the cases and you can pick it up any time you want it."

They were still patrolling in the subchaser, so Anton said, "I'll see you next time we're in."

When he got back to the ship he looked around for a spot to stow the booze, and he settled on a nice space behind the battery boxes on the outboard side of the engines. Anton was rated as chief motor machinist's mate, and that made him second highest officer below the skipper. Ordinary deck sailors, gunners, cooks and others were not permitted in the motor room. So he took some measurements for the boxes to stow the liquor, went up to the local lumberyard and bought some nice pine boards, and he and the ship's carpenter put those boards together into boxes that fit against the hull of the ship and were big enough to stow two rows of bottles. As soon as they finished the boxes they painted them with government issue navy gray paint.

By the time the subchaser arrived back in Puget Sound, Rudie had arranged, with some of his friends, to get the booze off the ship. Rudie and one of his friends were still in their army uniforms, and they had borrowed a big touring car, and when these guys went up to Everett to meet Anton they were carrying eight suitcases. Even at that they barely got all that booze stowed in those suitcases. When they later told me about this incident, Rudie said, "How in the world we ever walked the full length of that pier, through that big crowd of people, and not a single one of those suitcases lost its handle, I'll never know." He said that they had put some extra lashings around some of the suitcases because they were afraid they might break, but none of them did.

So they drove down to the house in Wallingford, where Rudie had made a special cache for all this liquor, and he had disguised it some way or other so no one would suspect anything was there. Their liquor supply never ran low. Rudie, who had gone back to work at Fisher Flouring Mills after he was discharged, was always able to buy booze all through Prohibition from crew members of the foreign steamships that visited the mill to load finished products, so they never even had to use the liquor that came through the Panama Canal courtesy of the United States Navy.

After the war Anton went to work for the Seattle Fire Department as a machinist. Those guys were just totally self-made in every respect, and after Rudie was discharged they decided they wanted a bigger sailboat that they could cruise in. They wound up purchasing a boat called the *Imp* in Vancouver, B. C., which they probably got for about $1,500 or maybe even less, because right after World War I things were more depressed in Canada. Canada had entered the war in 1914 and had lost many men, and the market was weakened up there just when it was beginning to be good down here.

So they had the *Imp* for about three or four years — it couldn't have been much longer than that — and they sold it. A few days after they sold the *Imp* they were having breakfast, and Ma Peier said to the boys, "You take that money you got for the *Imp* and you split it down the middle 50-50 and you invest it. When you have each made that money work until you've got $10,000 apiece, then you can start saving for another boat." She was a strong woman, and she really had a great influence on her boys.

Around 1927 or '28 a little 32-foot sloop that Ted Geary had designed, which had been built down south, was shipped up here. Rudie and Anton really liked the looks of that boat, and it had just about the amount of accommodations they were looking for. They thought things over for a while, and had Ted design them a 34-foot sloop, and then let the contract to my dad to build it for something like $4,000. This was in the fall of 1929, and things had been pretty tough at the Blanchard Boat Company, even before the Crash. Dad had had very good years up to and including 1926, but 1927 was pretty thin compared to the earlier 1920s when he had built the big gals like the *Wanda* and the *Samona*.

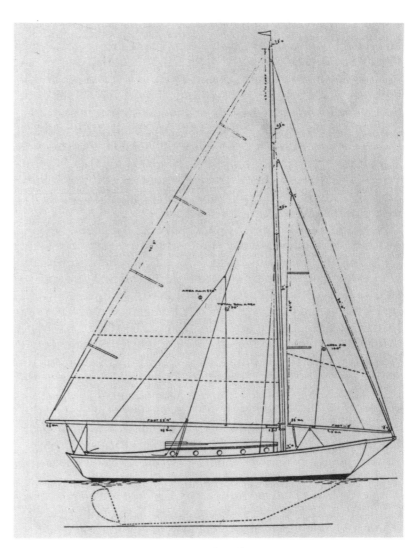

The Outboard Profile and Sail Plan of the first NEOGA. (WILEN COLLECTION)

The sloop IMP, CA. 1921. (BLANCHARD COLLECTION)

Dad really liked the Peier brothers, and he made a deal with them that they could have a key to the shop, and they'd come in Saturday afternoons and Sundays when the crew wasn't there. Everyone still worked Saturday mornings at the boat company, but that ceased somewhat later. The only things Dad contracted for in building their boat were the hull, to make it weathertight, and the mast.

The Peier brothers did all the interior and finishing work, and all the painting and varnishing, either at home in their basement or in our shop on weekends. Of course, they could use any of the machinery that they wanted to. That whole arrangement worked out just beautifully. I remember once during the building of Rudie's and Anton's boat, we were all going home, and Rudie said to Dad, "You know, Norm, we try to be economical, but we use quite a few lights. Put this $20 in your pocket." And that's just exactly what my dad did. The Peiers considered eight or ten different names for the boat, several being local Indian words. They chose *Neoga*, which means northwest or fairweather wind.

Now among many other things they accomplished, the boys had dug a basement under the house where they grew up. They dug this basement by hand when they were still pretty young. You had to enter by a cellar door outside; there was no stairway inside the house. It was paved, though, and they undoubtedly mixed all the concrete by hand, and it was a full basement, although the headroom was a little short.

In their back yard there had been a big black walnut tree. It was so big that it overhung the yard and house next door. When the boys were still in their 20s, or even younger, Ma Peier said to them, "That tree had better come down because we don't want the next big southerly wind to blow it down on the neighbor's house or ours." So Rudie and Anton took down that tree limb by limb, and almost all of the interior finishing, all the interior brightwork, drawer fronts, cabinet doors and dining table on the *Neoga* came from that black walnut tree. They only had to buy a few boards from the lumber yard. Not only that, they had saved all the curved limbs from that tree that could be used to make sailboat tillers, and quite a few sailboats that we built later at the Blanchard Boat Company were presented with a black walnut tiller made by the Peier brothers. The sailboat community was pretty small in the late 1920s and early '30s, when sailboats had not been popular for quite a while following World War I.

They gave a very nice launching party for the *Neoga*, but I was still in my teens and I can't remember much about it. Prohibition was still in effect, and I was too young to drink, but I did actually work on launching the boat, and that was

The first NEOGA. (Courtesy of Seattle Yacht Club)

really the beginning of my long and very close friendship with Rudie and Anton Peier. When I first was friends with them I was not fully aware of their many accomplishments, but as our friendship grew I realized that they were the most knowledgeable and devoted sailors that I had ever met. All of their boats were absolutely tip-top, really Bristol fashion. The brass was always polished, and they sailed just as hard when they were just sailing as they would when they were racing.

When my brother, Wheaton, was about 14 the Peier brothers invited him to go cruising with them on the *Neoga*, and I think by the end of that cruise he was a little tired of adult company. I remember one later occasion when the three Peiers — Rudie, Anton and Anton's wife, Jac — circumnavigated Vancouver Island in the *Neoga*. This was when there was nothing on the west side of the island but lighthouses, and they entered every inlet on that cruise.

Sometime around 1935 or '36 they decided to lengthen the *Neoga*. She was originally 34 feet, and we lengthened her stern overhang so she could carry a permanent backstay, and she ended up being 39 feet.

On March 1, 1940, Rudie and Anton sold the *Neoga* to Alan Engle. The boys' father had died before the launch of the *Neoga*, and they both still lived at home with Ma. Anton was the first one to marry, but this was after the launching of the *Neoga*, so I figure he was pushing 40, if he wasn't already past 40, when he married. His wife's name was Lulah, but we always called her Jac. Rudie didn't marry until much later; he was still living with his mother. Anton and Jac lived in the family home at 35th and Densmore, and Rudie and his mother lived in the house right behind them, so they were all more or less living right there together.

Earlier than that they all shared a big house in Laurelhurst for a time, on top of the hill looking east, a very nice home. All four of them, Rudie, Anton, Jac and Ma Peier, lived there. Eunice and I were invited once for dinner. While we were eating the phone rang and Ma Peier answered it. We could hear her talking: "No, he's not here...no...well, maybe tomorrow, but you can't have him tonight." It was one of their renters calling to complain that the toilet was plugged up, or the hot water tank was leaking, or some damned thing, but that's just the way the old lady was. She sure brought her boys up right as far as handling money was concerned.

Time went on, and they had enough money to have the *Neoga II* built. Rudie and Anton always subscribed to magazines like *The Rudder* and *Yachting*, and anything in the way of a new idea they would be more than happy to try out, usually building up whatever the thing was themselves. By the time they sold the little *Neoga*, Ben Seaborn had already designed

the *Tola* and the *We're Here*, which were sister ships, 42 feet overall, which the Blanchard Boat Company had built, along with the *Romp I* and *Romp II*, now called *Mistral*, for Keith Fisken, and the *Nautilus*. Keith also had us build the *Sunda* for him, which was a 35-foot boat, launched the same morning as the *Neoga II*, and these were all successful designs.

Rudie and Anton worked with Ben Seaborn; I'm sure they had many conferences, and he designed the *Neoga II* for them in 1939. In the early fall of 1940 the Blanchard Boat Company got a contract similar to the one we had had ten years earlier, and we commenced building the *Neoga II*, and we were happy to have the contract. She was built at our yard at 3201 Fairview Avenue. The contract called for the boat to be weathertight when we launched her, and the Peiers did all the finishing work themselves. It was during this time that my friendship with the Peier brothers really began to develop into the close relationship that Eunice and I enjoyed for the rest of their years.

The *Neoga II* was 52 feet long, and she was launched at the Blanchard Boat Company in 1941. June Hellenthal Vynne, who was still in school at the time, christened her. The Hellenthals and the Peiers had been great friends for many years, probably from before June was born. June was pretty close to my age, and I can remember that she was really dolled up when she sponsored that boat. I'd built a sponsor's platform for the launching, and I had used some red, white and blue bunting to decorate it.

Previously, I'd developed a process for decorating the champagne bottles used for boat christenings, and this was quite an undertaking. It usually took me about three nights at home to decorate a bottle of champagne. After removing the label I would score the glass with a carborundum stone and make a criss-cross pattern all around it so it would break easily. Next I would wrap it in muslin or some kind of cover, like a dish towel, sewn on skin tight. Then I'd wrap a spiral of one-inch-wide red, white and blue satin ribbons over that. Each ribbon had to be tapered and basted to the muslin cover. At the top of the bottle I'd stitch the ribbons together in a barber pole effect. Because of the curve of the bow of the *Neoga II*, June had to strike upward with the bottle, and she missed and it didn't break, so that boat was christened after she was in the water, which was supposed to be bad luck. The *Neoga II* launching was quite a party, nonetheless. There were at least 200 people, and lots of people had brought their kids. There was a beautiful punch bowl, and I'm sure my wife helped out with that.

The launching took place a little earlier in the year than it normally would have, because the Blanchard Boat Company had already received our first navy contracts, and it was a real push to get her rigged. One of the things that was an innovation when we built the *Neoga II* was her rectangular sectioned mast. It was the biggest one we had built up to that time, and it sure looked tall and heavy to me. Ben Seaborn had designed it to be pretty damned stout. I think the original wall sections were inch and a half. Normally the Peiers would wrap their mast in the fall to protect the varnish, and varnish again in the spring; they always varnished the mast twice a year. The first time we took the mast out of the *Neoga II*, about the third or fourth fall — we always did this on a Saturday morning, just Dad and me and the Peier brothers — they stripped all the hardware off it and planed by hand a good quarter, maybe three-eighths, inch off it to reduce the weight. This was probably done with the approval of Ben Seaborn, who was studying to be a naval architect, and who by then undoubtedly knew a little more about the strength of spars than he had when he designed the boat. The whole labor-saving idea of rectangular spars was quite new, and there was always more new data coming out.

All the steel standing rigging for the mast was stainless 1-by-19 wire, with fittings which screwed together and clamped onto the end of the wire. This was a good solution, because nobody around here except the Boeing Company had any swedging machines, and that was the only other good way to handle 19-strand wire. There is a way to splice 1-by-19 wire, but very few riggers have that expertise. I even made one of the patterns for what we called the boom bale that the mainsheet block fastens to, and they were pleased with it.

I don't recall for sure what the power was in the *Neoga II*, though it was a six-cylinder, straight six. My father used a lot of Kermath engines, but I am sure that the *Neoga II* did not have a Kermath. I think that probably Anton had picked up some second-hand engine and rebuilt it himself.

In July of 1941 the *Neoga II* was ready for her inaugural cruise, and Eunice and I were invited to go along. There was also a guest on board from the Boston area, Jac Peier's godson. He had just lost his mother, Jac's closest chum, and the boy's father had been able to talk the draft board into not calling him up until he had had this cruise with the Peiers. The boy was just out of prep school and at the stage when most boys think they're all grown up and they really aren't.

The Peiers were waiting at our dock at a quarter to six, and we were at the Fremont Bridge right at six o'clock; the bridge went up, and we got as far as Hansville, just north of Point No Point, that first evening, running under power. We were up at first light the next morning, and Jac and Eunice had breakfast on the table by six o'clock or earlier. I was designated to eat first, and then I took over the helm when we were off Point Wilson and Rudie gave me the course for Cattle Point. Rudie was the ship's navigator, and I wasn't yet that knowledgeable myself, but I sure learned a lesson that day. When you go out on a big ebb, and this one was the biggest that season, you don't head for Cattle Point, you head for Race Rocks. That way you're staying in the main, favorable current.

Jac and Anton Peier on the NEOGA II, *1941.* (BLANCHARD COLLECTION)

As we passed the lighthouse at Point Wilson I called below, "You girls better start securing the galley because I can see a lot of rough water ahead." They were still eating, and when we got off Partridge Bank we started to bounce, and apparently the young lad from Boston began to feel seasick almost as soon as he had finished breakfast. Jac sent Eunice up on deck after they had cleared the table. Anton had kind of a nervous stomach, and he was concerned about his guests and about the new boat, so he was feeling a little queasy.

Rudie was always the one with the cast-iron stomach, but after we had been in this rough water for, I suppose, a half hour, Rudie came up on deck looking a little green himself. He stood up on top of the house and told me, "I'm going to hoist the main. I think it might steady this thing down." So he cranked up the main, using Anton's new wire-reel winch for an all-wire halyard — Anton had made beautiful winches for the *Neoga II* that worked like a charm — and said, "I think

N. J. Blanchard at the helm of the Neoga II, *pursued by Keith Fisken's* Sunda, 1941. (Blanchard Collection)

Anton, left, and Rudie Peier with June Hellenthal sponsoring the Neoga II, *Blanchard Boat Company, 1941.* (Blanchard Collection)

that's helping a little." You could feel the boat had just the slightest angle of heel, and so he said, "By God, I'm going to get up the jib, too."

I said, "Rudie, you take the helm and I'll get the jib up."

The boat had no life lines on it; they were kind of a new thing at that time and very few boats had them. However, she had a good toerail, although it was only about four inches high. The decks were all raw teak, and they weren't slippery, so I went forward and the first problem was to get the jib, which was cotton and in a sail bag, up through the forward hatch, which had a scuttle. It was a very heavy bag of sail, and by the time I got the sail out, the breeze was beginning to pick up a little. I got the toe of the jib shackled down at the deck end, and then I straddled it and kept pulling the jib to me from where I had it alongside the hatch between my legs. Every time I pulled on that sail I realized that I was putting a lot of pressure on my stomach, and my stomach wasn't too happy, either.

In the meantime, we were taking solid water over the bow and the stern every time the boat pitched, because the tide rips were that steep, and much higher than our freeboard. I got the halyard on and jumped to the mast, and it was quite a jump, but I grabbed that winch handle and I wound that jib up in a matter of 60 seconds or less. My wife could see that something was bothering me, and when I got back in the cockpit I lost my breakfast, and then she lost hers, too. But we were sailing, and we were making better time; we kept the engine on, and pretty soon we were out of the tide rips, and we shut off the engine.

The next thing I remember about that cruise happened after we had cleared Customs at Sidney on Vancouver Island. Coal Island, which was nearby, belonged to Captain Fred Lewis. He was quite a character in his own right, and he made his home there on his island, and invited us all to come up to the house after dinner. So, after dinner we were all sitting around in his living room having a discussion. Fred had the most beautiful working model steam launch over the fireplace. He was just crazy about steam power of any kind, and his mother had given him a steam yacht for not taking up smoking before he was 21. Fred had grown up on an estate on Long Island, New York.

We were sitting in a circle, and the young chap from Boston was sitting next to me on my right. I was sitting next to Fred on Fred's right, and Fred was telling about cruising in the South Seas, and how he came to own his yacht, the *Stranger* — all of Fred's yachts were named *Stranger*. Then Fred told a story about Vincent Astor, who had been a friend of his from their college days.

We were all fascinated; Fred was a good talker. He told about how, a year earlier in New York, Vincent Astor had approached him and said, "I think I can sell that boat for you," meaning the biggest *Stranger* Fred had ever owned. Astor had

gone on, "But, I'm not going to do it unless you will promise to come with me on my South Seas Islands cruise next fall."

Fred said he didn't give this too much thought, things will usually come up and promises don't get kept, but he said, "By golly, he sold the boat and held me to my promise. I got a telegram saying, 'Join me in Miami on such-and-such a date,' or I could join him later in Panama. I joined him in Panama," and he continued, "You know, Norm, dressing for dinner every night and all that sort of crap..." After he had finished his story, Fred said to me very quietly, "You know the vessel, Norm, it's the *Nourmahal*," which was a 264-foot diesel yacht that had been built for Vincent Astor in 1928.

The youngster overheard him, and he was a very polite and well-trained kid, but when we got back aboard the *Neoga II* and the lights on the dock went out, he sputtered to me, "Who the *hell* does he think he is? Even President Roosevelt jumps at an invitation to go cruising on the *Nourmahal*."

The plan for that first cruise was that Eunice would go with the Peiers for the whole cruise, and I would catch the steamer back from Victoria, which I did the next day, after we left Coal Island, as there was work to be done at the boat company. That same cruising plan was followed for the next three summers during World War II, so Eunice got a lot of big-boat sailing experience that she hadn't had before.

Eunice was working as secretary to Dean Herbert Condon on the University of Washington campus. He was kind of semi-retired, keeping an office open at the university because they needed him. He was their oldest employee — that is, he had the longest tenure — so Eunice was able to get summers off, and cruising with the Peier brothers she developed into a good enough sailor that they could both be out of the cockpit, working at the mast or anchor, and she would do the right thing with the tiller. She could even shift the engine into reverse, which was done with rope the first season. So that was a very happy relationship, and it just got better as the years went on.

It was an interesting thing, cruising with the Peiers. You might go three or four days, especially if the weather was pretty cool, and never be offered a drink, except one that you could always depend on, and that was the morning "eye-opener," which was just one thimbleful of booze. I wasn't that sophisticated in those days, and couldn't appreciate it, but finally Eunice asked them, "Do you have liquor at home every morning before breakfast?"

"Most mornings, yes, we do," was their reply.

Another time during World War II the Peiers had made arrangements to meet Mr. and Mrs. Paul Webb of the 54-foot, ketch-rigged motor sailer, *Blue Water*, at Coal Island. The Webbs lived on the north end of Mercer Island and cruised on the *Blue Water* every summer. Paul Webb's younger brother, George, was the owner of the *Katedna*, and was the one who changed her name to *Red Jacket*.

Jac Peier and Mrs. Webb were friends, and Mrs. Webb had called Jac in Seattle from their farm at Genoa Bay and told her, "Eggs are dirt cheap up here. Save your cartons for when you're up here on your cruise, so we can take some eggs home."

Jac always saved her egg cartons. That woman just saved everything. So when they got to Genoa Bay, Jac went right over to the Webbs' boat, and in addition to the half dozen or so egg cartons she took for herself, she took some extras for Mrs. Webb.

The plan was that the Peiers and the Webbs would all meet at Coal Island, but the Webbs weren't ready to leave Genoa Bay. The Peier brothers wanted to take advantage of the nice northwest breeze; they didn't want to spend any more time in the Gulf Islands than they had to because they intended to get up north of Seymour Narrows. They said that they would sail over to Coal Island that afternoon. They hoisted sail and didn't use the engine at all that day; they sailed all the way to Captain Lewis' place, right up to the dock. As soon as the *Neoga II* was secured at the dock, Jac Peier grabbed her egg cartons and marched up to the farm manager's wife.

This gal said to Jac, "Oh, gosh, do you want some eggs? We'd just love to get rid of some, because the hens are making them faster than we can use them. But I don't have the faintest idea what I should charge you."

Jac said, "Well, you've got the newspaper from Victoria. Let's look in the paper." So they checked the produce column and noted that eggs were selling for so much per dozen. Jac got her eggs and paid for them, and everybody was happy.

The next day Mrs. Webb showed up and wanted her eggs, too. After she'd gone up to the farm, she came back to the *Blue Water*, which was moored right across the slip from the Peiers, and obviously she was just madder than the dickens. "All you rich Americans," she sputtered, "coming up here and spoiling a good place."

Now, I never knew that anyone could be more economical than the Peiers. They were so economically minded that a lot of people would call them penurious, but they weren't. They were honest and fair with everybody. Mrs. Webb, on the other hand, wouldn't hesitate to pick the pennies off a dead man's eyes, if she had lived in the days when they did that.

On another of Eunice's cruises on the *Neoga II*, Rudie and Anton decided that they wanted to have a good look at the rapids going into Sechelt Inlet. They anchored near the north entrance at the time of the afternoon ebb, and took the dinghy ashore and all walked up the beach to see the spectacle. The tide doesn't run any faster than it does there at Sechelt Inlet. When they got back to the boat Rudie and Anton checked the tide tables. Since World War II the tide and current tables have been much better, and errors, if any, are most unusual, but in those days they were not too reliable. The Peiers calculated the time they thought would be slack water and were planning to power through the entrance next morning.

For some reason, when it came time to leave, the engine wouldn't start. Anton was the machinist; he knew that engine inside and out, and he couldn't understand why it wouldn't start. Eventually he found the source of the problem, but when he did get the engine started it apparently ran just a little bit and quit again. During this time Rudie had shortened the scope on the anchor line, and the anchor came loose, so he had to haul it up. Time and tide wait for no one, so Rudie said, "C'mon, Eunice, we've got to sail this thing out of here."

There was a pretty light breeze, and Anton was still down in the cabin, cussing and swearing at the engine. He thought the boat would be lost. But Rudie got the sails up, and Eunice could sail the boat, and they were able to sail fast enough to buck the current and get out of there. It was a headwind, too, and the wind wasn't fair; it was right on their nose.

Much later, Eunice and little Norm and I went into just about the same place and anchored, and went ashore at low tide. We looked around, and thought, "Gee whiz, it looks like there might be clams here." Our boy was big enough that we could send him back to the boat to get a bucket, and with just our toes and a clamshell we had half a bucket of clams in less than half an hour.

One of the places that the Peier brothers always stopped on a cruise was Hardy Island, where Tom Brazil, the caretaker, was quite a character and a friend. Tom had been a deep-water seaman, and he took the job as caretaker of Hardy Island because he knew he had a booze problem. It was a lonesome job. From October 1st until June any of the five or six local neighbors around Blind Bay might see him occasionally at the post office or the local store in Pender Harbour, but the only other callers, other than yachtsmen, were tugboat men, and they rarely had time to do much socializing. To relieve the boredom he'd scout the beach and find an interesting root and carve it into something. One of them, after he'd carved it into a monkey, he put up in a tree, and it was good enough at first glance to fool a child.

Marion (Mrs. Harbine) Monroe with the driftwood monkey carved by Tom Brazil, caretaker on Hardy Island, 1946. (BLANCHARD COLLECTION)

Rudie and Anton had not only woodworking tools in their basement, but also a metal-turning lathe and all sorts of things. It wasn't a very big basement, and it did get pretty crowded. They had made all the sheet winches for the jib on the little *Neoga* from scratch, by borrowing a Merriman Brothers winch and taking it apart and making the patterns. As they worked with these things they were always figuring out improvements, and were very innovative with their first wire halyard winches. When we built the first *Neoga*, stainless-steel wire was a very rare thing, and few people would pay the price for it. The little *Neoga*'s mast was round and had galvanized wire eye-spliced around the mast; Rudie and Anton did the splicing themselves, and each eye-splice was served with seine twine and then parcelled with gray leather. They made patterns and took them to the foundry for casting, and then filed up the rough castings nice and pretty, and then buffed them with rouge. They really developed quite a home business when sailing began to catch on again, as the Depression was drawing to a close.

Then World War II came and you couldn't get any more castings in new bronze, so one day Rudie asked Red Stewart, their foundryman over on Westlake Avenue, "What about scrap? Old valve bodies and things like that. Could you make these castings for us if we could furnish enough scrap?"

Red said, "Hell, yes, it's just as good metal as buying new."

So that year, 1942, Rudie and Anton made arrangements with their jobs — Rudie being one of the oldest employees at Fisher Flouring Mills, and Anton principal machinist for the Seattle Fire Department — to take off July and August. They packed their hacksaws and a supply of extra blades on the *Neoga II* and sailed north, scrounging for scrap brass, and they were far more successful picking it up off the beaches where logging camps had been than in their most optimistic dreams. I think that one trip kept them supplied with metal until the war was over.

All they needed was those few extra hacksaw blades, and then after they got home they could finish the job of separating any ferrous metals. The *Neoga II* had an enormous space under the main cabin sole; it would take a thousand pounds easily, and, boy, you could make a hell of a lot of sailboat winches out of a thousand pounds of scrap brass. That's just another example of how resourceful and thrifty they could be. All the custom sailboats we built at the Blanchard Boat Company needed winches, and we always bought the Peier brothers' winches.

I think that the Peiers originally conceived the idea for the *Neoga II* because they wanted a good, big sailboat for the Trans Pacific (Honolulu) Race. They still had plenty of strength to sail her for a long time, but after World War II was over, and Eunice and I had acquired our own sailboat in 1949 or '50, I think they realized that they were getting to be a little bit long in the tooth or a bit weak on the physical end for an arduous ocean race. There was a very good market for boats at that time, so they sold the *Neoga II*, and that was their last boat.

I had a telephone call from the present owner of the boat in Florida in the spring of 1995. He told me that he was planning to take the boat to a wooden-boat festival in South West Harbor, Maine, that summer, and told me, "I can't think of anything better than to have you on board for a sail." He

The NEOGA II *at Chatterbox Falls, Princess Louisa Inlet, 1941.*
(BLANCHARD COLLECTION)

had purchased her in what a lot of people would have called a hopeless condition, and he had to put a whole new horn timber in her and a stern post. I flew back and saw her that summer, and while he didn't have her ready for a sail, she looked just wonderful.

Returning to Rudie and Anton, one incident of considerable interest to me was that they suddenly, in the early post-war period, resigned from the Seattle Yacht Club. It seemed to them that the house committee was spending money much faster than they approved of. Rudie could get mad and stamp his feet and swear and be very expressive. He didn't want "any goddamned new carpets in the club. I want a floor that I can spit on, just like the Blanchard Boat Company has." That's one thing that the boys were just poles apart on. When something upset him badly, Anton would upchuck whatever was in his stomach, and lie down for a while, but Rudie would get to raving for two or three minutes. You'd have thought the world was coming to an end, but five minutes later he was perfectly normal again.

The Peiers' houses were just a few blocks north of Vic Franck's yard. After Eunice and I got the *Aura* — our own "33" — and became involved in parenting with little Norm, we didn't see as much of the Peier brothers as we had earlier. The Blanchard Boat Company was involved with navy contracts again during the Korean War, so Vic Franck's yard got quite a bit of business that normally would have come our way. They built two nice sailboats, one from a Sparkman & Stephens design called *Jandy*, a 46-footer. There's a nice, fully rigged model of it at the Seattle Yacht Club. The *Tatoosh* followed, designed by Ben Seaborn, and she was the biggest sailing yacht that had been built around Seattle in quite a long time. The Peiers rigged both of those boats for Vic Franck.

One time I had a set of four Peier brothers winches for a job, sitting on the counter at the boatyard, just delivered, and shiny as could be. John Bowman came in with two friends from Manitowoc, Wisconsin, and they immediately started to examine those winches, and said to me, "Hey, where can we buy winches like these? Where did these come from?"

I said, "Well, they're made locally."

They asked, "Can we buy some?"

"Oh, I imagine you can," I said, "but don't just buy the winches, buy the business."

They looked at me, puzzled, and I explained that Anton wanted to get out of the business, that he had all the patterns and they were in perfect condition, and he would be willing to sell, I thought, for just about what the patterns would be worth if you had to make them. There were cleats and all kinds of things, cast bronze cowl ventilators. The thing was, every time the patterns came back from the foundry they got carefully sandpapered and another coat of shellac applied, so they looked just like new. Those guys made a deal with the Peiers, and I think they paid $2,000.

Eunice and I moved into our house at 2724 Boyer Avenue in 1958, and sometime after that the Peiers called up and said they wanted to come over and talk to us. They arrived, and told us that Jac, Anton's wife, had been diagnosed with terminal cancer, and they asked us, "We want to know, if we left our house to you in our will, would you live in it?" This was the house those boys had grown up in, with its wonderful basement, but Eunice and I just couldn't accept their offer.

Ma Peier died in 1960. Jac lived another nine years, and died in 1969. Not too long after Jac's death Anton remarried. His new wife was named Emma, and it was apparently a very happy marriage, but he moved out to where her family lived, south of Southgate. I think she had one daughter from a previous marriage. He moved most of the shop out there. Everything the Peiers had was excellent equipment, nothing very big or heavy. Rudie had married much later than Anton; his wife's name was Margaret. They soon got divorced and Rudie married a gal named Ann.

Sometimes sad things happen in families. The next time I saw Rudie, his brother had already died, and Anton's widow's family hadn't even told Rudie. They didn't let him know about the funeral or anything. Rudie had gone out to Anton's because he needed something, or wanted to make something, and he found that they had already sold all of the equipment. That was in 1975.

Rudie died in 1979, and I was very surprised when I called on his widow in Magnolia to find that the house is a treasure-trove of his work. Much to my surprise, Rudie did quite a lot of local landscape painting in his old age.

So that is the story of the Peier brothers, Rudie and Anton; they really sailed more than almost any other yachtsmen that I am aware of. Of all my friends, it was really about my most interesting and educational experience to have known the Peier brothers and their family for all those years, especially from about 1929 to 1958 when we were all the closest of friends.

THE WIDOWER SAILMAKER,
GEORGE BROOM, AND HIS SON, RUPERT

I'D LIKE TO tell you about George Broom and his number two son, Rupert. George Broom was a Scotsman, born in the British Isles. He was a commercial sailmaker when there was still a market for commercial sails, having learned his trade in England. George and his wife lived over at Port Madison on Bainbridge Island, and George commuted to his sail loft at the old Pier 8 on the downtown Seattle waterfront in a 40-foot commercial troller-type boat, which he named the *Dunlin*. She was built by my father before World War I, and was listed as a yacht, but she was really his commuter.

George and his wife had two sons, but I never knew Rupert's older brother. I imagine Rupert was born around 1916 or '17, because I always remembered him as being about four or five years younger than I am. He had one slight birth defect, I guess you would call it, and that was that even after puberty if he got the least bit excited, his voice would go way up high like a girl's. As a boy Rupert was small, and when he was just a few years old his mother died. The story goes that George Broom, being hard put for taking care of two small boys, and needing a housekeeper — and he had probably tried a couple — sent to England for a mail-order bride.

His new bride had two girls of her own, and, coming to a strange country, just try to imagine what she was up against. She had probably had very little education, geographically at least. George footed the bill for her coming to America, and undoubtedly she had pretty nice accommodations on the ship. I don't think that a man in George's position would have brought a future wife over in steerage. Well, when the poor woman got to New York City, which was a pretty dismaying experience to start with, she discovered that she couldn't get to Seattle on one train: she had to change trains in Chicago. And of course the situation was compounded when the porter on the train turned out to be black, and she undoubtedly had never been exposed to an African person before. She also learned that she had to sleep on the train, even going to Chicago, so she and the girls must have been pretty exhausted when they arrived at King Street Station in Seattle.

George Broom was a tall man, and he was anything but what you might call a fancy dresser, although he undoubtedly had his best clothes on when he met his bride at the train. He probably made arrangements for some kind of express wagon to take their bundles or suitcases down to the sail loft, and he walked his new family right up to the old County-City Building, which we now call the King County Court House, where he had already purchased the marriage license. One of the judges there was a friend of George's, so they were married, just like that. Then they all went to a very popular restaurant near the County-City Building and had a fine meal. When they had finished their lunch they walked down and inspected the sail loft. George showed his new bride how he made sails, and sometime in the late afternoon they went on the *Dunlin* over to Port Madison.

Now you can imagine this poor woman's mind when she discovered that her new house was surrounded by woods. The house itself was nice enough, and quite big enough to accommodate six of them, but the smell of the salt water and the tide flats was probably totally unfamiliar to her. Not only that, but just across the bay, she was told, was an Indian reservation with *red Indians* living there. Well, to make a long story short, whether it was three months or three years I don't know, but the arrangement just didn't work out, so George paid for all the transportation, put her and the girls on the

George Broom, CA. 1924. (ASAHEL CURTIS PHOTO, COURTESY OF SEATTLE YACHT CLUB)

train, and sent them back to England. George never even bothered to divorce her. I guess he figured that that was just an unnecessary expense.

So from that time on George Broom raised his two boys himself, and somehow those boys were damned nice kids. Rupert and his brother worked in the sail loft. At some point George moved the business out to Commodore Way near the locks, and, for the most part, I don't imagine there were more than one or two other people on the payroll, depending on the workload.

When he was a boy Rupe was a great friend of the real sailing kids, like Johnny Adams, Bill Garden, Otto Rohlfs and the Dreyer boys. Johnny Adams and Bill Garden spent a lot of weekends over at the Broom place when they were all growing up. Bill Garden built himself a sailboat called the *Gleam*, and one winter he lengthened the bow and the next winter he lengthened the stern.

Rupe joined the Seattle Yacht Club in 1938, and in 1947 he had a 36-foot cutter built to a design by William Atkin, which he named the *African Star*. She was supposed to be a sister ship to the *Tenderfoot*, which was built in 1937, although her cabin trunk was quite different. Rupe had that boat for 18 or 20 years, and then, as I recall, he had Atkin design him a bigger boat.

It would have been a number of years before World War II, I imagine, that Rupert's older brother married and started a family, so Rupe bought some property immediately west of the family place at Port Madison, although it was not adjacent property. Both boys had pretty much taken over running the sail loft, when, sometime before we entered the war, Rupe's brother died, and that left Rupert sole owner of the business. Of course, all through the war there was plenty of work, and I think sometimes he had five employees besides the woman who looked after the books and kept the office going.

I recall one Sunday morning Eunice and I were alone on the *Aura* over at Port Madison. We had left the boat at the Seattle Yacht Club outstation and gone for a walk on that particular side of the bay when we ran into Rupert getting his Saturday mail out of the mailbox, so he invited us into the house. I remember how amazed we were because everything was as neat and tidy as if he had a very devoted wife. Even the quarter or maybe two quarters of a waffle on the plate were arranged neatly, and I guess they had been a little too much for his breakfast that morning. Rupert had been married once, but it was not a happy marriage, and he remained a bachelor for the rest of his life.

Rupe called our attention to the property that we had passed on our left as we walked north to his house. It had a very good, standard, barbed-wire fence, and he told us that he'd just had that fence built, undoubtedly had let a contract to somebody, and it was down in the ground three feet so that when he turned a sow and her piglets into the big piece of property they wouldn't get out. The pigs would eat up all the undergrowth and I suppose they even killed some of the smaller trees by eating the roots. Eunice and I enjoyed that visit immensely.

Rupert was unquestionably a diamond in the rough, but he was a good businessman. He died in the spring of 1995, I believe it was, and I was quite pleased when I attended a kind of wake for him at his loft on Salmon Bay, to see that his grown nephew has taken over the business. Rupert Broom was a real sailor, commuting under sail from Port Madison over to his business in Seattle every day of the year.

Rupert Broom at the helm of the African Star. (Courtesy of PSMHS)

BILL HEDLEY, THE FIDDLING SAILOR

BILL HEDLEY MOVED to Seattle in 1903, when the Elliott Bay Yacht Club was housed in a little floating clubhouse near Duwamish Head in West Seattle. Bill joined the club in 1909, which was the year it merged with the Seattle Yacht Club, and he was involved that year in quite an event that helped bring about a new clubhouse. Mayor Hiram Gill, who was crooked as hell by anyone's standards, had a major role in helping the club negotiate a lease on a waterfront site about a block south of the old clubhouse, but this plan was challenged by the local lumber company that had its eyes on that site for an expansion.

One Saturday morning, when the mill was closed, a group of club members, including Bill Hedley and Quent Williams, sailed over on Adolph Rohlfs' yawl, the *Aquilla*, accompanied by a pile driver and all the equipment necessary for driving the pilings for the new clubhouse. The *Aquilla* had mounted four shotguns on her rails, I suppose to influence any opposition that might have been there to meet them. Well, the opposition was there, but I guess they didn't have the forces necessary to prevail, so the pile driving began and went on day and night until Monday morning, when the lumber company got a court injunction to halt it. After some negotiations, the injunction was lifted, and the clubhouse, which was designed by the architect, John Graham, Sr., eventually did get built.

Bill Hedley was born in Nova Scotia in 1877. He was a violin player all his life, and as a young man went to Europe and

Seattle Yacht Club's second clubhouse near Duwamish Head, CA. 1912.
(COURTESY OF SEATTLE YACHT CLUB)

studied in Germany, France and Switzerland. He eventually settled in London, where I believe he was first violinist with the London Symphony for a few years. He probably took up sailing when he was living in England, because sailing was far more common in the British Isles at that time than it was here. He moved to Vancouver, B.C., and a short time later to Seattle.

Bill's first boat in Seattle, as far as I know, was the *Norn*. She was a yawl, about 30 feet, relatively shallow, low free-board, not as low as the *Myth*'s, but for her time she was a pretty good little cruising yawl. The *Norn* only had sitting headroom, three bunks, no toilet, a galley of sorts, and an inboard engine that I believe was called a Doman, which was half of a Model T Ford engine. They'd saw the Model T engine in two and make a marine engine out of half of it. I'm pretty sure she was built by Mojean & Ericson Boat Shop in Tacoma, who also built Bill's later boat, the *Sindbad*. He also owned another yawl, named the *Milissa* before he acquired the *Sindbad*.

Sometime around World War I Bill had a brief marriage, and was divorced, and subsequently he became quite a woman-hater. He was one of the first members of the Seattle Symphony, and was concertmaster for many years. He opened his own studio in 1928 in the Fischer Studio Building downtown on Third Avenue, where he taught violin students for years.

When I first became acquainted with Bill Hedley in the 1920s the *Sindbad* was quite new. She is a beautiful 40-foot auxiliary schooner, now owned by Dick Wagner of the Center for Wooden Boats. Anyhow, for a long time Bill wouldn't bring the *Sindbad* into the lake because the thinking at that

Bill Hedley. (COURTESY OF SEATTLE YACHT CLUB)

time was that fresh water made for rot, which was true, but the fresh water that made boats rot generally came down from the heavens and through the decks. The boats that were kept in salt water usually were more active and therefore better kept up and had fewer leaks. So, in the early 1920s, after the Seattle Yacht Club had built its present clubhouse on Portage Bay, some of the members would say to him, "Well, Bill, why don't you come out to the yacht club?"

He would reply, "Well, you *know* I don't own a *motah cah*." And, as far as I know he never did own a car, or he may have briefly. Most of the time he'd get along with the streetcar, but he would never consider parting with his boat.

By 1928, when I became an active junior member of the yacht club, Bill must have changed his opinion about fresh water because he was keeping the *Sindbad* on a mooring in Portage Bay. He would race the *Sindbad*, especially in the Pacific International Yachting Association (PIYA) regattas, but he never did very well, and lots of jokes were made about him. In 1932 C. B. Blethen, publisher of *The Seattle Times*, resigned as commodore of the Seattle Yacht Club because the Depression had brought about his financial collapse, and Bill Hedley finished out his term. He was elected a life member of the club in 1945.

Seattle Yacht Club's new clubhouse under construction, 1919. (COURTESY OF SEATTLE YACHT CLUB)

Bill remained an active yachtsman up until his death, and the *Sindbad* became quite an ambassador for the Seattle Yacht Club up and down the coast. His friend, Dr. Clarence Veasey of Spokane, often went sailing with Bill, I think always on the basis of Dr. Veasey paying all the expenses, and especially after the Crash of 1929. Back in those days during the Depression, when sailing was barely kept alive, Bill Hedley had a big hand in keeping it going. Eventually, Dr. Veasey persuaded Bill to sail the *Sindbad* down to San Francisco and back, and, according to Dr. Veasey, it was mostly he and his friend from Spokane who did the sailing, because Bill spent a good deal of time lying in his bunk not feeling very well.

In 1909 the first of the Seattle Yacht Club's annual Barnacle Bill cruises started. These were end-of-the-season, all-male cruises, generally to Kingston, or Port Madison or some other place on the west side of the sound. Bill Hedley and Fritz Hellenthal probably became the most active organizers of the cruises until they were halted for a few years during the depths of the Depression and World War II. Those early Barnacle Bill cruises were pretty rowdy affairs. Of course the Seattle Yacht Club was about 98% male back then, no lady members, although there were a few women who liked to sail and were willing to put up with those roughnecks.

Bill was always popular with the men. He would never bring his violin from his apartment to the boat, but he was very involved in the singing of sea chanties and that sort of thing when the party really got going on the Barnacle Bill cruises. When the cruises started up again after the Depression, Bill filled the role of Barnacle Bill for the last 15 years of his life. From that point on Barnacle Bill's Last Cruise was always held at Point Monroe near the east approach to Port Madison, and Bill Hedley was always referred to as Old Barnacle Bill.

In 1939 Bill sailed the *Sindbad* to Victoria, B.C., where she and Captain James Griffiths' motor yacht, *Sueja III*, anchored in the Inner Harbour to help welcome King George and Queen Elizabeth on their cross-Canada train trip.

In time Bill had to give up his studio in the Fischer Studio Building, and that was a tough blow. During his last years he lived onboard the *Sindbad* at the Seattle Yacht Club, and she

was his greatest asset. Bill died of cancer in 1948, and shortly before he died he phoned a friend one day from the old Marine Hospital on Beacon Hill. He said, "I've just had the worst news I've ever had. I've discovered they're keeping me alive with *female* hormones!"

Everybody was sorry to lose Bill Hedley. He was very popular and a wonderful yachtsman for many years. In October, 1949, the year after he passed on, the Seattle Yacht Club officially dedicated the spit at Point Monroe as Hedley Spit in memory of Bill Hedley.

The auxiliary schooner SINDBAD. (COURTESY OF SEATTLE YACHT CLUB)

CAPTAIN JAMES GRIFFITHS AND
THE *SIR TOM* SYNDICATE

IN 1913 A syndicate made up of ten wealthy Seattle businessmen, some of whom were Seattle Yacht Club members, contributed $100 each and commissioned Ted Geary to design the *Sir Tom* to compete for the Sir Thomas Lipton Perpetual Challenge Trophy. She was built by my father and his partners, Dean and Lloyd Johnson, and Joseph McKay. Of course, the *Sir Tom* went on to become the most famous sailboat in the entire history of the Seattle Yacht Club. Of all the various syndicate members who supported her over the years, even though he was not one of the founding members, it was Captain James Griffiths who really made sure that she remained in active competition as long as she did.

Captain James Griffiths was one of the most prominent people around the Seattle waterfront in general, and the Seattle Yacht Club in particular, where he served as commodore three times, in 1921, '22 and '28. He was the first person who was made an honorary life commodore in the club. He was a Welshman, born in 1861. He had the characteristic British small stature, with red hair. I always thought he was about the same age as my grandfather, although I suspect he was actually younger.

He emigrated to Victoria, B.C., around 1885 and set up a stevedoring and towboat company. He settled next in Tacoma, where he formed James Griffiths & Company Ship Brokers, and founded the Tacoma Steam Navigation Company. He later moved to Seattle, where he began a towboat operation on Puget Sound, and formed Griffiths & Sprague Stevedoring Company. He had either a branch of that company, or perhaps a second stevedoring company, which he continued to operate in Vancouver, B.C. He also owned, or was a partner in, the Coastwise Steamship & Barge Company and the Seattle-Everett Dock & Warehouse Company, and acquired his own shipyard, the old Hall Brothers yard, which he renamed Winslow Marine Railway & Shipbuilding Company, at Eagle Harbor over on Bainbridge Island.

Later, Captain Griffiths became involved with James J. Hill, the "Empire Builder," in the business of importing silk from the Orient, and Griffiths is the man who is credited with bringing the Chinese silk through Seattle. He simply went to China and contacted the right people there, who were with the Nippon Yusen Kaisha Line. Of course he had to work through interpreters entirely, but he convinced them that they could get the silk to market a lot faster if they came to Seattle rather than San Francisco. This was a huge gamble on his part, but it paid off for Captain Griffiths: his company became agents for the Nippon Yusen Kaisha Line. Hill's "silk trains" met the ships at the pier and rushed the silk express on specially cleared tracks all the way from Seattle to New York City.

In spite of his active involvement in heading up the syndicate that financed the building and campaigning of the *Sir Tom*,

Captain Griffiths himself seemed to be only interested in power boats. He had a little boat, around 35 feet, that he called the *Sueja*, based on his and his wife's combined names, and I think he owned that boat before World War I. He kept her moored over at the Seattle Yacht Club in West Seattle. The only name I can recall ever having seen on her transom, though, was *Griffnip*. This was because after Captain Griffiths had a larger yacht built for himself in 1919 he wanted to name her *Sueja*, too, but without the Roman numeral. So he changed the name of his 35-foot boat to *Griffnip* and that way he was able to avoid using the Roman numeral on his new yacht. If you look carefully at the famous launching photo of the *Sueja II* out at Ballard Beach, you can easily see her name on the transom is just *Sueja*, although she was always thought of as the *Sueja II*.

The *Sueja II* was lightly built; not quite as light as Geary designed them later, but she could keep up a cruising speed of 15 knots with her pair of big eight-cylinder Speedway engines. Captain Griffiths kept a full-time engineer and full-time cook onboard. Frequently he would leave his office around 3:00 or 3:30 on a Friday afternoon, or any afternoon for that matter, and start out through the locks on the *Sueja II* and run all night to his regular mooring at Coal Harbour in Vancouver at the Royal Vancouver Yacht Club. That practice continued throughout the early 1920s, even after his first wife had died and he had married Ethel Ayers, who was an office manager in his Vancouver company. She also happened to be the mother of Arthur Ayers, who later became my very good friend.

By 1925 Captain Griffiths had commissioned Ted Geary to design a bigger yacht, and in 1926 the 117-foot *Sueja III* was launched at the captain's own yard, Winslow Marine Railway & Shipbuilding Company. *Sueja III* was, and is — because she is still in the charter business on the east coast, now

The Blanchard-built SUEJA II *photographed July 4, 1920.* (GRIFFITHS COLLECTION, COURTESY OF PSMHS)

Captain James and Ethel (Ayers) Griffiths, on the bow of the SUEJA III, 1928. (COURTESY OF SALLY AYERS)

known as *Mariner III* — much more heavily built than the *Sueja II*. All of her woods were Oriental. She was largely built in China and shipped in knock-down fashion to Captain Griffiths' yard, where she was assembled under the supervision of Geary.

There are many stories about the *Sueja III*, but one that I recall in particular occurred about 1927, which would have been her first full cruising season. Captain Griffiths had invited my friend, Doug Egan, to go with him on the *Sueja III* to California, because Doug had either his first or second mate's papers and knew celestial navigation. The captain was afraid they'd get driven offshore and if that happened he'd be in over his head. Arthur Ayers, the captain's stepson, was also on board. One morning, when the yacht lay at anchor in

Wilmington harbor, Art was standing up on the deck. He'd just finished breakfast when he saw a launch heading toward the *Sueja III*, and he couldn't figure out who this would be, as their own launch was moored on a boom alongside. Well, this launch pulled up alongside the gangway and out jumped two fellows, and one of them came bounding up the gangway ladder. Art walked over to meet him, and the stranger asked, "Is the owner aboard? I want to meet the owner. I'm going to buy this boat."

Art replied, "Well, I'll tell the captain you want to speak with him," and went to find his stepfather. Naturally, Art hung around to hear what was said.

The captain was really pretty short, and the stranger was pretty tall, and he said to Captain Griffiths, "I want to buy your boat," or something to that effect.

Captain Griffiths drew himself up to his full height, and, jabbing a forefinger at the stranger's chest, he sputtered, "Young man, this boat is not for sale, but if you'll keep a civil tongue in your head I'll introduce you to the man who designed her, and he can design you one and you can build it."

Well, the stranger was none other than John Barrymore, and so that's the story of how the 120-foot, Geary-designed *Infanta* came to be built in 1930. She, of course, is now known to us as the *Thea Foss*. She has been the Foss Maritime Company's corporate yacht for many years, and is still a beautiful yacht.

To get back to the *Sir Tom*, she was really the latest thing. Before the Lipton Cup arrived in 1912 Quent Williams had designed and built the *Myth* in 1907, thinking he could outguess Ted Geary. Quent never had any education as a naval architect, though. The *Myth* was of a design similar to boats being built considerably before World War I and maybe even before the turn of the century, which were largely called "skimming dishes." This was because they had very little freeboard, as well as very flat floors, and therefore were really on top of the water. They were fine under light weather conditions, but as soon as it began to blow at all they heeled and had to be reefed.

The R Class Rule had been developed by Nathanael Herreshoff in Rhode Island, and when Geary returned from the Massachusetts Institute of Technology and was commis-

above: The SUEJA III. (COURTESY OF SEATTLE YACHT CLUB)

right: The THEA FOSS, *originally the* INFANTA, *designed by Ted Geary and built by Craig Shipbuilding of Long Beach, California, in 1930 for John Barrymore.* (COURTESY OF PSMHS)

sioned by the syndicate to design the *Sir Tom*, he created a really fast hull shape. The *Sir Tom* was the first Seattle R Class sloop and easily won the right to challenge other candidates for the Lipton Cup, which she did, and she held it continuously from 1914 until 1928.

On a related note, Geary and Nathanael Herreshoff's son, L. Francis, were classmates at M.I.T. and somehow or other came to cordially hate each other. Geary always claimed that L. Francis Herreshoff killed the R Class when he designed the *Live Yankee*. I can remember him saying on more than one occasion, "Can you imagine the kind of son of a bitch who would design a boat just to make a horse's ass out of his own father?"

The *Live Yankee* was a radical design, and certainly the largest R Class design. The lead in her keel alone was more than the total weight of the *Sir Tom*. It looked almost like Herreshoff had turned the boat upside down and put the keel on the wrong side, because the hull rounded right into the deck radius.

Crew of the SIR TOM *photographed at the Blanchard yard, foot of Wallingford Avenue, June 21, 1921, all wearing* SIR TOM/SEATTLE YACHT CLUB *sweaters by Octoneck Knitting Company, Seattle. Left to right: Bert and Stanley Griffiths, Ted Geary, Norm Blanchard, Colin Radford, N. J. Blanchard.* (COURTESY OF MOHAI)

Her construction was totally different than anything else, although that was an idea that he borrowed from his father. The boat had transverse molds and they were laminated, but they had all been glued up right in the boat shop; they were about three and one-half feet apart, and then there were two bent frames between each of these. She was triple planked — two layers diagonal and a fore-and-aft layer of varnished mahogany on the outside — and no caulking except on the garboard seam. The other thing that was very radical was that she had a stem, of course, and a horn timber, but she had no wooden keel. When you were standing in the cabin you were standing right on top of the lead. I suspect that all of this must have been done for a client who had said something like, "Look, Francis, I want a boat that's going to win in the R Class, and as to what it looks like, you've got a free hand." She was built by Britt Brothers; they were a small shop in which a good share of the work was done probably by just the two brothers and maybe one apprentice. Anyhow, the damned boat just really was a flyer.

C. W. "Cully" Stimson hadn't been having much luck racing against the Canadians, and by the early 1930s it was pretty obvious that the poor old *Sir Tom* really wasn't competitive anymore. The men in the syndicate who had had her built had pretty much all died by then, and Captain Griffiths couldn't afford to spend money like the Canadians up in Vancouver, so it must have been about 1934 that Cully bought the *Live Yankee* and brought her out to Seattle from the east coast. Under Cully she didn't do very well at first, but, interestingly enough, in 1935 Geary came up from California and sailed her for Cully at the PIYA Regatta at Bellingham, and won. Geary and the *Live Yankee* gave the Canadians a hell of a good race. Cully was getting a little long in the tooth, and just hadn't been sailing her properly, and that's why they hadn't been winning any races with her. But it wasn't too long before the Lipton Cup competition changed from the R Class to the Six Metre boats; Cully lost interest in the *Live Yankee* after that, and pretty much left her sitting on our dock.

To return to the *Sir Tom*'s more competitive years, my first memory of her dates from right after World War I. We did all the practice racing on her in Lake Union right offshore from the Blanchard Boat Company at the foot of Wallingford Avenue, where the Seattle Police Harbor Patrol dock is now. Captain Griffiths had two sons who were both younger than my dad. Stanley was the older, Bert was the younger. In those days Stanley Griffiths would be in the cockpit with Geary, and Bert Griffiths was the mainsheet man. My dad was the foredeck man. I don't recall who was his partner up there with him initially, but Roy Corbett joined the group in, I think, 1922, and that year was the first time the *Sir Tom* had her famous curved Marconi mast and new sails. Up until 1928 she never entered a race that she didn't finish first. She didn't always win because sometimes races consisted of a mixed fleet and there would be time allowances, but she was a very, very fast R Class sloop, as well as one of the smallest boats in the class, at 39 feet, 8 inches.

Well, I think Bert and Stanley Griffiths were the first ones to leave the *Sir Tom* crew, and they were replaced by Roy Corbett and Swift Baker. Colin Radford also joined the early post-war crew. Later John Graham, Jr. became a regular crew member, and when Geary took over as sailing master on Don Lee's big schooner, the *Invader*, in the Trans Pacific Race, which many people refer to as the Honolulu Race, he turned the helm of the *Sir Tom* over to Jack Graham.

Originally the *Sir Tom* was single planked, but she worked so badly that the canvas on the cabintop would be wrinkled diagonally, this way on one tack, and the other way on the other tack. Swift Baker used to love to talk about how they were racing in Royal Roads up there in the strait, where the wind frequently got pretty strong, and two of them would be down in the cabin, bent down bailing, and they could watch the competition through the windward seams. So Ted Geary put her into Lake Union Dry Dock and they took off the original planking and replaced it with double planking, so you couldn't watch the competition anymore, but it certainly improved her watertight integrity!

The syndicate stuck together and paid the *Sir Tom*'s bills pretty much for years. Captain Griffiths was recognized as the manager of the syndicate, and as various members of the original group died he would either find the money from somebody else, or dig into his own pockets, because he really

felt that the *Sir Tom* and Ted Geary were head and shoulders above the gang at the Royal Vancouver and Royal Victoria yacht clubs. He was always the perfect host aboard the *Sueja II* at these races, especially PIYA regattas, from 1919 to 1926, and later on the *Sueja III*.

About the time I became a junior member of the Seattle Yacht Club, Captain Griffiths' stepson, Art Ayers, was the youngest vice-commodore of the junior club, and we became very good friends. I raced with him on the *Sir Tom* because Geary had moved to Los Angeles in 1930 and Art continued campaigning her. During the mid-1930s, around 1934 to '36, I went with the *Sir Tom* up to British Columbia to race on several occasions. We always stayed on the *Sueja III* during these races.

There is one story about the *Sueja III* that I remember that really gave Art and me a scare. We had been racing the *Sir Tom* in the PIYA Regatta in Vancouver in the summer of 1934. I'm positive of that because I wasn't married yet. We'd had a nice regatta, a good northwest wind, but we'd been beaten. The morning we were to start for home the rain was coming down. The wind had changed from northwest to southeast. Now Captain Griffiths was first and foremost a businessman, and he wouldn't let anything short of a hurricane stop him. So we got under way on schedule at, I think, seven o'clock in the morning. Captain Griffiths always towed any raceboat that he was towing on a long line, and he hardly dropped his revolutions down at all on the *Sueja III*. He was *always* in a hurry.

Art and I had the first watch on the *Sir Tom* during the trip home to make sure everything was all right. The ship's cook had fixed a couple of box lunches for us and we had a couple of decks of cards so we could play double solitaire or rummy, and we also had some paperback books. The water was rough as we left English Bay, and Captain Griffiths was towing us fast enough so that the last 18 or 24 inches of the *Sir Tom*'s stern were under the waves and the water was coming together over her deck. Our job, of course, was to keep the water out. Well, right alongside the companionway there was a great big hollow in the wave, so if we were careful we could get the little bilge pump going and a regular garden hose discharge on it, and hang it over the side so that the water in the bilge was higher than the outlet, and it siphoned out beautifully, and we didn't have to work.

Of course we had the hatch closed, but we didn't have the dropboards in, and when twelve o'clock came we were sitting down in the cabin, or slouched down or bent over because of the low headroom. We had long since eaten up any grub that was in those boxes, and pretty soon we could see the trees on Galiano Island through those little two- by eight-inch windows, so we knew that soon we'd be in Active Pass and the captain would send the launch back with the other two crew members to take our place.

I was sitting looking toward Galiano Island, and all of a sudden at the first window I saw a flash of red. I slammed open the companionway hatch and stood right up, and there was a big buoy less than a foot from the side of the *Sir Tom*. We were making at least 11 knots, but the tide was setting us sideways, both the *Sueja III* and the *Sir Tom*. Of course, the *Sir Tom* had a very narrow transom, no more than 24 inches wide, and a big taper. We were really drifting sideways on the tidal current as we approached that buoy, and our clearance of about 12 inches shrank down to about four inches by the time we passed it. We could so easily have hit that buoy, and it would have been just like hitting a rock. It was all steel and most of it was underwater.

When we got aboard the *Sueja III* Mrs. Griffiths said, "Well, boys, that was a pretty lucky break," and we replied, "We think so too."

She said, "I had just come up from checking to make sure all the staterooms were made up, and I stood there in the aft door where I could see what was happening."

Mrs. Griffiths knew all about tides and everything, and she could run the *Sueja III* herself, so Art asked her, "Well, Mom, what did you do?"

She replied, "I just stood there and prayed." So somebody was looking after us.

The *Sir Tom* eventually became, I guess by survival mainly, the property of Captain Griffiths. During World War II all international competition ceased, so she was stored at his shipyard in Eagle Harbor. Captain Griffiths died before the Armistice, on June 29, 1943, and for a while his son, Stanley, ran the companies, but he soon passed on. His son, James, became head of the Washington Tug & Barge Company, and

The SUEJA III, *shortly after World War II. Note the extension of her deck level saloon aft and the reconfiguration of her pilot-house windows. These military modifications have since been reversed.* (COURTESY OF PSMHS)

his brother, Churchill, was right in there as vice-president of operations. After World War II Churchill would turn up at some of the Seattle Yacht Club's events in one of the company towboats, even though the family owned several power boats over the years.

When my brother, Wheaton, came out of the navy about the end of World War II, he was at Officers Candidate School on the University of Washington campus, and in 1946 he persuaded my dad to go 50-50 with him and buy the *Sir Tom*. That summer Wheaton actively campaigned the boat at the Seattle Yacht Club races, but the R Class was dead by that time. After he got married he couldn't afford to pay his half of the boat bills, so the *Sir Tom* came to sit on our dock at the boat company for quite a few years.

In 1956 a young fellow came into the boat company and told me he wanted to buy the *Sir Tom*. I asked him, "Do you think you can repair her and put her back in condition?" Well, yes, he thought he could. I questioned him, "What kind of experience have you had?" Well, he replied, he hadn't really had any experience, so I said, "I'll tell you what I'll do. I'll write to Ted Geary and get the exact weight of the lead keel, and the day that you're ready to write a check I'll sell the boat to you for just what the lead is worth on that day. We can check the paper for the quotation on the price of lead. I'll give you five more years of free storage on the mast. If you haven't come to get it after five years, why if it's still up there and you want it we'll have to negotiate a new deal on the mast."

And I undoubtedly told him how much we usually charged for mast storage up in the rafters. But, I warned him, "You'll have to be here — and we'll launch her on a Saturday if you wish — but you'll have to be here with some kind of towboat to tow her away, and you'll also have to have at the very least a contractor's gasoline pump, two inches in diameter or bigger, to keep her afloat, because she's going to go down like a sieve when we drop her in the water." He eventually went through with the deal, and as he was getting ready to leave I said to him, "Now don't sell the lead keel for a honeymoon!"

About five or six years later — I know it was at least five years, because he never came back for the mast and I sold it after five years — I was lying in the large lock in my "33" sloop, *Aura*, and a Senior Knockabout came alongside and rafted up. The owner, or skipper, was at the tiller, and another fellow with him, and this other fellow said to me, "You don't remember me, Mr. Blanchard?"

I said, "Well, I don't recognize you, although I certainly couldn't say for sure that I don't know you."

He said, "Well, I'm the guy who took the lead keel off the *Sir Tom* and sold it for a honeymoon — and that was a *bad* mistake, too." It seems his marriage had failed. After he bought the *Sir Tom* he had her hauled out someplace and trucked to his parents' back yard, and, after he sold the lead, I suppose the boat was simply broken up for kindling.

So that's the story of Captain James Griffiths and the *Sir Tom* syndicate. Wells Ostrander, the son of one of the early syndicate members, gave his father's certificate, or membership paper, in the *Sir Tom* syndicate to the Seattle Yacht Club a few years back, and we still have that at the clubhouse. It's sad the way we lost the *Sir Tom*, but, as I've said about other former grand boats, sometimes when they fall into such a neglected condition it's maybe best to just let them slip away.

The Sir Tom *in the 1940s near the end of her long career, Wheaton Blanchard at the tiller.* (COURTESY OF SEATTLE YACHT CLUB)

THE GENIUS OF TED GEARY, AND HOW A RACE ON THE *SIR TOM* RESULTED IN A COMMISSION FOR THE LARGEST MOTOR YACHT EVER BUILT BY THE BLANCHARD BOAT COMPANY

I NEVER HEARD from my father — or anyone else, for that matter — when or how he and Ted Geary and the Griffiths boys all got together as young sailors, but it must have been shortly after Dad built the *Winona*. Ted Geary, whose full name was Leslie Edward Geary, was born in Kansas in 1885. When he was still a boy the Geary family moved to Portland, and soon on to Seattle, and Ted grew up around the waterfront. Two of his childhood friends were Dean and Lloyd Johnson, who later became my dad's partners. In fact, Ted and the Johnson boys circumnavigated Seattle in a sailing canoe sometime before the turn of the century, and at that time, of course, that kind of feat required portaging between Salmon Bay, Lake Union and Lake Washington.

Ted went to high school at the old Broadway High on Capitol Hill, and I think he was probably designing boats even before he graduated, which was in 1904. After he finished high school he enrolled at the University of Washington, and in 1907 he joined the Seattle Yacht Club when it was still known as the Elliott Bay Yacht Club.

The first yacht design that really brought Ted any acclaim was for the *Spirit I*, launched in 1907 — or just *Spirit*, as she was known until the *Spirit II* was launched two years later. Ted designed her while still at the university, and she was built mostly by the Johnson brothers in a former firehouse on the top of Queen Anne Hill. A fire station bay in those days was about the right size to build a fairly good-sized boat. The *Spirit* was a 42-foot sloop, built to challenge the Canadians for the Dunsmuir Cup, and, skippered by Geary, she beat the Vancouverites' entry, the *Alexandra*, and won the cup from the Canadians in 1907.

The next year, however, the *Spirit* lost to the *Alexandra*, so the Seattle Yacht Club commissioned the *Spirit II* in 1909. Well, this second design was to the then-new Universal Rule, developed by Nathanael Herreshoff. And what Geary did was design the *Spirit II* with a keel that went from nothing and then was not totally straight down, but steeper than most. Practically all the English keel designs, like the Canadians' *Alexandra*, were the long, sweeping profile. So the *Spirit II* beat the Canadians the next season.

In fact, I heard that they got so badly beaten that the measurer demanded that the *Spirit II* be hauled out so he could measure it, and he called this slight variation in design a notch in the keel. The first measurement was made in the notch. Of course, it wasn't a notch at all, it was just kind of a corner. There've been thousands, tens of thousands, of boats built like this since. But this episode caused a rift between the Canadians and the Americans that was not patched up until 1912 when Sir Thomas Lipton visited Seattle and brought about a truce.

Around 1907 Geary left Seattle to study naval architecture at the Massachusetts Institute of Technology. He returned to

above: The SPIRIT I of 1907 tacking to windward in a Canadian race, CA. 1907 or '08. (COURTESY OF PSMHS)

top right: Ted Geary, 1925. (COURTESY OF SEATTLE YACHT CLUB)

right: The Canadians' ALEXANDRA and the Americans' SPIRIT I, probably during the Dunsmuir Cup of 1907 or '08. (COURTESY OF PSMHS)

above: The beautiful, fast and controversial SPIRIT II *ready for launching, 1909.* (COURTESY OF PSMHS)

left: The ALEXANDRA *in 1907 or '08.* (COURTESY OF PSMHS)

Seattle in 1910 with a degree in naval architecture, and soon had many commissions for yachts as well as work boats.

Ted Geary was a very colorful guy, and of course he was not exactly a shrinking violet. I remember one story about him, where he'd been out sailing with some of the fellows, and they'd had a party of girls with them. Of course, all sailing at that time, before the Lake Washington Ship Canal was built, was in salt water. So later that afternoon, after they'd taken the boat back to the old Seattle Yacht Club, one of the girls said, "Well, gee, I sure wish I could invite you all up. My folks live right up there," pointing up the West Seattle bluff. There was a cable car that ran from the old West Seattle ferry dock up the hill, and then just a regular trolley car on the top — West Seattle was still a separate town then.

And Geary probably replied, "What's holding us up? Why can't we go?"

"Well," she said, "there's nobody home."

So Geary said, "I don't understand. What's wrong with that?"

She said, "Oh, people might talk."

And Ted said, "I don't give a damn what people might say about me, just so they *do* talk about me." And, of course, he even used the word "damn" in front of the young lady, which was considered highly improper.

Ted Geary could make a sailboat sail faster than anybody else. He was probably the most savvy helmsman on the west coast. He could sense changes in wind, things like that, with incredible accuracy. So for a good ten or eleven years the *Sir Tom* was never beaten.

Ted did a lot of commercial work, as well as sailing and motor yachts. One of these jobs was the *Kuskokwim River*, which I talked about earlier.

World War I interrupted competition in sailing, so when the war was over these guys were all very anxious to get sailing and racing going again. I recall it must have been in the early spring of 1919, when one Sunday a bunch of the fellows came over to get my dad and go down and have a look at the *Sir Tom*, which was sitting on the ground leaning against a fence at some commercial shipyard down on the waterfront. I was included in this expedition, and I don't remember why, because I was still pretty young. So we went down to this

Crew of the SIR TOM *in 1915. Left to right: Fritz Hellenthal, Dean Johnson, Ted Geary, N. J. Blanchard, Lloyd Johnson.* (COURTESY OF SEATTLE YACHT CLUB)

shipyard, and the *Tommy* was sitting there with the entire first 18 or 24 inches of her bow missing. During the winter of 1916 and '17 there had been a record-breaking northwest wind and freezing conditions, and quite a few of the fleet at the Seattle Yacht Club over in West Seattle had broken loose. Some of them wound up unharmed on sandbanks, but more of them were badly damaged, and the *Sir Tom* had pounded her snoot off on her mooring float.

This was a big shipyard, but at the time it was more or less down to a maintenance crew. They had steam locomotives in those yards and it was no problem for the yard to fire up one of the steam locomotive cranes on a weekday and set the *Tommy* back in the water. Quent Williams or somebody with a power boat picked her up and brought her up to the Blanchard Boat Company. They built a new nose on her, and that first year, 1919, she still sailed with her gaff rig.

The Vancouverites had a brand new boat called the *Lady Van*, and she was a hard chine design. She was designed by somebody up in Canada, and Geary was successful in shipping both boats down to California, so right away he could see the handwriting on the wall, and he had to put a new rig on the *Tommy*. At that time, the early 1920s, the original syndicate that owned the *Sir Tom* was pretty much

The very fast express cruiser WINIFRED, designed by Ted Geary and built by N. J. Blanchard in 1920, shown at flank speed. (COURTESY OF MOHAI)

intact, and old Captain James Griffiths would say, "C'mon now, you're going to put up another $150 so Norm can build a new mast for the *Sir Tom*."

In 1922 the Pacific Coast Championship Regatta was held in Newport Harbor, California. My dad had built a cradle for the *Sir Tom* and she was towed afloat down to the Pacific Coast Steamship dock for the trip to California. I think they put her on the *Emma Alexander*. We were there and the boat did not have lifting eyes at that time, so they used automobile slings and spreaders and lifted her into her cradle.

The races were off Newport Beach, which was nothing much but a beach. Newport Harbor had been made by

dredging out a natural salt-water marsh. The big red interurban cars ran on standard railroad track out to the end of the peninsula, where they made a circle and stopped. About 50 or 100 yards from the end of the peninsula was the Newport Harbor Yacht Club. It was about the size of a triple garage, big enough for a bar and not much else.

Each day, as they were going out between the jetties, the guys in the *Sir Tom*'s crew could see a great big stone house up on the Balboa bluff, and somebody standing behind a big pair of tripod-mounted binoculars in the window, and they'd wave at him and he'd wave back. After the race on the third day there was quite a lot of partying going on. Somebody let go of the main halyard, so they hoisted the spinnaker and were sailing out between the jetties with an offshore breeze. Dad, being far and away in the best physical condition of any of the five men in the crew, was hoisted up to the top of the jib halyard because it had a two-part purchase, and it was all straight muscle power. Then Dad had to shinny up from the spreaders, which were about 60% up the height of the mast from the deck, get hold of the block and send it down. Apparently the old gentleman with the binoculars watched this whole thing.

The *Sir Tom* won all three races and was still the west coast R Class champion. It was quite a distance in through the jetties and then around the corner to the Newport Harbor Yacht Club, and on the way back in somebody had found a bottle, so these guys were all feeling pretty good by the time they got to the yacht club. When the launch brought them ashore, the manager of the club was standing there on the float and he said, "Mr. Geary, there's a uniformed man waiting for you out back."

Geary was the only bachelor — he'd been divorced and a bachelor for a long time. So the four married guys were kidding him about how some innocent girl had probably gotten him in trouble with the law. They all trooped out to the parking lot — Dad said there was room for at least eight cars — and here was a great big Bentley or Rolls or something like that, and a fellow in a very sharp chauffeur's uniform with polished leather boots leaning up against the fender. Geary went over to him and said, "Are you the guy looking for Ted Geary?"

"Oh, yes, sir, are you Mr. Geary?"

"Well, I guess I am," or some damned remark. Ted was awfully quick with a sharp remark.

The chauffeur said, "Mr. Hole would like to talk to you."

"Who in hell is Mr. Hole, and when does he wish to see me?"

"Oh, at your convenience."

So Ted turned to his crew and said, "How about it, gang, is it convenient?"

Dad said they all piled in the back of the car and there was what we now call a microphone to talk to the chauffeur, and Dad said he hoped the driver had it turned off because they were all taking turns making ribald remarks where they should go and where were the good places. Finally they got to a long driveway up on the hill, and here was this little man, Mr. Willits J. Hole, standing out on the steps waiting for them. He shook hands with all of them and said, "C'mon in, boys, I've got something you'd like here."

Dad said there wasn't one of them that had had a taste of *good* whiskey in years. Mr. Hole, as they soon learned, owned most of the Signal Hill oil fields; he'd been in failing health, and his doctor had recommended that he take up boating and deep sea fishing to regain his health. So, Mr. Hole went on, "Well, you know, I don't know when I've enjoyed three days as much as I have watching you fellows out there and envying you. And I got to thinking, maybe I could have some fun with a little motorboat for fishing. Nothing very big, but I do have a male nurse who goes with me wherever I go, so I'd have to have somebody to run the boat and look after it."

Geary's wheels shifted into high gear at the sound of that, and he got on the train that night, rushed back to Seattle, got out the plans for the *Wanda*, plus photographs of her, put all this stuff together and within 24 hours was on his way back to Los Angeles with preliminary drawings of a stretched-out *Wanda*, a 115-foot, triple-screw diesel yacht.

Mr. Hole took one look at the drawings and said, "Mr. Geary, this is a *yacht*. I can't afford a yacht."

And of course Geary had already gotten a Dun & Bradstreet rating on Mr. Hole and knew he owned most of Signal Hill, so Geary said to him, "Why, Mr. Hole, have you learned a way to take it with you?"

And that's just the way he sealed that deal for Mr. Hole's new motor yacht, which he called the *Samona*, by combining the names of his two grandchildren, Samuel and Ramona. Mr. Hole must have been very much impressed with my dad, too, and I suppose he had done a little snooping around on the waterfront, so the upshot of all this was that Ted completed the design and Dad gave an estimate, and a contract was signed to build the boat for cost plus ten percent, which was usual at that time. Geary got ten percent for designing it.

The *Samona* got built, but not before a fire destroyed the new plant at the foot of Wallingford Avenue. So Dad wired

inset: Willits J. Hole, left, photographed during a chartered fishing trip in Mexico. (BLANCHARD COLLECTION)

above: C. D. Stimson's WANDA of 1922; Ted Geary, designer, N. J. Blanchard, builder. (COURTESY OF MOHAI)

Mr. Hole: "Disastrous fire has levelled the plant, but suitable premises and location is available on lease basis for one year. What is your pleasure?" And, if I remember correctly, a wire came back within an hour or two at the most, which was terribly fast in those days, with just one word: "Proceed."

One evening at dinner, during the building of the *Samona*, Dad said, "You can't guess what happened to me today."

In a chorus, we said, "What happened?"

"I talked on the telephone to Los Angeles for half an hour."

That was at least a $100 telephone call, when you could still buy a Ford for under $900. Dad said Mr. Hole asked him, "Norm, do you ever use any rosewood in the boats?"

And Dad said, "Not very often, Mr. Hole, because it's a very heavy wood, you know, and they don't sell it by the board foot like other lumber. Rosewood sells by the pound."

"Oh, really?" Mr. Hole didn't know that. He said to Dad, "A few years ago we were down in Central America and spent quite a bit of time there one winter with a Señor so-and-so who has a big coffee plantation, but he also has a little logging business there, and he sent me a gift of seven rosewood logs. The damned things have just been lying down here on the wharf where they arrived, and I've been paying a monthly rent on them, so I'm going to send them up to you. I think you can find some use for them on the boat."

I was there with my dad on a Saturday morning, and those logs had arrived. The shortest log was bigger in diameter than I was tall, and I was 11 years old. The yard had a big circular saw, about five feet in diameter, and they made one cut in this log and decided it was too tough. I remember how surprised I was, because the end of the log was just about the same color as strawberry jam, but the sawdust that came out was exactly the color of grated orange peel. So they talked to C.D. Stimson, the owner of the *Wanda*, and they got the logs sawed up over at the Stimson Mill. Of course, they didn't have semi rigs in those days, but that one log, bigger than five feet in diameter, was a full truckload. The longest log was only about two feet in diameter on the big end, but it was 40 feet long, and how they ever hauled that one over to Stimson's I don't know. But every man in the shop who wanted to make a rosewood plane got a nice block of that rosewood.

The entire inside of the *Samona*'s deck saloon aft, and the entire interior of the dining saloon, were nothing but rosewood. They even had some of it sliced up and made into small panels to go between the deck beams. Ted's father, W. S. Geary, owned a piano shop up on Broadway, and he made a piano for that aft saloon that had a solid rosewood case.

And the next thing that happened that really impressed this little boy was that Mr. Hole came up to Seattle in a private railroad car; he had a very fancy limousine on a flatcar behind his private car, and the chauffeur came up with the car. It was a beautiful spring day and Dad had to get to the shop early because there were a lot of things to take care of before Mr. Hole got out there to inspect his boat. He was expecting them around ten o'clock, but they showed up at nine. Dad said they hung around and hung around. The boat wasn't far enough along that they could go aboard it. There was a lot of material that had been dumped outside the delivery doors and hadn't been taken inside yet.

Dining saloon on the SAMONA. Her interiors were all finished in rosewood.
(COURTESY OF PSMHS)

Twelve o'clock came and Dad was wishing they'd get out of his hair. The nearest restaurant was way over on 24th Avenue Northwest, about a block north of Market Street. The man who owned this restaurant had built a canopy over the box of his Model T pickup truck, and he would come down to the yard about a quarter to twelve, back his truck up to the delivery door of the shop, and sell pints of milk, in glass bottles, of course, and individual pies. Well, the truck showed up and Dad walked over and got himself a pie and a bottle of milk, so Mr. Hole went over and got himself a pie and a bottle of milk. He bit into his pie and said, "Gee, Norm, that's a mighty nice pie. I haven't had any better in a long time."

And Dad said, "Yeah, I understand this man's wife gets up at two or three o'clock in the morning to bake these pies, and some of them are still warm when he gets down here."

Mr. Hole finished his pie and milk, and beckoned the man over. He asked Dad to get the information from the book-keeper on how many men there were on the payroll, and Mr. Hole added a few more to that number, and then he asked, "Can you have 60 pies down here tomorrow?" And, yes, the man could do that. So he said, "OK, tomorrow the milk and the pies are on me."

So the next day, just before the bell rang to go back to work after lunch, the men gave three cheers for Mr. Hole, and he thanked them and said, "OK, every Thursday between now and whenever the boat's finished the pies and milk are on me."

And they even built a better place for this man to deliver his pies and milk, where he could back in over a ramp up to the building, which was on pilings, and they had a little counter there where he could set his stuff up — tobacco and things that didn't need refrigeration — so that he didn't have to haul it in off the truck each day. So that was a very happy deal.

There was no place out there on Ballard Beach where they could keep a boat the size of the *Samona* once she was launched, so as soon as she was in the water — and I'm pretty sure I rode down the ways, I remember it was late in the afternoon, around 5:30, because that was when the tide was at the maximum flood — she had to be towed right away through the locks and up to the Seattle Yacht Club dock, to what is now Dock 4. The yacht club immediately received a complaint about all the workmen working on that yacht taking up all the parking spaces. The nearest corner lot was

Launching of the SAMONA, *1923.* (BLANCHARD COLLECTION)

vacant at that time, there was no house on it yet, so Dad got in touch with the owner of the lot and rented it for 60 days for the men to park their cars so they wouldn't have to park on the street.

I didn't get over to the yacht club to see the *Samona* until maybe two or three weeks after the launching, but I was there one Saturday when two Frederick & Nelson delivery vans came up, one right behind the other, and parked. There were three men in each truck, two of them being the boss decorator and one of his helpers, and the boat company furnished some help to them, too, and those trucks were full of furnishings, draperies, all kinds of stuff. I don't know who made the dining saloon set, but it was also solid rosewood.

I'd just love to see that boat again. She was triple-planked Alaska cedar, so it's possible she's around somewhere. She was in San Diego after serving in World War II, but she was sold to Mexican ownership, and it's just about an impossible task to track a boat in that country.

Well, to get back to Ted Geary, his career just blossomed. In addition to commissions to design working boats, he had considerable success with bigger motor yachts after the *Samona* was built, and they were, to name a few, the *Electra*, the *Canim*, the *Principia*, the *Blue Peter*, but those yachts were all built at Lake Union Dry Dock. He also turned out some fine sailboats, like the schooner *Katedna*, which we know as the *Red Jacket*. And in 1927 he designed a new class of small sailboat for the juniors. These Flatties, as they were called, were built at the Blanchard Boat Company.

Ted had always been awfully nice to me; he was really my boyhood hero, and it was very hard for me to understand at the time, although my mother tried to explain it, when he began to push the work to Lake Union Dry Dock, following the disagreement with my dad over Dad's refusal to pay Ted a sales commission. Samuel Rindge, who was married to Mr. Hole's daughter, Agnes, had had Geary design the *Gosling* for him, another one that was built at Lake Union Dry Dock.

One of the most beautiful motor yachts to emerge from a Seattle yard, Willits J. Hole's SAMONA *of 1922-'23 was the largest ever built by the Blanchard Boat Company.* (COURTESY OF PSMHS)

above: C. B. Blethen, publisher of THE SEATTLE TIMES, *commissioned Ted Geary to design the* CANIM, *built by Lake Union Dry Dock Company.* (COURTESY OF PEMCO WEBSTER & STEVENS COLLECTION, MOHAI)

left: The ELECTRA, *almost identical in profile to the* CANIM; *both are 96 feet and were built in 1930.* (COURTESY OF PSMHS)

Ted Geary's daughter, Sharon, later married the Adamsons' son, Merritt. A few years after Merritt Adamson died she married her current husband, Geoffrey Gee, who is a contemporary of mine and grew up sailing on a Senior Knockabout.

Ted continued to work in Seattle as a naval architect until after he married for the second time in 1927. He was elected commodore of the Seattle Yacht Club in 1930, and by that time I think he had one daughter or at least was expecting one. He had had a lot of success in Seattle with the larger yachts, but he finally decided that he had to get out of little old Seattle and go down where the money was in Los Angeles. In 1930 he moved his main office to Southern California, but he maintained an office in Seattle, too, for a few years.

Ted continued to have considerable success in Southern California. He designed the big, steel-hull yacht in 1930 for John Barrymore, which we now know as the *Thea Foss*, and apparently the *Samona* had restored Mr. Hole's failing health

to the point that he ordered a bigger *Samona II* from Ted. This was another steel-hull yacht, 147 feet, built in 1932. Ted had plenty of work all through the years of World War II, but of course he was beginning to get pretty elderly by that time.

After my father had his heart attack in California, he reconnected with Geary. It's strange, but I always thought that if anyone was ever a good candidate for a heart attack it was Ted Geary. He was a heavy smoker all his life, unfiltered Camels. To the best of my knowledge, my father never once smoked a cigarette in his life.

The last time I had a good contact with Ted was when he came up here to design the new rig for a Malabar VII, an Alden-designed schooner. I had redesigned a 22-foot Phil Rhodes sloop into a 25-footer, so Ted came over and laid out the sail plan for me, and we had a nice visit. Ted passed on in 1960, and he was undoubtedly the finest helmsman I ever sailed with and had the pleasure of knowing.

The PRINCIPIA of 1928. She was one of four 96-foot motor yachts designed by Ted Geary and built by Lake Union Dry Dock Company between 1928 and 1930. (COURTESY OF PSMHS)

SAILING WITH RAY COOKE
THE EXTRINSIC YACHTSMAN

RAY COOKE WAS, I think, a little younger than my dad, having been born probably around 1890. He was a Buick salesman, working for A. S. "Pop" Eldridge, as he was known, the Buick distributor for the entire Pacific Northwest region. Ray had been doing well enough in his work that he had purchased a small schooner, the *Clarabel*, and when my father incorporated in 1924, Ray purchased about ten shares of stock in the boat company. For a while he moored the *Clarabel* at our place, and I suppose my dad gave him a little cheaper moorage rate than the Seattle Yacht Club would have charged. Ray was pretty tight with a dollar.

Clarabel was a little unusual as far as her sails were concerned, because she was Marconi rigged. I think my dad may have rerigged her, which would have been how my friend, Ray Fletcher, got acquainted with Ray Cooke. Ray Fletcher was six years older than I was, and worked for my dad. He and I started to sail with Ray Cooke on the *Clarabel* when I was in my mid-teens. Ray Cooke was not the easiest guy to sail with, because you were expected to contribute time and work, and you also shared in all the expenses, especially the food. Ray Cooke was the opposite of what you would call a gourmet, just 180 degrees in the other direction. His idea of a nice breakfast on a cruise was to mix up a big can of tomatoes with about half a dozen eggs. Ray Fletcher and I sailed on the *Clarabel* in the Tri-Island Race — Protection, Hat and Vashon islands.

In 1924 I went with my parents in the first of the Blanchard 36-foot stock cruisers to the Pacific International Yacht Association (PIYA) Regatta in Vancouver, B.C. After the regatta Ray Fletcher was planning to go for a cruise in the Gulf Islands on the *Clarabel*, and Ray Cooke asked me to come along. The Cookes had a foster son, I guess you'd call him, because they had not adopted the boy. The boy was seven or eight years old, and while I was crazy about sailing, this youngster was pretty much of a dry land boy, and I always

Ray Cooke, CA. 1924. (ASAHEL CURTIS PHOTO, COURTESY OF SEATTLE YACHT CLUB)

thought the kid was very lucky that Ray didn't adopt him. I don't know where the boy was from, or whatever happened to him. Ray's first wife, who owned the Pembroke Hotel on Marion Street in downtown Seattle, later divorced him. To return to that cruise, my parents agreed that I should go. Ray Cooke loved to swim, and somebody had told him that there was some nice, warm swimming in the Gulf Islands. Right across from Crofton, at Booth Bay on the west side of Saltspring Island, we found the water beautiful and clear, and every bit as warm as Lake Washington. You could see your anchor in 50 feet of water. We stayed at Booth Bay for two nights, maybe three, and returned to Seattle.

In 1925 the PIYA Regatta was held in Tacoma, and there was just no wind over there. Ray had taken the *Clarabel* over, but he couldn't stay with the boat, so Charlie Seaborn and an old friend of his who liked to sail, and we three boys, meaning Ben and Jack Seaborn, the twins, and I, all drove over in Charlie's Studebaker. In 1925 I would have been 14, and the twins about 12 or 13, so if all three of us tailed on a line we could do pretty well, but we certainly weren't grown men by any stretch of the imagination.

Ray and Ben were continually experimenting with the sails on the *Clarabel*. Ray Cooke always insisted on buying his sails from Sunde & d'Evers, a sailmaking firm in Seattle. They had a pretty fair quality of workmanship, but a very poor quality of material, 50 if not 100 years behind the times, and this hampered Ray, who, even if he had really good sails, was more or less challenged as a real yachtsman in his efforts to win.

Ray's chief rival at that time was the *Gwendolyn II*, Fritz Hellenthal's 48-footer. The 1926 Vashon Island Race was held in the late summer, probably about a week before Labor Day weekend and the beginning of school for us boys. Mrs. Seaborn brought the twins and came on the race with us. It was a beautiful day, but the wind was light, and it was about two o'clock before the race got started. The *Clarabel* and the *Gwendolyn II* were the only two contenders. Fritz was playing the tides, but Ray didn't really know the tides the way Fritz did, so the *Gwendolyn II* got way ahead of us. We did eventually get up to Blake Island, favoring that west side of the sound, which, of course, was the wrong place to be; the Seattle

side would have been much more in our favor. Eventually, I got sleepy, and asked permission to turn in.

About halfway through the night Ray came below and woke me up. "Norm," he said, "we're at anchor right here at Vashon Heights, and I'd like you to come up now and stand anchor watch while the rest of us get some sleep."

The twins and I had been in the forward stateroom, which was pretty small, and Ray Cooke and Mrs. Seaborn were sleeping together in the main cabin. Ray's first wife had divorced him by then, and Mrs. Seaborn had been widowed the previous year. Ray had begun courting the widow Seaborn. Nonetheless, I remember thinking at the time that that just wasn't right, two people who weren't married shouldn't be doing that, although I never told my parents about it. Later that winter, I think, Ray Cooke and Mrs. Seaborn got married. It was kind of a strange union. Ben told me that all Ray contributed financially to the family was $50 per month, even before the Depression, when he was doing pretty well selling Buicks.

Whether Sunde & d'Evers finally started using better material I don't remember, but eventually Ray got the *Clarabel* so she was doing pretty well. The twins were by then around 17 years old, and I wasn't sailing as much with Ray because I was racing my Flattie. Around 1929 Ray was sailing the *Clarabel* off Royal Roads, Victoria, and a photographer by the name of Miller managed to get a really gorgeous picture of her. It was largely through that photograph that Ray later was able to sell the *Clarabel* to a man in California.

After the sale of the *Clarabel* Ray turned Ben loose on the design of a new boat. This was 1932, and Ben was still a senior at Broadway High School. Ray was enamored of a boat named the *Nina* that had won the Trans Atlantic Race to Spain in 1928. Ben ended up designing the *Circe* for his stepfather, somewhat along the *Nina's* lines, and I remember that everybody at the Seattle Yacht Club and along the waterfront was really excited about this project, because, at 58 feet, *Circe* was a really big sailboat.

Ray had stumbled across a good buy on some second-hand teak down at Todd Dry Docks. This teak had come out of one of the big battleships, and there were two, possibly even three, truckloads of big timbers and planks. However, it was all covered with black pitch and red lead, and that entire summer Ray and the twins worked every Saturday afternoon and Sunday scraping that teak. It was a dirty job. The scraper would break and splatter the pitch all over them, and then the sun and body heat would melt it. Their clothes were always a terrible mess, but they stuck with it. A lot of us came to feel that summer that Ray Cooke had probably married Mrs. Seaborn because he wanted those two boys more than he wanted her.

Now since Ray had stock in the Blanchard Boat Company, my dad fully expected to be awarded the contract to build the *Circe*.

Ray Cooke's CIRCE, *designed by Ben Seaborn in 1932.* (COURTESY OF SEATTLE YACHT CLUB)

However, he came to find out, and I suppose it was Ray who told him, that Lake Union Dry Dock had given him a bid to build the *Circe* that was way below what he had been expecting. This was a big blow to my dad, who had been counting on that contract. We learned in time that Jim Chambers, who formerly worked for my dad, and four of the top men at Lake Union Dry Dock were going to be laid off on a "we'll call you when we get some work" arrangement. Even though two of those guys were officials in the union, and that was just the worst thing a union man could do, they wrote up a labor contract. That's how desperate people got during the Depression.

One of those men, the joiner boss, had earlier been hired away from my dad by Lake Union Dry Dock. Larsen was his name, and he had been trained in the old country and was an excellent worker. Larsen was busy building all the furnishings and interior fittings for the *Circe*, and the other three guys were building the hull, when the joiner shop caught fire and the whole project burned up. All of the interior furnishings were lost, so Ray came to an agreement that for rebuilding the boat, the interior finish would include more enamelled surfaces than natural wood finishes. By today's standards, this is really nicer and lighter for down below in a sailboat.

Eventually the *Circe* was launched, and Ray was still buying sails from Sunde & d'Evers, even though George Broom was making all sorts of commercial sails, and Otto Sturham, an old Scandinavian, made excellent sails, doing 85% of the sewing himself. Anyhow, Ray had some kind of tie-in with Sunde & d'Evers and he just stuck with them all through his sailing years.

An experience that made Ray Cooke really aspire to enter the *Circe* in the Honolulu Race was his having been invited some years earlier to crew on the *Invader*. The *Invader* is a beautiful steel-hull schooner, 130 feet long, and, she's still in existence down in San Diego. She was owned by Mr. Don Lee, who had the Cadillac distributorship for all of California, and was based in San Francisco. Ted Geary was invited to be the sailing master for the Honolulu Race, and he was directed by Mr. Lee to bring as many really good sailors as he could from this part of the country. Swift Baker was one of those, along with Lloyd Johnson, and they had an enormous union crew of about 30 altogether, made up of both professionals and amateurs. This must have been one hell of an expensive trip for Mr. Lee.

Well, that experience on the *Invader* led Ray to enter the *Circe* in the Honolulu Race; this was probably around 1936 or '37. The crew was made up mainly of friends of Ben's and Jack's; Mayor Dore's son, John, who later became a prominent attorney in Seattle, was in the crew. The *Circe* didn't do particularly well in the race, but some photographer did manage to get some awfully pretty pictures of her. One of them is hanging at the Seattle Yacht Club, but the sails are all baggy.

Ray and the twins sailed the boat back from Hawaii by themselves, and the boys did most of the sailing because Ray was seasick much of the time. Whenever Ray went on an extended cruise he would inevitably become seasick. Of course, it's really a downwind race going over to the islands, but a hard beat to windward all the way back. What they did was to beat to windward until they caught the northwest trade winds, which in summertime are pretty good, and by then they were about as far north as Queen Charlotte Sound and could square off and come in on a broad reach, and from then on it was a really lovely sail. I remember the twins talking about how they could smell the fir trees two or three days before they sighted land.

Ray entered the *Circe* in the Honolulu Race twice more prior to World War II, never doing particularly well. Eventually he and Mrs. Seaborn were divorced; this was either right before or during World War II, as I recall. Ray had the *Circe* until he died, and he lived aboard her at Marina Mart on Lake Union. Much to Ben's disgust, he cut the top of the mast off. I think that he was always kind of afraid of the boat. He just never had it in him to be a natural, really top-rate yachtsman.

In time he got to the point where he could no longer drive a car, so he started riding a bicycle everywhere. It was really quite amazing, considering he was getting along in years by then. Toward the end of his life I'm sure that Ray was pretty much down to his last nickel. Ray Cooke died within a few years of my dad, and he left the *Circe* to his stepson, Jack. Eventually someone did get the boat away from Jack, and took her over to Beaux Arts on the eastern shore of Lake Washington, where she sat summer and winter for years, decks leaking and getting really down at the heels. Finally she was brought back to Lake Union and put up on the beach where the Center for Wooden Boats is now located.

The owner had to replace a hell of a lot of frames, which required him to pull a lot of planks around the turn of the bilge to get at the frames. He tore off the original house, which was a damned good one, and built a much larger house, because he thought he was going to put the boat in charter work. My friend, Bob Lamson, persuaded me to come down and look at the boat one day. I had been down on my own to inspect her a couple of times when she was still open, and I certainly didn't think the work was first class by any means. When Bob and I looked at her the *Circe*'s hull was closed up, and she had the bigger house on, but down below she was wide open, no cabin sole, open right down to the bilge and keel.

I asked, "What condition did you find the old keel bolts in?"

He asked me, "What do you mean?"

I said, "Surely you've checked the keel bolts?"

"We don't think so," he replied, "not while we've been working on the boat."

Well, I knew from what Ben had told me that they had had a lot of trouble getting the bolts through. The iron keel was so big and heavy, and shaped like a keel should be, that where the gate came in, the hottest metal, the cores floated up and the holes weren't straight. They had really had to work like hell to get the holes straight enough so that they could get any kind of bolts through them, and the result was that sometimes the bolts used were smaller than originally specified. So I hope that someone has replaced those keel bolts in the years since I looked her over. After all, she's about 70 years old, and it would be just amazing if those original keel bolts are still all in good condition.

Anyway, the *Circe* was a wonderful design, especially for a kid who was still in high school when he designed her, and we have Ray Cooke to thank for her existence. Ray Cooke was never the yachtsman that he aspired to be, but he was a man who played a big role in my early years of sailing.

A MEMORABLE DAY WITH FRITZ HELLENTHAL
ON THE *GWENDOLYN II* AND SOME MUSINGS
ON DROWNINGS AND OTHER TRAGEDIES

FREDERICK C. "FRITZ" HELLENTHAL owned Hellenthal Plumbing & Heating on Rainier Avenue South, and served as commodore of the Seattle Yacht Club in 1925 and '26. He was the youngest man on the crew of the *Sir Tom* during the second year of her career, which would have been 1915. I don't know about any racing he did prior to crewing on the *Sir Tom*, but he must have had some experience. Fritz was of German descent, and he looked German, but he was very popular, and this was during the years of World War I. Fritz did not serve in the war, to the best of my knowledge, although he was the right age. He was very much involved with his business, and quite possibly had started his own family, which eventually consisted of three girls, so I suppose that kept him out of the service in World War I.

The *Gwendolyn II* was a 48-foot yawl. My dad built her for his two partners, Dean and Lloyd Johnson, in 1907. Dad worked every day planking her, and all those planks on that boat were full length. Dad really must have had some ingenious methods of hanging those long planks with ropes and shores because clamps and edge sets were scarce. The Johnsons took *Gwendolyn II* in the first Trans Pacific Race, San Francisco to Honolulu, and won second place.

There was a hell of a bad northwest blizzard the winter of 1915-'16, and most of the boats moored out at West Seattle in those days were taken up the Duwamish River or to some other snug harbor, such as Winslow or Port Madison. In fact, there is a good photograph of the boats moored in the Duwamish River at the Johnson Bros. & Blanchard yard with the snow piled up about 14 or 15 inches deep on their decks. The *Gwendolyn II* got pretty badly damaged, and the Johnsons were out of town, so somebody took pity on them, or on the boat, and took her up the river a little bit above the old jack-knife bridges and put her up on a sandbar. She lay there all during the war until about 1919, with the tide running in and out of her. Gradually, she was pretty badly stripped of bronze hardware and anything else the junk dealers would buy.

Fritz Hellenthal bought the *Gwendolyn II* in that condition, probably for something around $1,000 or less, and gradually he got her back into service again, and she was really the dominating sailboat from the Seattle Yacht Club fleet in competition throughout the 1920s. Fritz was very active with the Canadians; he always went to the PIYA regattas, and it was always with a stag crew. However, every summer he took his wife, Nora, cruising, along with his three daughters, who were quite small at that time. He had an agreement with Nora: "If you will come with me cruising on the boat and take care of the children, I'll do everything else, all the cooking, all the washing up, all the sailing, everything." This is how the girls learned to love sailing, on those cruises of two weeks or more each summer.

left: The GWENDOLYN II *with original gaff rig.* (COURTESY OF SEATTLE YACHT CLUB)

below: The GWENDOLYN II. (COURTESY OF MOHAI)

I had my only sail with Fritz on the *Gwendolyn II*, just the two of us, from Port Madison back to West Seattle on October 7, 1928, when I was a half-grown teenager. The Seaborn twins, Ben and Jack, were about 14, and the three of us were sailing with Ray Cooke as regulars on the *Clarabel*. The event was to be Junior Day on Senior Boats, a Sunday race that was supposed to start off Port Madison. As it turned out, I did have a remarkable sail with Fritz that I remember to this day, but it was also a day laced with a tragic drowning.

Fritz already had the *Gwendolyn II* anchored in Port Madison, and Quent Williams was going to be the committee boat. We left the Seattle Yacht Club on board the *Clarabel* at 6:30 or 7:00 AM. It was blowing so hard that I think we waited a little while at the locks; it was a very bad blow. All we put up for the crossing was the foresail, and we sailed across to Port Madison with the engine going. She had a four-cylinder Buick engine that had been converted to a marine engine, because Ray Cooke was a Buick salesman.

There were two other junior members with us, who were probably around 24 or 25 years old. The twins and I were pretty much down below out of the way because there was a lot of spray and it was pretty cold. I remember I didn't have any oilskins of my own, which we wore in those days to keep dry. Except for the fact that the wind was very strong, it wasn't such a bad day, and we got into Port Madison and found the *Gwendolyn II* anchored just about where the Seattle Yacht Club outstation is now. There was a kid standing in a flatbottom skiff, hanging onto the *Gwendolyn*'s rail.

Fritz called over to Ray Cooke and said, "Quent called George Broom from the yacht club and George sent his boy Rupert," motioning to the kid in the skiff, "over here to tell me that none of the juniors who were going to come over and race with me showed up, what with this wind. He also talked to the Weather Bureau and we think that we should cancel the race. Could you let me have one or two of your fellows to help me sail the *Gwendolyn* back to West Seattle?" And that's how I got my one and only sail with Fritz Hellenthal on the *Gwendolyn II*.

Fritz enjoyed cooking, and in a working man's sort of way he was something of a gourmet. Ray Cooke was absolutely the opposite of Fritz in that respect. Ray's idea of a meal on a boat

was *anything* out of a can. In those days we didn't have any frozen stuff, and a lot of the canned stuff has been greatly improved since then. Fritz got me down in the cabin, and he asked, "Are you warm enough? Do you have enough clothes on?" I pulled up my navy blue surplus bellbottoms and showed him that I had on my long underwear.

He said, "Well, we've got plenty of clothes on board *Gwendolyn*," and, as I recall, he even outfitted me with oilskins. He asked, "Are you hungry?"

I said, "Well, as soon as we doubled the spit the Seaborn boys and I ate our sandwiches."

"Sandwiches?" he asked.

I said, "Yeah, on Mr. Cooke's boat we always bring our own lunch."

"Well," he said, "I'm going to have some ham and eggs and hashbrowns. You could eat a little ham and eggs, couldn't you?" I allowed as how maybe I could, and so Fritz got out two big spiders — the stove had been going all night — and he asked, "Do you drink coffee?"

I said, "No, I don't drink coffee, Mr. Hellenthal."

"How about cocoa, chocolate, do you like that?" he asked, and I said, "Well, sure, that's great." Immediately he reached into the icebox, which was a top-opener, and got out a glass quart bottle of milk, and dumped the whole thing, cream and all, into a saucepan to make hot chocolate just for me. I've forgotten if the eggs were over easy or scrambled, but it was sure good.

Fritz had provisioned the *Gwendolyn II* in anticipation of having five or six hungry juniors as guests. I was just finishing my hot chocolate when he opened the oven door and with a spatula brought out an Augustine & Kyer Grocers butterhorn. They were good-sized butterhorns and were a real treat at our house. If we kids got a quarter or even an eighth of an Augustine & Kyer butterhorn we were lucky. Fritz plopped this whole butterhorn right on my plate, and I thought to myself, "Gosh, I don't know where I'm going to put it, but I'm going to eat it even if it kills me."

As I started to eat it Fritz asked me, "What's the matter, don't you like butter on it?"

I answered, "Well, Mr. Hellenthal, my father says they're called butterhorns because they're made with butter."

"Oh, really?" he replied. "On the *Gwendolyn* we have butter on them," and he took one sweep with his knife across the top of a half-pound of butter sitting in a nice, warm bowl that had been in the oven, and he put about three squares of soft butter on my butterhorn in less than one second.

Just about then the thunderous flapping of a sail caught our attention, and we looked out and here were these two fellows in a small sloop, 25 feet or so. It was Harold Yetterdahl's boat, the *Codger*, a raised-deck sloop very much like the east coast Victory Class, designed by Ted Geary.

Harold Yetterdahl was a student at the University of Washington and a junior member of the Seattle Yacht Club who was somewhere in his early 20s, and his friend and mate on the boat was Professor Hugh Frame, who was the professor of transportation at the University of Washington. They had a reef in the mainsail, and had dropped a little stock-and-bar type kedge anchor, probably not more than 25 pounds, and the wind was blowing so hard that they were dragging the anchor like it wasn't even there.

Fritz called out to them, "Don't monkey with that damned little pick. C'mon and tie up to the *Gwendolyn*. We've got 200 pounds down, all chain, and we've been here all night and haven't moved." So they were glad to do that because they were soaked to the skin. Fritz gave them each a shot of whiskey, and then he proceeded to fix the same meal for those guys that he and I had eaten, and all the time he was telling them that there was too much damned wind and it was too rough out there for their little boat. He said he could loan them a good anchor, a 40-pounder, and that Mr. Broom would be very glad to have one of his boys check the *Codger*'s bilge every day, and they could come back on the following Saturday or Sunday and take the boat back to Seattle. However, Harold and Professor Frame were stuck with appointments and had to get back that afternoon, so they put in a second reef and set a tiny little storm jib, and they started back for the locks.

This incident had delayed our own departure, and Fritz was very anxious to get going, so he didn't even bother to clean up the galley. We had to hand crank the windlass to get the chain up, and I think he started the engine. It was a two-cylinder type, more or less what is called today a heavy duty engine. As soon as we got a little way out I steered while he got up the main, and this was heavy work on a 48-foot yawl with a gaff rig: two halyards were required. A short way out Fritz took the peak halyard up about a quarter of the way and then he took both halyards at once, and he got it about 25 or 30% up, and he had to belay one of those halyards while he took the other one up.

We had a fair wind out of the bay, and Fritz looked at his watch and said, "The goddamned ebb has started, so we'll have to run the power when we go through Agate Pass." Then he gave me a little lecture about how the exhaust of the *Gwendolyn II* came up through a gooseneck and then went out both sides. It was a real advantage on a sailboat in a situation of this kind because you could sail on either tack and still have the engine helping. We got through Agate Pass — of course there wasn't any bridge there then — and the mainsail began to tear, so Fritz said, "Well, we'll have to go into Manzanita and drop the hook again and reef the main and put up the mizzen and put on the outer jib." We'd been sailing with just the club staysail or inner jib. So we did that and got underway again, and when we got around Battle Point it began to get dusk.

By the time we got to Rich Passage it was dark, but it was the first broad reach sailing and easier and faster than beating all the way up the backside of the island. The weather started to clear and the moon came out. I sure remember that sail across Puget Sound to Duwamish Head. We just *tore* across there, picked up the mooring buoy by the old West Seattle Rod and Gun Club, which had been the Seattle Yacht Club before World War I, and Fritz took me in his car to the post office downtown, where I caught the Ravenna car that was delivering the morning papers. I think it was pretty close to three o'clock in the morning.

I was very much surprised when I woke up to discover it was well past noon. My mother brought up the morning paper, and there was an article on the front page that Harold Yetterdahl had lost his friend, Professor Frame, overboard. The *Codger* got caught in a trough off Point Monroe, and Professor Frame was pitched overboard. Harold tried to find him, but the wind was blowing the *Codger* in the opposite direction. Quent Williams came to Harold's rescue off West Point, and towed the *Codger* back to the locks. That was a hell of a thing. I don't suppose Frame was married, although he might have been. No body was ever found, and you're not legally dead for seven years in a situation like that when there is no *corpus delecti*.

Later that year Fritz brought the boat into our yard and my dad put new bulwarks on it. I don't know who made the spars, but the next season Fritz came out with the Marconi mast and jib-headed rig, and from that time until after World War II the *Gwendolyn II* was one of the most active sailboats in the Seattle Yacht Club.

That reminds me of another similar situation that occurred a few years before Professor Frame's drowning. Charlie Seaborn, Ben's and Jack's father, was my dad's foreman, and he went overboard from a 110-foot converted subchaser named the *Pandora* just west of Four Mile Rock in Puget Sound. This was in the fall of 1925, I think. As soon as the rest of the party onboard the *Pandora* discovered that Charlie was missing, they turned around and came back through the locks to report it, and the news was reported in the morning paper.

Sometime later I was standing on the pier alongside our drydock with John Wilson, the president of National Steel Construction Company, whose boat, the *Maureen*, was being hauled. John Wilson had grown up in Port Blakely during its boom years, and had gone to school with Charlie and Henry Seaborn. While we were standing there, John said to me, "You know, I've been thinking about this for quite a long time, and I think I ought to tell you. You recall when Charlie Seaborn drowned it was determined to be an out-and-out accidental death. Well, I knew better, and when I read about it the next

The motor yacht PANDORA *was converted by N. J. Blanchard from a World War I subchaser in 1917. Charlie Seaborn jumped off this boat and was drowned, CA. 1925. (COURTESY OF PEMCO WEBSTER & STEVENS COLLECTION, MOHAI)*

Fritz Hellenthal at the helm of the GWENDOLYN II, CA. 1930. (COURTESY OF JUNE HELLENTHAL VYNNE)

morning in the paper I immediately threw some stuff in a bag, told my wife I had to run down to San Francisco and didn't know when I would be back, got in my car and drove downtown.

"I went to a restaurant where a deputy sheriff friend of mine ate pretty regularly. I found him there, and I sat down and said to him, 'Now look, you owe me a favor.' He looked at me and said, 'Yes, I know I do.' So I told him, 'I've got my ticket, I'm leaving on the 8:30 train for San Francisco, but while I'm gone I want you to keep your eyes open, and if they bring in any stiffs out of the salt chuck I want you to look carefully at the hands. If you see the letters C S tattooed on the middle finger just keep it to yourself. When I get back I'll contact you, and I don't want you to say anything to anybody about this conversation.' "

What John knew, and it was pretty common knowledge on the waterfront, was that Charlie Seaborn had taken out a large life insurance policy shortly before his death, naming his wife as sole beneficiary. It wasn't known for sure if he even knew how to swim. So the talk was that Charlie had actually committed suicide.

When John got back to Seattle, sure enough, they had found a body in the sound that was badly eaten by crabs, but it did have the telltale C S tattoo, and there were lead sinkers

in the pockets. In the meantime, Mrs. Seaborn had gotten her double indemnity accidental death insurance payoff, and that kept her in pretty good shape for a while, which was good, because she had three kids to raise.

The daughter, Dorothy, was the first born, and I remember Mrs. Seaborn once told me, and I was kind of amazed because I was still just a teenager, but she said, "You know, Norman, Dorothy was a planned-for baby, but the twins were just an accident. Nobody's ever been able to figure out why it happened, but Charlie came home from town one night drunk, and the twins were just an accident." Dorothy was just fine mentally, even pretty talented at picking out a tune by ear on the piano with her tiny hands, but she never weighed more than 14 pounds. Twins are hard to raise, anyway, and to have been raised with this living doll of an older sister, poor Ben and Jack had two strikes against them from the beginning.

Charlie had made a lot of money in Tacoma building sailing ships during World War I. He had always had a strong interest in drinking, and if it hadn't been for the booze he would have had a fortune. As it was, he always boozed and partied away his money. In 1924 my dad hired Charlie as foreman at the

The five-year-old Seaborn twins, Ben and Jack, in a studio portrait of 1920. No one but their mother could tell them apart. (COURTESY OF PATRICIA SEABORN)

Blanchard Boat Company, and, because his boozing was well known, it was with the very clear understanding that if he came to work with alcohol on his breath, that would be the end of it. I remember that when my dad was building the *Highway*, a Leigh Coolidge design, Charlie was the foreman on that job. He was also the foreman that year for the building of the *Hermina*, designed by Ted Geary.

My dad had a pretty good year in 1924 and Charlie bought some stock in the Blanchard Boat Company in his wife's name. Either that year or the following year the company was incorporated under the name N. J. Blanchard Boat Company, and that year was the only one when my dad could ever pay a dividend.

One time I was at the shop, I'm pretty sure it was on a Sunday, and Charlie had a big block of red cedar, at least two and a half feet long. I came in about the time he was flattening one side of it on the joiner, and the twins were there watching him. Charlie went over and started up the big bandsaw and started sawing out the block by eye for a toy schooner for the twins. My uncle by marriage, Val Vassar, was there. Uncle Val looked after the machinery. He liked to just fuss around in the shop, and I think my dad slipped him a bottle of booze or a five dollar bill now and then. Well, that day Uncle Val was nervous as hell because Charlie was staggering drunk, but he was sawing that block of wood by eye and it was just as perfect as could be.

Eventually Charlie said, "OK, kids, let's go upstairs." He had his toolbox up in the joiner shop, which was above the boiler. He got the head of his adze out of his toolbox, threw the block on the floor, got out his slipstone and sharpened the adze up to perfection, a job that took him about ten minutes, and then started roughing off the extra meat on the block of wood on each side of what would be the keel. My Uncle Val was watching this and shaking his head, because he figured that at least Charlie wasn't apt to hurt himself or us kids with his handtools, but Uncle Val had really been worried about the bandsaw. I've seen that bandsaw break, and when that happened the broken end, about an inch and a half wide, could fly out with such force that it could easily inflict severe injury, or if you were standing in the wrong place it could kill you. So Uncle Val was well justified in being concerned, but

with the adze Charlie only had to work about ten minutes and he had all the meat off that he wanted.

That was as far as Charlie got with the toy schooner that day, and he took the twins and went home. Much later they finished the schooner rig on that model, and they would sail it on Portage Bay right at the foot of East Hamlin Street; they could just barely catch it when it was sailing right. I've often wondered what became of that toy boat.

Keith Fisken was really a patron of Ben's when Ben's skills as a budding yacht designer were beginning to emerge. I think Keith realized that the twins needed to help their mother. Keith was a financial wizard, and I suspect he had some inside information about her financial condition. Eventually Ray Cooke married Mrs. Seaborn, but I think he did this as much to gain a crew for the *Clarabel* as to gain a wife. Ray was something of a frustrated father.

Booze also played a large part in Ben Seaborn's eventual downfall. There may well have been mental problems, too, depression, that contributed to his drinking, but we didn't have much information about those types of things at that time. Anyhow, when Ben's daughter, Patricia, was 15, she came home from Roosevelt High School one day in early December 1959, to find her mother on the floor,

Ben Seaborn, CA. 1955, on the TWINKLE *of 1948, the first of what he hoped would become a class of Seaborn "30s."* (COURTESY OF PATRICIA SEABORN)

semi-conscious from a stroke that had evidently happened as the result of her falling downstairs and hitting her head. Within a few days, Tink was dead. She and Ben hadn't been getting along for some time. Ben had gotten to the point where he couldn't keep a job because he was too drunk most of the time, and he was in financial trouble.

Within a matter of weeks, in late January 1960, Patricia went looking for her father and found him hanging in the basement, just outside his drafting room. He had hooked a piece of hose from the car's exhaust pipe into the back window, but the damned car ran out of gas before the fumes could kill him. This was such a sad situation.

Patricia had a school chum whose father was an FBI man, and when he had heard about Ben's suicide, he asked her where Patricia was.

"Well, she's at a neighbor's home," the girl replied.

Her father said, "Get in the car," and they drove over to the neighbor's house, found Patricia there, and this man said to her, "Get your clothes together. You're going to come down to our house." So Pat went for a while to live with her friend. They had lived on Webster Point in Laurelhurst, but by the time Patricia went to live with them they had moved to North Seattle. This fellow worked directly with the Pacific National Bank, which had all of Tink's funds in trust, just as if he was Pat's uncle. In fact, in time he and his wife did become Patricia's legal guardians.

That summer Patricia was sent east to stay with relatives somewhere in upstate New York, but after the FBI man talked with her relatives by phone a couple of times to check on her, it was decided that she'd be happier in Seattle, so she came back and lived again with her friend, whose dad had been transferred by the FBI to Walla Walla, and Pat completed her high school education there. She now lives in San Jose, California.

I last visited with Patricia when Bill Baillargeon, who owns the *Mistral*, which was originally Keith Fisken's *Romp II*, had a big party for the 50th anniversary of the boat's launching, and invited Patricia. That was a wonderful reunion with well over a hundred people for a sit-down dinner on the lawn of the Seattle Yacht Club, and it was especially good to renew an old friendship with Patricia. After the party several people said that if old Ciebert Baillargeon was able to communicate from the afterlife and knew about that party, he'd probably have rolled over in his casket until he was round as a cylinder!

A few more words about Harold Yetterdahl might be in order. As I said, Harold was a junior member of the Seattle Yacht Club, about six years older than I was. He was one of the big kids among the junior members, while I, at the time, was still very much a "junior junior." Losing Professor Frame off the *Codger* was a terrible tragedy, and it changed Harold's whole personality. I ran into him downtown one day on Second Avenue, and, while he was very civil, it was obvious that he didn't want to stop and chat. As I recall, eventually he became an architect, but he remained very self-conscious all the rest of his life about having lost Professor Frame.

Whether Harold had built the *Codger* by himself or had had professional help, maybe from Quent Williams, I don't know, but she was a well-built boat. After the accident he got Ted Geary to redesign the sail plan. He cut the rig way down, shortened the main boom and the mast, and continued to sail her. It always seemed to me, though, as if he was trying to avoid the yacht club crowd. Of course, it wasn't much of a crowd in those days. I remember seeing Harold from the boat shop out on the lake on a weekday, or I might run into him out on the sound someplace, but I never had any other personal contact with him after that encounter on Second Avenue. Eventually Harold just more or less disappeared, and the *Codger* with him. What became of him or the boat I simply do not know. It's sad how one tragic event could have shaped the entire rest of a man's life.

RAYMOND FLETCHER
BIG BROTHER, BOATBUILDER
DISCIPLE OF CHARLES ATLAS

IN THE FALL of 1923, the year that my father purchased four lots and began construction of the plant on Fairview Avenue, he said, one evening at dinner, "Well, something happened today at the plant..." — or shop, he always said shop — "...that hasn't happened in years."

And, of course, we older kids asked right away, "Oh, what was that?"

"A young man walked up to me. I'd never seen him before, and he said, 'Mr. Blanchard, I want to apprentice myself to you,' " and, of course, there was nothing like an apprenticeship program at the time. Dad went on, "So I talked to him, learned his name is Raymond Fletcher, he's 19 years old, he came from Portland, Oregon, where he worked for the Vanderworths, and he looked like he might be pretty handy. So finally I asked him how much he expected to be paid. And he said, 'I'll work for a dollar a day.' So I said to him, 'If you're not worth two dollars a day you're not worth anything at all.' "

Well, the next day was either Saturday or Sunday, and I was down at the shop with Dad. He had a wonderful big bandsaw at the time with a 42-inch wheel, and I remember that a salesman from some company had left a 12-inch bandsaw for him to try out, and he really wanted that smaller bandsaw. I was using the small bandsaw to make little animal figures or something of that nature, probably toy boats, too. Pretty soon I became aware of a young man standing beside me and

watching me, and it wasn't long before he made a suggestion, and that was my introduction to the young Raymond Fletcher from Portland.

So Raymond started his apprenticeship program at the Blanchard Boat Company, and everybody liked him. He was certainly a willing worker, and he only knew one speed, which was full speed ahead. Raymond already knew how to splice rope and tie quite a few good knots, and other similar things, and he was a quick learner.

The 36-foot raised-deck cruiser DORLEON *with Raymond Fletcher on the bow.* (BLANCHARD COLLECTION)

When Dad had a layoff that included Raymond — and that was not often — he would go back home to Portland and spend some time with his folks, helping them. Shortly after Raymond started his apprenticeship at the Blanchard Boat Company his father decided to go back into placer mining, in which he had had pretty good luck in the past. The Fletchers had a placer mining operation down near Grants Pass, Oregon.

It wasn't too long before I had my first trip away from home unchaperoned, all by myself. I was 13 or 14, and went on the train down to Grants Pass to visit Raymond and his family. The Fletchers' mining operation was on Onion Creek, a number of miles from Grants Pass, and, because they got their mail deliveries so rarely, it was difficult for them to coordinate their trips into town. So I stayed in a small hotel in Grants Pass, which was owned by a couple, and they told me where to eat, which was at a boarding house around the corner and a block away. I stayed in that hotel for three nights, I recall, before Raymond and his younger brother, Milton, who did most of the driving in the family although he was just a year or so older than I was, came into town with a shopping list.

We raced around Grants Pass trying to find the things that they needed, and we bought a lot of groceries, including a 100-pound sack of flour, and then we drove out to Wonder, which was their post office. The post office and store were the only things I saw in Wonder, although there were probably a few houses back in the trees. Then we took off again up a logging road that had many switchbacks, and finally we came to the top of a ridge where there had once been a logging camp. Like most hilltops, it was reasonably level, and the boys had fixed up an old shed so the car wouldn't be out in the weather. After about a hundred yards the trail dropped about 2,000 feet over the next mile and a half before coming to Onion Creek, where the Fletchers were living.

I stayed with the Fletchers for ten days, and most of our efforts during my stay were confined to building a cabin for Raymond. The logs had already been cut, and the way we built the cabin was to stand the logs on end. Then Raymond would find a log that was practically knot-free, and he would split it like a pie and nail the V-shaped pieces between the cracks in the vertical logs. Actually, he did most of the vertical V-shaped pieces after I had left. When I started helping him Raymond had one wall almost finished, and by the time I left to go back home we had the walls 90% or 95% completed and the dirt floor levelled.

Whenever he returned to Seattle Raymond would come to us first for employment. Some of the boats we were building at that time included the *Hermina* in 1924, an express cruiser designed by Ted Geary for Bert Jilg, and certainly the *Malibu*, also designed by Geary, and built for Mrs. Rindge and Mrs. Adamson. And Dad was building several 36-foot standardized Blanchard raised-deck cruisers, as well as the usual types of repair work. As I recall, it was only once or twice during the Depression, when we didn't have enough work for him, that Raymond went over to Grandy's or someplace like that for a while. Much later he confided to me that he would have really had a hard time making it on a dollar a day, which was the offer he had first made to my father, because he had found it was pretty tough going at the two dollars a day that Dad was paying him.

Well, over time Raymond and I became close friends. He was very much like a big brother to me. Raymond had a tremendous physique, tremendous shoulders, but he was short. By age 15 I was as tall or taller than he was, and I still had some growing to do. Raymond was no more than five feet, six or seven inches. And he was a real disciple of Charles Atlas, the great body builder. Raymond and I would often go camping out at Sand Point, when it was still a wilderness, but belonged to the navy, and we'd fix up a camp on the beach. We made these trips in a 16-foot company skiff, and we didn't have sleeping bags, just blankets, and very sketchy supplies. As soon as we got our shelter set up Raymond would fix up a sapling between two trees for a bar, and he would chin himself. He could chin himself with both hands for ages — 40 times was not at all unusual — but he could also chin himself with either hand singly five times. Atlas would have been proud of him!

In fact, Raymond's muscle density was such that, even though he only weighed 130, never more than 135 pounds, when he jumped off our dock into the water to try to swim — it was 12 or 14 feet deep there — he would just struggle to keep afloat. We would struggle to try to teach him to swim, but he always ended up walking ashore.

We had great fun on those camping trips to Sand Point. Raymond taught me to splice rope, and later, by watching him, I learned to splice the wire shrouds for the Knockabouts. I can remember clearly returning from one of those camping trips at about two o'clock on a Sunday afternoon, April 6, 1925. My dad saw us coming, and he walked out to where we were landing and said, "Well, son, you've finally got a baby brother." And that was my mother's sixth child, my brother, Wheaton.

Raymond worked with me on Saturday and Sunday afternoons, and sometimes even in the evenings, helping me build my Flattie, and then he raced with me, especially during 1928, the first year of the Flatties. And, of course, the following fall was the big Crash, so I sold my Flattie to Mr. Deming of Bellingham for sailing on Lake Whatcom.

Raymond and I did a lot of sailing together. Once we even sailed a 36-inch-wide, heavily constructed, 20-foot canoe with a sail that he picked up someplace in Lake Union, and I remember there was snow on the ground and it was well below freezing. Before I was even out of the eighth grade we were sailing with Ray Cooke on his schooner, the *Clarabel*. He

really couldn't afford a boat like the *Clarabel*, so he was glad to have Raymond and me because we could do varnishing and painting and things like that for him. We were willing to do it free in order to go on the overnight races and up to the regattas in Victoria and Vancouver. Raymond was a highly desirable crew member on any boat, and sometimes, when things slowed down in the summer, he would go as a deckhand on Pop Eldridge's 85-foot motor yacht *Alarwee*. It had been designed by Ted Geary for the blind lumberman, Jesse Ives, and was originally called the *Jesimar*. The summer I was 19 years old I crewed on the *Alarwee* for Pop Eldridge for $50 wages, and a most generous tip of $50. Raymond always had plenty of stories to tell about the Eldridge family.

On December 7, 1941, the Japanese bombed Pearl Harbor, and, even though he was way older than most of the fellows who were enlisting, the next day Raymond volunteered for the navy because he really wanted to fight the Japanese. Of course, he had been handling all kinds of guns since he was a very small boy, and he was an excellent shot. He was immediately attached to a specialized bunch of Seabees. There were about 40 of them

above: Raymond Fletcher on the BLUE BOOT, *Star boat #908, CA. 1932.* (BLANCHARD COLLECTION)

right: "Pop" Eldridge's ALARWEE *showing the full-length, deck-level saloon added by Eldridge abaft the wheelhouse. Photographed by the* SEATTLE POST-INTELLIGENCER, *August 22, 1929.* (COURTESY OF THE SEATTLE POST-INTELLIGENCER COLLECTION, MOHAI)

in the outfit and they were all journeymen of one trade or another — a couple of electricians, two or three house carpenters, a steelworker, a welder — but Raymond was the only boatbuilder. They were rushed through basic training and sent down to San Francisco, and from there shipped to the South Seas just after Guadalcanal was considered secure, even though there were still a few Japanese hiding out in the mountains.

These Seabees were strictly a support group for the Marines, and Raymond spent the years of World War II on the big island of Nouméa, which was a French possession, and also on Bougainville. The navy had many enlisted men who had been farmers and office workers, people like that who had never run a boat before, and after 14 months Raymond was so frustrated that he decided if he was ever going to get a shot at a Japanese he was going to have to do something drastic. So he literally went on strike. He refused to work. One example was his story about a brand new, wooden, drop-door landing craft. It had just been dropped in the water from the transport ship, and some yay-hoo lieutenant in gold braid smashed right into the side of it, bow on. Well, he figured he knew how to repair the landing craft, and they immediately got Raymond over there for his opinion, because he was the only boatbuilder, and he said, "You can't repair this boat that way."

The lieutenant said, "Of course you can. All you've got to do is get some of the right kind of goop, and screw a panel of four-by-eight over the damage." Raymond looked it over and told them he wouldn't have anything to do with the repair work. He was constantly getting himself on report for incidents like that.

Raymond did bring back one remarkable story. He told me that a bunch of the guys were gassing around the fire late one night on the beach on Bougainville, and one of the young Marines happened to mention how he had lived all through one winter in a cabin in the Siskiyou Mountains, and it was the most comfortable cabin he'd ever experienced, but it was very different. The logs, instead of being horizontal and notched, were all standing on end. Well, Raymond knew that he was talking about his own boyhood cabin in Oregon, so he spoke up and astonished this young Marine because he said, "Oh, yeah, that was on Onion Creek near Wonder, Oregon."

When the war was over Raymond came back to Seattle. He never married. He told me once that he had had, as far as he was concerned, a very serious high school love affair with a classmate, and something went wrong. In fact, he didn't have anything to do with women unless he was properly introduced by somebody he knew and respected. Of course Eunice and I were married by that time, and my sisters were gone from home, but we had a female cousin living with my parents. Raymond would come by my parents' house, all dressed up, and ask, "Anybody want to go to the show?" And, as long as it was two girls, he was happy to take them to a movie and show them a good time, but he would never take just one girl. He was always quite shy about the fair sex.

Later, Raymond boarded with my mother sometimes, and he would have my old room. Eventually his parents moved up here from Portland, and bought a piece of land, a long strip, 100 feet wide, that ran down to the Sammamish Slough in Kenmore. Of course, Raymond built the house without any plans, and entirely according to his own ideas. One of the things he did that no one had ever seen before was to sink bolts into the top of the concrete foundation wall and bolt the plates down to the concrete. He was also determined not to have any cracks in the driveway, which was for a double garage, so it was wide. He formed it up, and the slab was 9½ inches thick! Raymond was driving either a big old Buick or Cadillac, and it was a nice, heavy, sensible car for him, but he was so small that lots of people, when they met him sitting in the car, thought that he was a kid.

Raymond lived in that house with his parents, and first his father died, and then his mother died, and he continued living there alone, cooking for himself and probably not eating right. Some time went by and the neighbors began to sense that maybe something was wrong, because none of them had seen Raymond for a while. They knocked on his door and got no answer, so they called the sheriff, who came and found Raymond dead on the kitchen floor. The sheriff's doctor, or forensic man, concluded that he had probably had a heart attack while trying to get the refrigerator door open. I don't think Raymond was more than 62 or maybe 65 when he died, and it was a loss I felt quite badly because so much of our younger life had been like an older brother-younger brother relationship.

CHARLIE FRISBIE
THE SILVERWARE COLLECTOR

CHARLES J. FRISBIE was a remarkable man in many respects. His father was a German and his mother a native of Paris, although they met in Grand Rapids, Michigan. His father had come to Grand Rapids because at that time, it was more or less the center where young men learned to become dentists. In fact, my own grandmother had travelled to Grand Rapids for her first set of false teeth, and that is where my mother was born. Charlie's father's express purpose was to learn dentistry and then settle in Paris, because Parisians were famous for their bad teeth. Charlie's mother was the daughter of a French hotel entrepreneur. Eventually, the young dentist and the wealthy young French woman were married in Grand Rapids, and that is where Charlie was born, because his parents wanted him to be an American citizen.

As a child growing up mainly in Paris, Charlie always had nannies, and they were German, French or Swiss. He could not remember a time when he didn't know how to speak French and German, as well as English. Later, after Charlie and I had become good friends, he showed me some of his early snapshot albums, and, honestly, this guy would have been a perfect model for the cartoon character, Boob McNutt.

Every summer, or maybe I should say most summers, the Frisbies would travel from France to Grand Rapids, so Charlie was in Grand Rapids when the United States entered World War I. He lied about his age and was inducted into the army. Nobody in the army could believe that he could speak fluent French. He was sent to boot camp somewhere in Pennsylvania, if I remember correctly, and was then shipped overseas to France.

As soon as they were ashore at Brest the soldiers went marching up the street, with the crowds cheering them. The French people greeting them were either very old or young women, so right away Charlie was fixing up all his soldier buddies with dates. The word finally got out to the top brass that this guy really could speak not only French fluently, but also German, and so they made him an interrogator of German prisoners of war. Charlie could speak German without any trace of an American accent. He was a great story teller, and could josh with the prisoners, and throw them off guard, and wind up getting all sorts of dope from them that they weren't supposed to tell. As a result, after the Armistice, Charlie was discharged as a second lieutenant.

After Charlie's maternal grandfather died, Charlie's mother's two oldest brothers came to his father and said, "We've got to have your help." Their father had left the brothers the hotels he owned, and they needed help to keep them running. In a very short time this became a big enough job and profitable enough business that Charlie's father did not continue with his dental practice. As it turned out, not only the sons, but also Charlie's mother inherited a very sizeable estate and considerable property.

Time went on and Charlie had returned to Grand Rapids. He and an army buddy, Stan Nelson, decided to drive a Model T Ford to Puget Sound by way of Snoqualmie Pass. Neither one of them had ever been out west. When they got to Ellensburg someone told them that they damned well better have a good sharp crosscut saw because they would find trees across the road in the pass, which they did. So eventually they reached Seattle, and the two of them began a Ford agency and garage in Ballard, and it wasn't too long before Charlie had met and married Capitola.

Some years later, in the late 1920s I think, Charlie acquired a funny little yawl called the *Norn*, which had been built for Bill Hedley, the concertmaster of the Seattle Symphony Orchestra.

My first real recollection of meeting Charlie was in 1928 when his daughter, Dawn, was only about six or seven years old. In 1929 Charlie invited me to accompany him up to the PIYA Regatta at the Royal Vancouver Yacht Club on English Bay. I'd been up there the two previous years, racing on the first *Gwendolyn* with Ellis Provine and John Winslow. In 1929 my Flattie was two years old, and I think there were about ten of us Flatties up there. The Canadian builders sold their boats for only $150. They even had square masts; can you imagine anything so horrible as a square mast on a racing sailboat?

That trip to the PIYA Regatta in 1929 was a great experience for me. Charlie had his wife, Capitola — everyone called her Cappie — and her sister, who was only in her late teens, as his crew. My crew for the Flattie consisted of Gary Horder. We all had ten days on the *Norn* that July, and on the way back to Seattle, after we cleared Customs at Roche Harbor, the crankshaft on the engine broke as we were trying to sail in Speiden Channel. Radner Pratsch came powering by in his new cutter, the *White Cloud*, but he couldn't stop to help us. He owned three motion picture houses in Tacoma and one of his projectionists was gone and he had to get back to Tacoma. But, right behind Rad came this big, old power boat, and the captain stopped to give us a tow. I still have a snapshot of all of us sitting with Charlie while under tow back to Seattle. That was really a great trip and we had a grand time.

Cruise on the NORN, *July, 1929. Left to right: Charlie Frisbie, Garrett Horder, Norm Blanchard.* (BLANCHARD COLLECTION)

Charlie's father had always told him that when a man was disgruntled with something, that was a good time to offer to buy it. One day Charlie, Cappie and their brand new baby girl took the Ford over to Fletcher Bay on Bainbridge Island. Charlie saw a man working on a little boat, and the guy was really mad and frustrated, and eventually he yelled, "To hell with it!" Charlie had fooled around with Fords for a while; he knew a thing or two about engines and liked working on them, so he went over and made the acquaintance of this man, eventually got the engine running, and then asked the fellow, "You want to sell it?" Well, I think he bought that first boat for $50 or $75. It had a little one-lung inboard, and the following weekend Charlie brought her through the locks, and kept her in Ballard. I don't recall what became of that boat.

After Dawn, was born, Charlie's parents came for a visit. His father said to him, "Charles, automobiles are nice, but it will be a long time before they are going to be a really big thing. What you want to do is get into some kind of business where everybody needs the product." So Charlie and Stan Nelson parted ways, and Stan eventually jumped from Fords to Chevies and opened Nelson Chevrolet, which is still doing business in Ballard.

Charlie's next venture was running a produce stand somewhere near where the Seattle Center is now. He told me several times how things were often so tough that he would have to open the stand and sell some fruit or vegetables to get enough money to go down to the store and buy some milk for the baby's bottle. It soon became obvious that Charlie was never going to make a decent living peddling produce, so he decided to try to sell life insurance. That opened up a whole new career for him, one that he stuck with throughout the rest of his working days, and eventually he joined the New England Mutual Life Insurance Company.

During the winter of 1922-'23, my dad was building the *Samona* for Mr. Hole and the income from that job allowed him to purchase a new car from Nelson Chevrolet. Charlie remembered meeting me at Nelson Chevrolet the day Dad bought his car, although I don't recall the occasion clearly. He was probably visiting his friend Stan. I can still remember that Chevy that Dad bought. It had windows that you let down with a leather strap, just like the ones my dad was installing in the boats he built.

Radner Pratsch's WHITE CLOUD, *1928.* (BLANCHARD COLLECTION)

Sometime in the early 1930s Charlie showed up at the Blanchard Boat Company one day. He was talking with my Uncle Cal for a while, and then came over to where I was working and said, "I've just been given holy hell."

I asked him what he meant, and he answered that Uncle Cal had said to him, "You call yourself an insurance salesman. Norm has been working here for over two years and you haven't ever said anything to him about buying life insurance." So I ended up buying a policy from Charlie, and later I doubled it, and after we got little Norm I increased it again.

Cappie was the perfect wife for Charlie. All the years I knew her — and, remember, Dawn was six or seven when I first became acquainted with Charlie and Cappie — she was just a trifle heavy. When she was really fixed up, dressed up for a party, she was as attractive as any of the women. At the same time she was great for Charlie because the two of them could go out in the boat, and Cappie would slip into a pair of pants and a sweater, which is all I remember she ever wore during the cruise I went on with them in 1929, and pitch right in.

The Frisbies had a summer home over at Quartermaster Harbor, right on the water on Vashon Island. The way that house had been built was unique because there were no studs or framing. It was a two-story house and the walls were full-length tongue-and-groove, or maybe double tongue-and-groove, but they stood vertical all the way to the top. It got its strength solely from the double-thick, full-length tongue-and-groove. I remember being over there one weekend when Dawn was about eight years old, and, having so many sisters myself, it didn't bother me at all to be around one more girl.

After he sold the *Norn*, Charlie got himself another odd little yawl, called the *North Star*. It was a trifle bigger, with more headroom, and he even kept her at our yard for a while. He kept the *North Star* for three years or so, then sold her, too. She was his last sailboat for a while because he decided to try power boats again. Victor Franck, Vic Franck's father, had a partner by the name of McCreary, and Charlie bought a power boat built by Franck & McCreary. It was their version of a stock cruiser, only about 28 feet long, and without full headroom. Charlie was over six feet tall, and was doing well enough in his insurance business that he was eating a little too well and was probably at least 25 pounds overweight. He had my dad put a trunk cabin on the cruiser so he could stand up straight. He kept that boat a year or two, then sold her and bought the *Alice*, which was a 40-foot navy motor sailer that had been converted to a pleasure craft.

One day in the fall of 1932 my dad was talking with Ben Seaborn, and happened to mention something that had been bothering him: "Why does a cruising sailboat have to look like a goddamned Gloucester fisherman?" Those may not have been his exact words, but he was of the opinion that they tended to look like tubs. Now, Ben was just a senior at Broadway High School that year, but, as a result of my dad's comment, he drew up plans for a 42-foot sloop. My dad was so impressed that he had Ben complete the plans, and this was Ben's very first yacht design commission. My dad paid him $50 for it, and, hell, $50 was a lot of spending money for a kid still in high school. There was even some type of provision to pay Ben extra if more than one boat was built from the design. So we had the plans there in the shop, and my dad and I were quite excited about them; we wanted to get a keel casting going as soon as we had enough money, and go ahead and complete the boat on speculation.

Well, one evening Charlie came into the shop. It was kind of late, around five o'clock, winter time, and he looked first at my dad and then at me, and said, "I'm never," and as he began to speak he hit his fist on the counter, where we had photos under glass, and I thought he might break the glass, but it was quarter-inch plate and didn't break. "I'm never going to be a streetcar motorman for a bunch of gin-swizzling poker players again!" he yelled.

I looked at Charlie and said, "You *sold* the *Alice*!"

"I sold the damned thing," he replied.

I smiled and said to him, "And you want a sailboat."

"I do!" he said. "From now on, anything that floats for me is going to have rags on it."

When we showed him Ben's plan, he fell for it hook, line and sinker, and that's how we came to build the *Tola*, which he named for his wife, Capitola. *Tola* won the Opening Day Class B Race for the Seattle Yacht Club in 1937, and, God almighty,

Charlie Frisbie and Eunice Blanchard on the TOLA, *1937.* (BLANCHARD COLLECTION)

Charlie was just ecstatic when the front page of the sports section of *The Seattle Times* carried the bannerline: "TOLA WINS OPENING DAY, owner Charles J. Frisbie." Ben Seaborn and I were both in his crew for that race, and I can't remember who handled the tiller, but Charlie wasn't a bad sailor by a long shot. Over the years he became a terrific silverware gatherer — by that, I mean he won a lot of trophies — and this got him a lot of publicity, and that's what Charlie liked and needed.

The Frisbies built their house in the 2700 block of Boyer Avenue East on the Portage Bay waterfront, and Charlie could keep the *Tola* right there at their private float. The house had the most dreamy space for a workshop hat you ever saw. He even put a third flue in the chimney for a forge. He had everything you could imagine in that shop.

In the summer of 1938, Eunice and I cruised on the *Tola* with Charlie and Cappie to Princess Louisa Inlet, and as we were coming back down through Sansum Narrows Charlie let out a whoop just about the time we got to the south end of Saltspring Island. "Got a great idea," he exclaimed. "We're not gonna go home tomorrow. Tomorrow is Sunday, so we'll take the boat to the Royal Victoria Yacht Club. We can leave her there for a week, and come back and get her the following weekend."

We all agreed that that would be fun, and then Eunice said to me, "If your father doesn't need you this week, we could

top left: Charlie Frisbie in his well-appointed basement workshop, 1938. (WILEN COLLECTION)

above: The TOLA. (COURTESY OF MOHAI)

left: The TOLA, *1937.* (BLANCHARD COLLECTION)

just stay on the *Tola*, and save the money that it would cost us for steamer fare going down to Seattle and then coming back."

It was August, always a slow month at the boat company, so that's exactly what Eunice and I did. We rode the streetcar several times that week into Victoria, where we generally had a supper of fish and chips, 35¢, and good, I mean *good* fish, and potatoes that were peeled, not like the ones you get now with half the skins still on them. The city of Victoria was dry, but the town of Esquimalt, where the Royal Navy yard was, was not, so one evening we rode the streetcar all the way out there to get a glass of beer, and the roadbed was so wiggly and out of level that you could sit in the back of the streetcar and watch it twist.

The result of our start with the *Tola* was that the Blanchard Boat Company was commissioned by Marcus Mayer, Sr. to build the *We're Here*, her sister ship. Mark Mayer, as he was

The 42-foot WE'RE HERE, sister ship to Charlie Frisbie's TOLA.
(BLANCHARD COLLECTION)

always known, and his brother had started the first wholesale jewelry-manufacturing business in Seattle, and his uncle had also built all the street clocks in Seattle, about a dozen of them in the early years. Mark had grown up in a house on East Hamlin Street, only one block up from the Seaborn home.

Shortly before World War II, Cappie Frisbie had a stroke. By this time Eunice and I were living right across the street from the Frisbies on Boyer Avenue East, and it was very sad to watch Cappie go down. The stroke didn't cripple her badly, but it turned her mind and personality inside out, and she became very religious. Charlie dealt with it for two or three years, but a parting of the ways was inevitable, and he and Cappie were eventually divorced.

On December 8, 1941, Charlie was walking down Second Avenue when he ran into a friend, who asked him, "What are you doing now?"

"Peddling insurance," Charlie replied.

The friend said, "You were in World War I, weren't you, and didn't you come out a second lieutenant?"

"That's right," Charlie said, so the friend said, "C'mon with me," and he took Charlie to the Exchange Building, and he enlisted in the navy.

Because of his rank in the army in World War I, and his age, he was immediately made a lieutenant commander and was sent to Alaska, where he became the commanding officer of the naval facility on Kodiak Island. The United States Navy had quite a repair base up there, and Charlie spent the entire war right there. I don't remember what his discharge rank was, but he might have been a captain. By the time World War II was over, Dawn, Charlie's daughter, had married, and her husband, Jack Bowen, was on a cable layer before and all through the war. Dawn and Jack also were eventually divorced. Jack still lives in Honolulu, after retiring as a captain of the Long Lines, and is still a good friend.

Charlie kept the *Tola* through World War II, but soon after the war was over he sold her to Alan Engle. He bought a Q Class boat, or maybe it was an Eight Metre, but at any rate, her accommodations were not nearly as commodious as the *Tola*'s. She only had an outboard for auxiliary power, but he did sail and race her for a while.

above: The TOLA, CA. 1949. (COURTESY OF SEATTLE YACHT CLUB)

above right: Charlie Frisbie in 1945. (COURTESY OF CORINTHIAN YACHT CLUB OF SEATTLE)

right: The ALOTOLA, *June 12, 1949.* (COURTESY OF PSMHS)

Eventually, Charlie bought the *Renegade*, which was a 57-foot Knockabout schooner rig, meaning she had no bowsprit, from Gardner Gamwell's estate, and renamed her *Alotola* — you spell it the same forward or backward. She was a George Wayland design, and had been built down in Stockton by Stephens Brothers in 1927. She came out on our drydock for a survey, and the surveyor didn't find much wrong with her except for a couple of rotten ribs. Charlie was in a hurry to cruise her, and although he intended to change her rig to a sloop, he took her quite far north with her schooner rig that first summer. In the fall he hauled her to repair what he thought were just a couple of ribs, but the story I got later was that he had a whopping big bill because nearly half of the frames in that boat had to be partially replaced.

It has always been my experience that white oak is an excellent wood for frames, but red oak, milled, is difficult to tell from white oak, and is not nearly as good. I think that some of the lumber suppliers down south were either ignorant or deliberately dishonest, and foisted red oak off for white oak. I suspect that that is what had happened with the *Alotola*.

Well, the *Alotola* had been designed as a staysail schooner for San Francisco Bay, and was a great competitor in their winds, but she was hopelessly short-rigged for Puget Sound. A little earlier Cully Stimson had had us build a new rig for the *Angelica*, and he was doing well with it, so Charlie got Ben Seaborn to design a very similar rig for the *Alotola*, and he was soon winning races with her. Charlie eventually sailed the *Alotola* all the way to Greece in 1960, where he sold her to a Greek shipping magnate.

When Charlie returned to Seattle he was too canny a businessman to have a new boat built twice, so he found a ketch that had been built in Los Angeles. There were quite a few of these boats built; they used the cheapest quality of fir lumber and plywood in them, and then covered them with two or three layers of fiberglass, which was beginning to come into popular use in boat construction. The damned things, hard chined and all, did manage to sail pretty well, and that was Charlie's last boat.

I should mention one other thing about Charlie. He remained an active member of the Seattle Yacht Club all his life, but after World War II was over he was instrumental in establishing the Corinthian Yacht Club in 1945, and he served two terms as its first commodore.

One evening in June of 1964 Charlie was leaving the Seattle Yacht Club, and he was driving a young man home when he had either a stroke or heart failure, and ran into a telephone pole, killing both the young man and himself. A very sad thing, indeed, and the end to a great career as far as Puget Sound sailing was concerned.

Cully Stimson's 52-foot ANGELICA on Opening Day, May 6, 1939.
(COURTESY OF SEATTLE YACHT CLUB)

CAPTAIN FRED LEWIS
MILLIONAIRE "BOATMAN"

CAPTAIN FRED LEWIS was one of the most intriguing guys you could ever meet. He was a millionaire many times over, and had just a fascinating life. All of his boats were called the *Stranger*, except his last one, which was called the *Stranger II*. By that time Fred was living in Canada, and under Canadian maritime regulations there cannot be two vessels with exactly the same name. Fred's vessels were *not* yachts — he would be very emphatic about that — although they resembled yachts in some cases. They were always painted white, because he mostly liked the warmer climates for cruising.

Fred was born in New York and grew up on Long Island Sound. I found out a lot about Fred's childhood from Stanley Seaman, who was our navy inspector during World War II and new to the west coast at that time. Stanley and Fred had been childhood friends and neighbors, and Stanley and I became good friends after he was sent out to Seattle. As a child, Stanley lived right across the road on the main highway on Long Island from the Lewis estate, and, as he put it, "My father's house was bigger than the Lewis gatehouse, but the Lewis gatehouse was a lot fancier than our home." Fred's father was a Wall Street banker, who had negotiated the merger between the Chase and Manhattan banks, and soon afterward he died, when Fred was a small boy. Fred could apparently just remember his father, but not very well.

As a boy, Fred had a playroom that seemed like heaven on earth. It was about 40 feet square, and, near as Stanley could remember, there was enough track and electric trains for them to have a switching yard in each corner of the room. But Fred didn't like electric trains. Real trains ran by steam. So the Christmas morning after his father died, Fred came out of his bedroom, and on the patio sat his new steam train, all fired up and ready to go. As Stanley recalled, there were at least five miles of track around the estate, and, boy, Fred didn't lack for friends after that.

As an adult, Fred became a Wall Street banker as his dad had been, but he had many, many other interests. For instance, prior to World War I he started a marine engine school because men who could run gasoline engines were scarce. The navy took that over as soon as World War I started, and throughout his life Fred always seemed to have a close association with the navy and the military as a whole.

Many years later, after I had made Fred's acquaintance, he and I were on the bow of the Peier brothers' *Neoga II* one day during 1941, sailing in a beautiful breeze on a warm sunny day — in fact, we even had our shirts off. Fred said to me, "You know, you're one of the few people in the world I could envy."

I looked at him and said, "It sounds to me like there's more to it than just that."

"Well," he said, "I can't imagine anything, if I had my life before me, as you do, that I'd rather do than run a boatyard catering primarily to the yachting public, as you and your father do."

I thought a second and said again, "But I think there's more to that story."

Fred laughed. "You probably never heard about it, but I once owned Luders Marine Construction Company. They were building a very special sort of vessel for me," — and I knew instantly that it had to have been a high-speed commuter to get him from Long Island Sound down to Wall Street. "The boat was just nicely started in frame," he continued, "and a few planks were on when the boss said to me, 'I guess I have to tell you, Mr. Lewis, that come Saturday the bank says it's going to close us up.' So I talked with their head accountant for a couple of hours and finally I grabbed a train and rushed down to New York to my office." And he arranged to buy that company, which was in Stamford, Connecticut, and a major east coast yard.

Fred went on with his story. "You know, Norm, I was recovering from a pretty serious illness," — only later was I to learn from Stanley Seaman that it was tuberculosis — "and I decided that the thing for me to do while I was recovering and needing something to occupy my mind was to make a study of the boat business, and I've made it my business to be personally acquainted with every major museum curator in the world."

"No," I said, "I was not aware of that."

He said, "Well, I really went into it. I went as far back as the ancient Phœnicians, and the truth is, nobody has ever made a profit in the boat business or shipbuilding business except in time of war. By a profit I mean a reasonable 10% or 15% average profit over a period of 10 or 20 years, such as Eastman Kodak or General Motors. That's why I couldn't afford to be in the boat business, and the other reason is because it is a profitable business in wartime, and I didn't want anybody to ever be able to call me a warmonger."

Fred had bought his biggest *Stranger* in Denmark in the very early years of the Depression, "when bottoms were going begging all over the world," as he put it. She was 230 feet

Captain Fred Lewis' first STRANGER, built in Sweden for commercial use.
(WILEN COLLECTION)

long, and had been built in Stockholm in 1916, a small, ocean-going commercial ship with twin steam engines, twin screw. And right away, when the ship was still in Denmark, I believe, he had the steam engines removed and replaced with diesels. The reason for that was that he wanted to be able to go around the world without refueling, and why that could be important to Fred I think we shall see. With the steam engines removed she could carry enough diesel bunker oil to do that. But he kept the boilers to run the steam auxiliaries for the ship's generators because steam made no noise when they were anchored at night. Up until the time he went around the world with the big *Stranger* Fred was not licensed, but upon his return from that trip he sat for his master's papers and got them, because, tonnage-wise, the *Stranger* had qualified him.

By this time Fred was living with his third wife out at the tip of the peninsula at Newport Beach, California, and I suppose the estate was small compared to his mother's place on Long Island Sound, but it was pretty nice. When you drove by on the highway you could see that big ship tied up there. The story goes that for his crew on the *Stranger*, Fred had an arrangement with the St. Louis school system for any Sea Scout troop that the school system would agree to let leave on or before the first of May and not return until the first of October to be his crew for his summer cruises. He outfitted those boys in brand new Sea Scout uniforms, underwear, everything. And of course he had a chief engineer, a boatswain, and probably a mate, as well.

He made three of those cruises to the South Seas, every other year, to gather specimens for museums, and on the odd years he went to the Arctic and gathered specimens. He had a taxidermist right on the ship, and he presented the Field Museum in Chicago with two dioramas: one of walrus and one of polar bears. I heard about this probably 40 or 50 years ago, and only recently did I actually get to see them. Since then I've learned that this whole operation — buying the ship, of course, was fun for Fred — was all a cover. What he was really doing was spying on the Japanese. Nobody on the ship at the time, including Fred's friend, Stanley Seaman, had any idea what was really going on.

Fred's legitimate business when he was living down there in Newport Beach was raising hogs. About 1930 he came up here to Seattle to observe how the conveyor belts worked on the Denny Regrade, when they were cutting down the remainder of Denny Hill that had been left after the first part of the regrade was completed in 1911. Then he devised a means of feeding his hogs using conveyor belts, and he got most of his feed, or at least a large share of it, from the garbage contracts in Los Angeles.

Left to right: Captain Fred Lewis, Mrs. Lewis and Ted Geary inspect the second STRANGER, 1938. (WILEN COLLECTION)

Captain Fred Lewis' second STRANGER, designed by Ted Geary and built by Lake Union Dry Dock Company in 1938. (COURTESY OF PSMHS)

About 1932 Fred bought Coal Island up in British Columbia, right off Sidney, with the idea of making it his permanent residence. He didn't leave Newport Beach immediately, but he spent a lot of money on Coal Island. He built a small, but beautiful, home, and as soon as his wife was pregnant he built another very nice home just far enough away so that he wouldn't be able to hear the kids cry. In time Coal Island came to be Fred's primary residence.

Fred joined the Seattle Yacht Club in 1934. Just when he got rid of the great vessel that was built in Sweden I have no idea, but he had Ted Geary design him another *Stranger* that was built at Lake Union Dry Dock in 1938. She was a wooden hull, twin-screw, ocean-going vessel, 134 feet. Fred called this his "hobby boat" and he didn't hesitate to experiment in her construction, but of course why should he? He couldn't begin to spend his money as fast as it came in. Well, Fred only had one cruise to the South Seas in the new *Stranger* because she was taken over by the navy in 1941. When she came out of the service after the war she returned to private ownership in Los Angeles, but in 1955 she was donated to the Scripps Institute of Oceanography and was removed from documentation the following year, and I don't know what's become of her.

The next boat of any size that Fred owned was a little steam towboat which he called the *Sea Puss*, and I had a role in events involving that boat. One day during World War II Stanley Seaman and I were standing on the front dock at the boat company on a warm spring day, when I looked out over the lake and said to him, "There goes an end of history, Stan."

"What do you mean?" he asked.

I said, "See that little steam engine coming out of that boat over there? That's the *Mercer*. She's been running on that engine since she was built at Mercer Island in 1916, and they're putting a gas engine in her to run across the East Waterway over at the new Todd destroyer yard."

"Do you know what they'll do with it?" he asked.

"I would imagine that it'll go to salvage, junk," I replied.

"Oh," he said, "I've got to get over there."

And he high-tailed it off, and, sure enough, Fred Lewis came down and bought that engine for his little towboat. He only had a two-cylinder compound engine for the boat. She had a good boiler, very modern, a fine boiler, but he needed more engine and he couldn't find one, so the *Mercer*'s engine went into the *Sea Puss*. Fred called the boat the *Sea Puss* because she moved about so quietly. Later, however, he came to the conclusion that a surplus "Jimmy" — a GMC diesel — was the best thing for the boat and he took out the steam entirely, which also made her a little bit more commodious, because with the boiler out he had more room for accommodations.

Another day Stanley was in our office when I was showing our bookkeeper, Lorraine Slingsby, some of my boat pictures in an album. "Oh," he said, "I've had several trips with Fred Lewis on his big *Stranger* that he sold a while back, and I'll bring a couple of my albums down." Well, eventually we got him to bring all five of them, and those albums were full of snapshots, each album covering a different cruise.

In 1945 a bunch of us were sailing up in Canada on the *Cavu*, which was a 40-foot ketch, designed by Ed Monk for Grover Tyler, and built by the Blanchard Boat Company. Grover had been a pilot for United Air Lines, and had left them to become a test pilot for Jack & Heintz in Cleveland. Well, about the time we cleared Customs at Sidney I discovered that we had an exhaust pipe leak. Grover was kind of chintzy about engine installation. The *Cavu* had a very common twin side outlet exhaust system, where the exhaust fed into a "T" and went out both sides of the boat. We stopped at Coal Island to fix the leak. The question was simply one of getting one of the fittings replaced, and the fitting was available, but Fred's biggest pipe tap was one inch. So after we got all the things ready to go on with our cruise, Fred asked me, "Do you think you could find me a proper one and 1¼- or 1½-inch pipe tap?"

I said to him, "I think I could."

He said, "If you could I'd very much appreciate it if you'd buy it for me."

I shipped them up to him without a bill. After all, he'd helped me out. Within two or three days, I think it was, Fred was down in the office and said, "Norm, I ordered those and I expect to pay for them." And pay for them he did, a matter of $25 or $30, but that's the way he was, a very unusual man.

Some years later, probably in the mid-1950s, I was in Victoria, B.C., for some kind of a yachting meeting one spring, and I was going over to Vancouver on the Canadian Pacific steamer, traveling alone. A young fellow came over to me and started talking, and pretty soon he said, "You seem to know a lot about this area up here."

I said, "Well, I've been cruising in small yachts since I was a boy."

He said, "I've got a friend up here who has an island called Coal Island. You wouldn't know that island, would you?"

I said, "Sure, that's Captain Fred Lewis' island."

"Oh," he asked, "do you know Fred?"

"Yes, I do."

"Well," he said, "I haven't seen him since, but a few years ago I was on a Matson Line ship going out to Singapore." He explained that the ship probably had no more than 100 passengers, and, as usual on those ships, a lot of them were widows or single women having a trip, and he went on, "I soon realized that this little guy who didn't impress me was my main competition, so I decided to get better acquainted with his technique. We were leaving Hong Kong, and we were on a first-name basis by then, and he asked me, 'You're not getting off in Manila?' 'No,' I said, 'I have to go on to Singapore.' 'Well,' he said, 'I understand from the captain that we'll be at least three days there, and we arrive tomorrow, and I thought maybe you'd like to do something for me, which I would very much appreciate, and that is to stand up with me when I get married.' And I told him, 'Naturally, I'd be honored.' Well, imagine my astonishment when I discovered his bride was a gal 18 years old."

It turned out that the girl's father had been a roommate of Fred's in college, so Fred had known this girl since she was born, practically, and she finally wanted to marry him, and her parents had no objection. She and Fred were still married at the time this conversation took place, so I pointed out Coal Island as we went by. I explained that we couldn't see Fred's house because it was located in a harbor on the northwest end of the island, and that the house we could see was the farm manager's house, which had been the home of the people Fred bought the island from.

Fred bought his last boat up in Canada soon as World War II was over, and she was the one he had to name *Stranger II*, with the Roman numeral. She was a surplus Fairmile, about 112 feet, as I recall; they were much more seaworthy and sea-kindly than our torpedo boats, but they didn't have quite the speed of ours. There were quite a few of them, ten or more, that had been built in Vancouver, B.C., and at least five or six of them went surplus after the war, and several millionaires purchased them. Of course Fred took out the big gasoline engines and replaced them with diesel, and he did all that work right there at Canoe Cove by hiring direct labor. The Danish Bendixen brothers — I think there were three or four of them — worked for Fred during this early post-war period, and one of them started the Bendixen yard on Portage Bay right east of the University Bridge.

The *Stranger II* was Fred's yacht, or boat, as he would have insisted, until he died in 1962. And that is pretty much the story of Captain Fred Lewis, certainly one of the most memorable persons I ever had the pleasure of knowing.

Captain Fred Lewis' STRANGER II *at Coal Island, 1946.* (Blanchard Collection)

HORACE W. McCURDY
BUSINESS LEADER, YACHTSMAN, AUTHOR

H. W. McCURDY was born in Port Townsend, Washington, in 1899. The "H. W." stood for Horace Winslow, but most people knew him simply as "Mac" McCurdy. He grew up in Port Townsend, and as a youngster had quite a bit of experience working on various small commercial vessels. He had an Uncle Will who owned a little Port Townsend shipyard called Madison Street Marine Ways, and no doubt Mac worked around that yard.

In 1915, after he graduated from high school at the age of 16, Mac enrolled at the University of Washington. This was many years before the university had made a name in football, but rowing was becoming quite popular, and Mac turned out for crew, which was then coached by Hiram Conibear, the father of modern college rowing. However, as the war was going on in Europe, and it looked like we were going to become involved in the hostilities, Mac decided that he would enlist in the navy. So, he went over to Bremerton to enlist, hoping to be sent to Europe, but this didn't happen, at least not right away.

You see, there was an elderly man named Ed Sims living in Port Townsend who had a fine ketch, 120 feet, called the *Anemone IV*. This man was sure we would get involved in the European war, and he probably figured his ketch could be put to use by the navy, so he made a deal with the then-admiral of the 13th Naval District, who was an old friend of his, to take over the boat. This was on the condition that Horace McCurdy would be the machinist's mate in charge of the engine on the boat. So immediately Mac got transferred from Bremerton to Portage Bay.

One of the first things that happened, once the U.S. got involved in the war, was that the lower campus of the University of Washington, the land now occupied by the medical school, became a big Naval Officers Candidate School, and training station. We were living in Laurelhurst at the time and, especially in the better days of summer, we'd see those boys in their blue uniforms on a forced march past our house.

The admiral was living aboard the *Anemone IV* in Portage Bay, and Mac's first job every morning was to row over to the south side of Portage Bay and pick up the admiral's secretary, Anne Bathurst. Now Mac didn't like this assignment at all; he wanted to go to Europe, so I guess every morning as he was rowing this gal to work he'd complain to her. Apparently she kind of liked Mac, and eventually she interceded for him and talked to her boss, so finally he managed to get transferred off the admiral's ketch, and he spent the rest of the war as a gob on a navy transport running back and forth across the Atlantic, with hardly any shore leave on either side.

Mac must have had a good work ethic instilled in him as a youngster. He sure didn't have any veterans' benefits when he got out of the navy, but he decided that in order to get the education he felt he needed, he would enroll at the Massachusetts Institute of Technology. So he went home and worked and saved his money, and, with that and what his family could give him, he entered M.I.T. in the fall of 1919.

However, before he left Port Townsend he managed to meet a young lady over there, Catharine McManus, who was the daughter of Colonel McManus of Fort Worden, and, to hear Mac tell it, I guess it was love at first sight. Catharine promised Mac that she would marry him the day he graduated from M.I.T., and, by golly, she did. Once, while Mac was still at M.I.T., Catharine was visiting him during a break, and they went to Newport where they rented a rowboat. Mac rowed Catharine around several of the huge steam yachts anchored there, including J. P. Morgan's *Corsair*, hoping for an invitation aboard one of these millionaire's pleasure yacht, but it didn't happen.

After graduation Mac got a job with Puget Sound Bridge & Dredge, but the job was not here, it was at the King Ranch, the biggest cattle ranch in Texas. Mac's job down there was to run an earth-fill dam to salvage the water that was just running down the river. So, Mac and Catharine had their early married life there on that job in a forlorn part of Texas.

When Mac and Catharine did eventually return to Seattle, one of his early jobs, if not the first one, was completing the building of the Wilsonian Apartments on University Way at 47th Street. He had to take over that job at a time when it looked as though they were going to lose money on the project. In those days, if you were planning to build rental property in the University District, you damned well had

H. W. McCurdy. (Courtesy of Seattle Yacht Club)

H. W. McCurdy's Moby-Dick *was built in 1914 as the* Olympic.
(Courtesy of PSMHS)

better have the job completed before the school year started. Otherwise, it would probably sit there vacant for months. Mac got the job completed on time, and that was, as far as I know, his only landlocked job for Puget Sound Bridge & Dredge. He stuck with that firm for life, and eventually was made president of the company. Before Mac died the company was purchased by Lockheed. They thought they could get navy contracts to build nuclear submarines, but when they lost their president that deal evaporated, and the property has been idle ever since.

As an adult Mac was never a sailor; he was always a power boat man. When his son, Jim, was about ten years old he and Mac did build a little sloop in their back yard down in the Mount Baker neighborhood. That boat was called the *Pequod*. The first power boat that he bought was called the *Macard*, and he bought that boat in 1930. She was a 50-foot double ender. He sold her in 1934 and bought a 62-footer, designed by Lee & Brinton that had been built as the *Olympic* in 1914 at the Heath Shipyard on the Duwamish River. She had served duty in World War I and was a well-known boat and highly thought of by everybody on the waterfront. Mac had her completely redone, and renamed her the *Moby-Dick*.

Mac was so notoriously pinchpenny at the time he bought the boat that a lot of people who worked at the Blanchard Boat Company, and who had helped build her, thought, well, that poor old boat's going to go to hell now. But that never came about. Mac had a full-time man on her named Otto, who'd been a deep-water man, and this fellow was just one of those jewels without price. He not only kept the boat up year round all alone, but he did all the cooking when they were out cruising. The *Moby-Dick* won the Pacific Motor Boat and Rudder Cup races in 1938. Mac kept that boat until she was commandeered by the army in December of 1941. He did actually buy her back after the war, and she was in a sorry state. He again completely re-outfitted her, but, as I recall, he did sell her fairly soon after that.

Mac joined the Seattle Yacht Club in 1934, and served as commodore in 1941. That was a tough job for him, because so many members were serving in the armed forces, or in some way got tied up with the war, and it took a great deal of effort on Mac's part, and that of several subsequent commodores, for that matter, to keep the club afloat during those years of World War II. In 1944 the club had an opportunity to acquire land over at Port Madison for an outstation, and Mac served on the committee that developed the outstation in 1944 and '45.

Mac had always admired the *Blue Peter*, the 96-footer that Ted Geary designed for John Graham, Sr. Old Graham had lost his shirt in the Depression and had to sell the boat in 1933, and she'd gone down to Los Angeles, where she'd been taken over by the army for the war effort in 1943. In 1948 Mac got word that there was an ex-yacht in the surplus fleet up the river above Vallejo. The army didn't even know her former name. Most of the boats that they had grabbed for the war effort and were now trying to get rid of didn't interest Mac at all. So he sent his son, Jim, down there to check this one out, and as soon as Jim saw her he realized that she was the ex-*Blue Peter*, and so he negotiated the purchase. Graham had had her originally powered with Hall-Scott gasoline engines, and either the fellow from Los Angeles who bought her from Graham, or the army, had repowered her with diesels, and of course she is still diesel. So in 1948 she came up the coast under her own power to be converted back to a pleasure yacht.

In reconditioning her as a yacht Mac only made a couple of changes to Geary's original design. The army had partitioned Graham's stateroom in the forward part of the deckhouse into two smaller rooms. Mac had the partition removed and returned this space to a full-width guest stateroom. For his own stateroom he enlarged the former chart room abaft the pilot house. Mac rechristened her the *Blue Peter*. That, of course, is the common name of the flag which, in the international code for signal flags, represents the letter P, and is raised 24 hours before a ship's departure. Mac kept Otto, the former deep-water man who had served him all the years he had the *Moby-Dick*, so this fellow continued to work full time on the *Blue Peter*.

For many years Mac hosted navy and Coast Guard brass on the *Blue Peter* for the Seattle Yacht Club's Opening Day festivities, and this continues to this day under Jim McCurdy's ownership. I'm very happy to say that after Mac died, Jim and his family decided that the *Blue Peter* should stay in the family, and she continues to be kept by Jim in beautiful condition, truly one of the finest classic motor yachts in this part of the country.

In 1963 Mac funded a project through the Seattle Historical Society to write a definitive maritime history of this area. Some important maritime historians in this country and Canada agreed to serve on the editorial board, which was chaired by Keith Fisken, who was retired by that time. Captain Adrian Raynaud was a member of that board. *The H. W. McCurdy Marine History of the Northwest, 1895-1965*, over 700 pages in length, was published in 1966. A second volume, covering 1966 through 1976, was published in 1977. These books have been out of print for years, and are prized by collectors.

Mac was a member of the group of men at the Seattle Yacht Club who were known as the "soupers." This group included "Doc" Harvey, Keith Fisken, Dietrich Schmitz and several others; they met every Friday for lunch and ordered a tureen of pea soup, which they took turns paying for. Well, when one member of this group died the others would erect some type of memorial to him at the yacht club. H. W. McCurdy was the last of the "soupers" to die, and he passed on in 1989 at the age of 90, a grand gentleman and a grand yachtsman.

Opening Day, CA. 1950. SEATTLE TIMES photographer Vic Condiotty is standing on the Chris Craft, right foreground, H. W. McCurdy's BLUE PETER is center, and the 125-foot Boeing yacht TACONITE two boats back.

The Guinness family's former yacht, the schooner-rigged FANTOME, is at anchor on the left. (COURTESY OF PSMHS)

ROY W. CORBETT
A CADILLAC OF YACHTSMEN

ROY W. CORBETT arrived in Seattle about 1920. He and his wife moved out here from Virginia, and, frankly, I don't have any idea what brought them here. I don't think Roy even had a job when he got to Seattle, but within a short time he did find work selling Cadillacs. Roy was a very good-looking man, very personable. Just how he got hooked up with Ted Geary and the *Sir Tom* gang is a mystery, because when he first arrived in Seattle Roy Corbett didn't know stickum about sailing or sailboats. Over time, though, he managed to become a pretty good sailor.

My acquaintance with Roy was made when he was having his first-ever sail with Geary on the *Sir Tom*. I think he thought that Ted was going to buy a Cadillac from him, and I'm just as certain that Ted thought that Roy was going to have himself a yacht. They remained good friends for life. It was probably around 1921, maybe 1922, when this occurred, and I think that Captain Griffiths' two sons, who had been part of the *Sir Tom*'s crew, decided they were getting a little too old for the game. Bert Griffiths was pretty heavy. So in the summer of 1922 Roy Corbett crewed on the *Sir Tom*, with Geary at the helm, and my dad, who was the foredeckman, Colin Radford, and one or two others.

Now this was during the time when the *Sir Tom* was being campaigned heavily. She always finished first, and her crew practised very seriously right off our company dock. Most of the fellows would just come down in their business clothes after work, and usually they didn't even bother to take off their neckties, although they might change their pants and put on a pair of white ducks, but just old, beat-up ones to practise sailing. I really got a kick out of Roy Corbett that day. All the rest of these guys were wearing pretty much any old thing, and here came Roy, who probably had never set foot on a boat before, and he was the only guy besides Geary who was wearing a yachting cap. In time Roy became a very adept sailor and was the mainsheet man on the *Sir Tom* under Geary, and later with Jack Graham at the helm.

Roy, to my knowledge, never sailed in any catboats, but when Ted introduced the design for the Flattie, Roy was one of the first ten to put up the $150 and order one from my dad. I think that Roy mainly wanted the boat for their daughter, Mary Helen, to race. She became a pretty good sailor herself, and was the 1929 Seattle Yacht Club Flattie champion.

In 1928, my dad launched a boat called the *Barbara Lee*; it was built for McDonald Smith, although I never knew anyone to call him anything other than Don Smith. Well, Mr. Smith hired me, and I got ten dollars a month for looking after that boat, checking the bilge, checking the oil, and keeping her washed down. Sometimes I'd come down and find the pots and pans and dishes all dirty in the galley, and I'd clean her up inside. One evening in the fall, after I had finished up on the

Roy Corbett. (Courtesy of Seattle Yacht Club)

Barbara Lee, I was walking to the streetcar to go home, and I saw a beautiful LaSalle phaeton parked.

Mrs. Corbett was sitting in it waiting for Mary Helen, who was down on the dock with some of the boys and girls. So I said something to Mrs. Corbett about having to chauffeur her daughter around, and remarked that I had thought somebody down at the Cadillac agency would have taught her how to drive. I think Mary Helen had just had her 16th birthday.

Mrs. Corbett said, "Oh, she can back it out of the garage and put it back in the garage, but she couldn't get along out on the streets."

So I asked, "Well, would you like me to give her driving lessons?"

"Would you?" she asked, and I replied, "I'd love to," so she said, "That would be marvelous."

It was agreed that one day a week, Thursday after school, I would go over on the streetcar to the Corbetts' home to give Mary Helen a driving lesson. The Corbetts weren't Catholics at all, but they lived just two blocks north of Holy Names Academy on Capitol Hill, and that's where their daughter went to school. One day I arrived for the driving lesson before Mary Helen got home from school, and her mother explained to me later that Mary Helen was terribly embarrassed because she never wanted me to see her in her Holy Names school uniform. Anyhow, I think that within about six lessons I actually had her driving down on Railroad Avenue, as we called it then, Alaskan Way now. There were a lot more railroad tracks along that street then than there are now.

In the meantime, I'd been saving the ten dollars a month I was getting from Mr. Smith, and, because I knew that the driving lessons were coming to a close soon, one day I asked Mary Helen, "Would you like to go to the show? There's a pretty good show coming up at the '5th Avenue'."

She said yes, she would. When the day of our date came I figured I would go to the Corbetts' house and call a taxi to take us from there to the movie, but Mrs. Corbett said, "Oh, no, Norman, you take Mary Helen's car, but *you* drive."

So we went to the show, and then we went someplace down on Second Avenue around Union or Madison Street and had some ice cream or something to eat. It wasn't the Pig & Whistle, but one of those restaurants on Second, which was still a pretty important street at that time, even though Frederick & Nelson and The Bon Marché had already moved uptown. Then we went for a little drive, and I think I probably gave Mary Helen her first real boy-girl kiss that night.

I was a freshman, or maybe a sophomore, at Roosevelt High School that year and feeling awfully green and young. Mary Helen was a good-looking redhead. She had dated other boys, I knew, and I had only had one date with her, but I started taking her out, and, oh my, I thought all my future was arranged. I soon learned, though, that we were really too young to be so serious.

Later, as young marrieds, Eunice and I saw quite a bit of Mary Helen when she was in Seattle. She had two kids, and we had young Norm. After World War II was over, square dancing started to become very popular, and I discovered that Mary Helen was learning very fast from lots of different teachers. She eventually moved to Coeur d'Alene, Idaho, and was divorced, got remarried, and then divorced that one, too.

To return to Roy Corbett, from all appearances he was doing very well selling Cadillacs. The Corbetts built a big house on the north slope of Capitol Hill at 2010 East Galer Street, one of the finest houses up there, especially if you don't count the really big ones below and west of Tenth Avenue East, and Roy finally bought a real boat from Ted Geary.

It was a Marconi-rigged ketch, about 50 feet long, which had been built on speculation down in California. She had been designed primarily as a racing boat with some cruising accommodations. She was deep, but not very commodious for extended cruising. Now that I look back on it, I'm sure Geary was able to sell this boat to Roy because Ted knew the details of the owner's distressed situation: that is, he had to sell it quickly, and Roy could have the boat shipped up here for probably about 60% of what it would have cost him to have my dad build one like it. My dad's and Geary's ideas of what a boat should be like were very much in harmony, even though they no longer had a working relationship. Roy had that boat for two or three seasons, and then Geary sold it for him.

His next boat had been shipped in from China, and she was, design-wise, as different from the ketch as she could be. She was a big sloop, very beamy and shallow, but she was a keel sloop, and the trunk cabin was a little higher than we were used to, and it had bigger windows. The boat had been built in Hong Kong, but the owner couldn't be here all the time to look after it, so Roy started looking after it for him, and pretty soon he owned a half interest in it, and then he owned the other half as well.

Well, after C. W. Wiley died, Roy bought his motor sailer, the *Alice*, and the Depression was on by this time. The *Alice* was very similar to Clare Egtvedt's *Navita*, about eight feet shorter, a little chopped off on the stern, with a gas engine rather than diesel.

After Roy got the *Alice*, he renamed her the *Mahero*, and she won the Seattle Yacht Club Opening Day Class A Race for him in 1932 and again in 1937. Roy was commodore of the Seattle Yacht Club in 1933, and active in the Barnacle Bill cruises that had been started by Bill Hedley. He kept the *Mahero* until early in World War II when she was taken over by the Coast Guard.

During the war Roy got out of the automobile business, and worked as vice president of Marina Mart on Westlake. It was around this time that the Corbetts sold their big home on Capitol Hill, and I've never been able to find out just what happened there. They moved back east shortly thereafter, and when they did return to Seattle in the mid-1950s they first lived in an apartment on First Hill and Roy was working for Lake Union Boat Sales. Later they bought, or maybe only rented, a very small house in the 9200 block of 35th Avenue Northeast, way out almost to Lake City, just before you start to go down the hill. There used to be a golf course there. I remember so well going out there once with Eunice because Mary Helen was coming over and Mrs. Corbett was going to have a little luncheon for her.

When Eunice and I got there the only thing I recognized from their big old house was the grandfather clock, which was a real good one. It could just barely clear the ceiling in this house by less than an inch, and they must have had a hell of a time moving it in there. Mrs. Corbett was a real lady of the old school, always the perfect hostess, and it was a small, but beautiful, lunch, just the Corbetts, Eunice and me, and our friend, Ray Fletcher from the boat company. Roy was not terribly well, and spent most of the time lying on the couch until three o'clock, when it was time for him to go to work. He was working at the time as a night watchman at Lake Union Dry Dock, and this never seemed to bother Mrs. Corbett at all.

Roy died in 1974, and we probably will never know the full story about the Corbett family.

EDWIN MONK, SR.
NAVAL ARCHITECT AND POWER BOAT MAN

EDWIN MONK BEGAN as an apprentice at the old Hall Bros. yard at Port Blakely toward the end of that yard's existence, and probably didn't finish his apprenticeship until the yard was moved to Winslow. His great-grandfather, grandfather and father had learned the shipbuilding trade in England, and later, after Ed opened his own office, he had a framed indenture that his great-grandfather had signed when he started his apprenticeship. I imagine Eddie Jr. still has it.

I first knew Ed Monk, Sr., when he came to work at our brand new yard on Fairview Avenue in the fall of 1923. At first I didn't really take much of an interest in him, nor he in me. It was a very gradual thing, but, as I look back on all my youth around the yard, Ed Monk was certainly one of my best friends among the crew. Lots of men would loan me a gouge or a spokeshave or some other tool if I was having a little trouble making one of my toy boats, Ed being very much among them, but he would not only loan me the tools. It never made any difference to him how much I abused the tools. If he saw that they weren't sharp anymore he'd take them away from me and sharpen them, and then hand them back. I'm sure he believed that a good, sharp tool was far less dangerous than a dull one, and that is certainly a theory that I subscribe to at this stage of my life.

The first thing I remember about Ed in particular was that he brought the unfinished hull of his boat into our yard because he didn't have space to complete the project under the temporary shelter that he had built at his home on Capitol Hill, and he undoubtedly paid some moorage. Ed was married, and his first wife's name was Blossom. They had two small daughters, who were somewhere around five and nine at the time. My sister, Pauline, was later in nursing school with one of the Monk girls.

Another recollection of Ed was that from a very early age he suffered from stomach ulcers. He was in the crew that built the *Samona* for Willits Hole in 1922 and '23. The story that went around at the time was that one day it seems Ed's stomach was bothering him a great deal, and he belched while he was grinding a chisel or plane or some other tool on the grinder wheel and making sparks, and all of a sudden the gas he belched from his stomach ignited. He probably had a blister or two on his lips from that experience.

One of the first yachts that Ed Monk designed was the *Silver King* for Mrs. Eskridge of Los Angeles, which we built in 1925. He did that project for Dad at home, working on the plans in the evenings. Shortly after that boat had gone to California Dad noticed that something was bothering Ed, and asked him what was wrong.

Ed said, "Well, I was going to come in and see you after 4:30," took off his glasses, pulled out a clean handkerchief and started polishing them, and continued, "well, dammit, N. J., Ted Geary's offered me a job as a draftsman."

Dad asked him, "What's the matter with that?"

Ed replied, "Well, I figured you gave me my first chance, and I owe it to you to stay with you," or words to that effect.

Dad said, "Oh, gosh, Ed, you'll learn more in a week with Ted Geary than you would with me in a year. You're crazy if you don't take it." So that's how Ed Monk left our employ.

Ed's leaving the Blanchard Boat Company cemented our relationship more than anything, even though in 1930 he and Geary packed up and moved down to Los Angeles. Ed stayed down there a few years working with Geary. He designed and lofted one boat in Craig Shipbuilding's loft in Long Beach, and when he finished that project he packed up his storypoles and other stuff he had there at Craig. He came back to Seattle and hung out his shingle from his boat as a naval architect.

Ed designed and started building a power boat called the *Nan*, which was Ed's mother's name, and he and Blossom and the girls lived the first summer on that boat out at Zenith, which is just south of Des Moines, where his mother had a beach place. The *Nan* was designed as a liveaboard, and, for a family, she was very comfortable, with a bathtub and lots of comforts. As soon as he got the *Nan* completed to his satisfaction they got a mooring at the Seattle Yacht Club, which Ed joined in 1934, and you might say he became a professional yachtsman.

The NAN. (COURTESY OF SEATTLE YACHT CLUB)

In his practice Ed designed a few sailboats, but his real interest was power boats, and all the boats he owned were strictly power boats. During the Depression he did design a sloop for a young couple, who had the boat built at the Edison Tech Boat School. The husband did a lot of the work himself, painting and other jobs. When the boat was finished the young couple lived aboard at the Queen City Yacht Club, and the wife was pregnant, when all of a sudden they got divorced. Well, Ed and Blossom took this young woman in — her name was Anna, although she was usually called Ann — and she lived with them aboard the *Nan* at the Seattle Yacht Club. By this time Blossom was ill, and I think she probably was aware that it was terminal.

About 1936 Ed moved his practice off the *Nan* and opened an office at Grandy's on Westlake Avenue, which, of course, was a much better location for a naval architect's office than our yard, and, consequently, he did a lot of work for people who had their boats built at Grandy's. But considering the circumstances, we got our fair share of his work. He and Blossom also bought a lot over at Port Madison on Bainbridge Island where he could moor a boat, but Blossom died at the end of the 1930s before they could move to the island.

After less than a year Ed and Ann were married, Ed sold the *Nan* to Art Russell, and he and Ann and the family moved to Bainbridge Island. Art Russell was later commodore of the Seattle Yacht Club. Of course by the time the family moved to Bainbridge Island it had expanded to include a boy, who was Ann's son. The boy was named Edwin Monk, Jr., and he was raised as if he had been Ed's natural son.

The *Sea Rest*, which had been designed by Ed for O. D. Fisher, was being built at our place in 1937, and Mr. Fisher owned some waterfront property on Westlake Avenue, which just had rental houseboat moorage. He got talking to Dad, Ed Monk and a few others and they started a new company — Fisher-controlled, of course — called Marina Mart, and Ed was very much involved in designing it, along with a licensed land architect.

During World War II Ed had to move out of Grandy's. I suppose that Grandy's, because of the war, needed the office space. They were running just as big a crew as we were, being very busy with navy contracts. Ed decided that Mr. Fisher would give him some space upstairs at Marina Mart to have an office. By this time his reputation was growing, so he was better off in a real office building. That arrangement was fine until they lived on Bainbridge Island, and Ed moved his office down to the National Building on Western Avenue in the mid-1950s.

After the war the first job we did for Ed was the *Miss Blondee*, and then a 46-foot power boat for Frank Hawkins, who owned Frank Hawkins Buick, and both boats were launched in 1946. Ed kept the office on Western Avenue for around ten years, and after Eddie Jr. finished his course of studies he began working there with his dad. Most of the time he was in that office I would say that Ed Monk, Sr., was in his prime, as far as his practice was concerned, and he usually had Eddie and two other draftsmen working there with him.

About the time the war was over there was a man living in British Columbia named George McQueen who had two sons who were near maturity. While this man could very easily afford to have put them through college, all these boys wanted to do was build boats. So Mr. McQueen got a place on the Fraser River at New Westminster and had his boys build him a boat, designed by Ed Monk, Sr., which turned out to be pretty good.

Mr. McQueen had connections, so they soon had another boat in the works, and each time a question came up he'd run down to Seattle to see Ed Monk, and they became quite good friends. The father, as far as I know, never was actually involved in building the boats, but was kind of like an inspector. He watched those boys pretty closely, and they developed a really fine reputation. So eventually Ed started having the McQueen boys build some of the boats he designed for himself. Labor was cheaper in B.C., the exchange rate was favorable, and he'd have the boats towed to Seattle unfinished. Then he and Eddie would finish them themselves, working evenings and weekends.

After about ten years on Western Avenue Ed moved his practice to Bainbridge Island. The family continued to live at Port Madison and the office was in Winslow, where Ed Jr. now continues his own practice.

Ed and Ann had a daughter of their own, Judy, and she has always been special to me because she had gorgeous, golden red hair, like my own mother. One day Eunice and I were walking south on the road that skirts the south end of inner Port Madison Bay, and we were just coming to approximately where the Edwin Monk home was when all of a sudden, without any warning, a little tot, who was only about two, came running out of the bushes and right across in the road. Both Eunice and I could hardly believe the beautiful color of red hair this child had. Her mother was chasing her, and we soon realized that this was Ed's youngest child.

Ed did a lot of cruising in his power boats. Two or three of them had flying bridges, but eventually Ann got tired of the difficulties in communicating with him up on the bridge when she was in the main cabin. So the last one or two boats they had were a little old fashioned at the time they were designed, in that you could also steer the boat from the pilot house.

Ed Monk, Sr., was certainly one of the most prolific naval architects working in Seattle. Because he worked with tools in his earlier life, and was primarily thought of as a boatbuilder and naval architect, one might be tempted not to think of him as a yachtsman, but he certainly was. Among other things, I was surprised to learn that he and Ann actually owned some property up on Saltspring Island, which wasn't exactly stupid. Good property up there is a sensible thing to own.

Ed Monk died in 1973, but the many boats designed by him that are still sailing and cruising throughout Washington and British Columbia are a testament to his work as one of the finest naval architects our area has produced. And his son Eddie is still carrying on this tradition.

A CRUISE ON THE *GADGET*
AND A LESSON IN COMPARATIVE ECONOMICS

DURING THE SUMMER of 1929, my 18th year, I had a job working for T. Harry Gowman on his new 48-foot motor yacht, the *Gadget*, launched that year from the Blanchard Boat Company. I don't remember just how I happened to get the job, but it paid $50 a month, which wasn't bad — pretty good pay in those days for a teenager. I lived aboard the boat and Mr. Gowman bought all my grub, so it was a darned nice summer for me. The *Gadget* had a tiny crew's quarters right up in the bow, which you could only get into through a forward hatch. We cruised north to Nanaimo on Vancouver Island on one occasion. Harry Gowman was national president of the Kiwanis Club, and we went up there so he could open the very first Kiwanis Club in British Columbia.

On Labor Day weekend, Harry Gowman decided to cruise to the south end of Puget Sound, and as we were coming between Eagle Island and McNeil Island, I said — and I pointed it out on the chart to him, by Longbranch — "That's a nice harbor in there, and there's a point that belongs to the McDermotts of The Bon Marché, and they have given a standing invitation to Seattle Yacht Club boats to tie up to their float." Frank McDermott was the president of The Bon Marché, and their summer home was there at Longbranch.

Mr. Gowman was skeptical and said, "We can't do that at a private home," but I told him, "Where the McDermotts are concerned, if we're flying the Seattle Yacht Club pennant on the bow we're welcome."

"Huh!" he said, "you'll have to go up to the house and ask."

As we approached the inner harbor I noticed that the McDermotts were flying the American flag on their big flagpole under several other flags. After we tied the *Gadget* up to their float I got cleaned up for dinner and went up to the house, and a lady came out and told me, "Oh, yes, all Seattle Yacht Club boats are welcome."

I kind of hesitated, and then I asked her, "Is Mr. McDermott here?"

She said, "Oh, yes, but he's napping."

"Well," I continued, "as we came by the flagpole I noticed there's no halyard at the gaff and the American flag is flying very improperly under several other flags, and if he's got a new piece of line I'll be glad to reeve it through there and get the American flag flying properly."

So she said, "I'll tell him when he wakes up."

Mr. Gowman and the rest of the party were just sitting down to dinner on the *Gadget* when Mr. McDermott called out to me on his megaphone, and so I hightailed it up to the front porch, and he already had quite a line right there. I said to him, "Well, I have to eat my supper now, and I wouldn't want to try and make that climb until it has had at least an hour to settle."

Launching of the GADGET, *Blanchard Boat Company, 1929.* (COURTESY OF MOHAI)

So I went back to the *Gadget* and Mr. Gowman and his party had their supper and we sat and talked. Even though I was the hired hand, I was treated like a guest. As soon as the meal was finished he would usually start a bridge game, and I generally cleaned up the galley. So when I had finished in the galley and it had been a full hour I put on my old clothes and went back up to the McDermotts' house. Mr. McDermott saw me coming and met me on the porch, and we walked up the hill to where the flagpole was near the edge of the bluff; he had a nice clearing where it stood.

Mr. McDermott said, "Now tell me what you plan to do."

"Oh," I said, "I'm going to tie the end of that line around my waist and you can feed it to me while I shin up this wire."

He asked me, "You think you can do that?"

I replied, "Oh, sure, when I get my hands around the yard there I can rest a little, and then I can climb right on up and stand on the top of the mainmast with my arm around the topmast and pull the gaff up to me and reeve the line through, and come down again."

So we proceeded and I accomplished the change, and when I hit the ground he said, "By golly, I'm sure glad to be here and see you do that. That was fantastic, I want to shake your hand," or something to that effect.

We shook hands and I felt a folded-up bill in his hand, and I held onto his hand and I said, "Mr. McDermott, you've probably forgotten, but I used to come over here with my mother and Lizzie Larson and my two little sisters and we picnicked on your lawn right here four or five, if not half a dozen, times. I just wanted to do this for you."

"Well," he said, "a young fellow like you can always use an extra buck or two. Put that in your pocket and buy yourself some cigarettes."

"Oh, sir," I said, "I'd never be able to make that climb if I smoked cigarettes," because even so I had had to stop to rest halfway up. And it's a good thing I had, too, because I had underestimated the height of the pole. I had been fooled by the second-growth trees around the clearing. They were 75 to 80 feet tall, and the flagpole had looked much shorter, but when I got to the top I was nearly as high as the trees, so I figure I was close to 70 feet up.

Well, I put the bill in my pocket and left, and when I got back to the *Gadget* and changed my clothes I looked at it, and it was a $20 bill. You know, in those days you could buy a fine suit of clothes for $20. Not the finest, but a good ready-made suit was $20 to $25. I told Mr. Gowman what had happened and said, "Golly, I can't accept this kind of money for a little ten-minute job."

He said, "Well, now, wait a minute. Let's think about this. You know, I have three or four flagpoles on top of my hotel, and I have to call people for service on those poles, paint them and so forth, and, believe me, they don't work cheap. You just wanted to do him a nice favor, and he appreciated that, and, you know, $20 to him is not anything like $20 is to you. I think that you should follow his advice and put it in your bank, or whatever you want to do with it." So that was the end of that incident, but it is a treasured memory.

Thomas Harry Gowman was a Canadian who had come to Seattle from Victoria. He owned the Gowman Hotel on the southeast corner of Second Avenue and Stewart Street, directly across from the old Washington Hotel, which was *the* hotel in downtown Seattle before the Olympic was built. Of course, the

Gowman was a much smaller hotel than the Washington, but it was very, very popular with Alaskans. It was later named the Stewart Hotel and was torn down in the late 1960s.

Harry Gowman had had one of the smaller stock cruisers Dad had built. If you can imagine this, he'd go out to the north end of Lake Washington on the eastern shore, a nice, deserted place, by himself, and dive overboard and swim in the nude. After he'd had the boat for a while he turned it in for us to sell, and the Blanchard Boat Company built him a 48-foot cruiser with pilot house amidships, his stateroom forward of the pilot house, galley aft, and then the main cabin with seat-backs that came up so you could sleep two couples back there.

Mr. Gowman was a young, middle-aged man at that time; he happened to be in the process of a divorce and already had his second wife picked out. It came out in the papers — which was very unusual in those days — in the divorce proceedings that he wanted children and his wife did not. So he was living the bachelor life there in his hotel, and I think he named his new boat the *Gadget* just because he thought it was kind of a cute name.

I've thought many times if I could really have anything I wanted in the way of a power boat it would be about 52 to 55 feet long, but otherwise just like the *Gadget*. My primary reason for the additional length would be so that you could give it some additional beam. The alley decks of the *Gadget* are so narrow, the rail is so close to the trunk, that it is a little difficult to walk along them. Four feet of length justify one foot of beam, so if you make her 52 or 55 feet long — and, of course, nowadays you'd let the topsides flare out a little all the way aft — that would give you another couple of inches, and that's really all we're talking about.

above: A dock party after the launching of the GADGET. *Owner T. Harry Gowman is near the center, in yachting attire.* (COURTESY OF MOHAI)

left: The GADGET *after her 1929 launching. T. Harry Gowman, owner, at starboard rail.* (COURTESY OF MOHAI)

J. L. PATTON AND
THE BLANCHARD BOAT COMPANY

J. L. "JOE" PATTON was a navy machinist's mate at the Naval Air Station in San Diego during World War I, so that made him somewhere near halfway between my father's age and mine. Aviation was in its infancy at that time, and after the war Joe came back to Seattle and opened his own business, the Seattle Marine Equipment Company. As I remember it, he made up 75% or more of the total workforce of his company. At one time during the 1920s he needed somebody to keep the storefront open, sweep out the place and answer the telephone, and this position was filled by Jerry Bryant, who later started Bryant's Marina, when he was still in Queen Anne High School. After Jerry got interested in outboard racing he made a deal with Joe to have a workbench in the back of the shop where he could work on outboard motors, and pretty soon he was doing work for other racers besides himself. So that's how Jerry Bryant got his start.

I first really got acquainted with Joe Patton when I was still in high school. He had a gas engine that had been outclassed by the newer models, so he wanted to use it in a boat. He had found a design for a boat by the designer, William Atkin, in an issue of *Motor Boating* and brought it into the Blanchard Boat Company. I redesigned the superstructure and increased the overall length for him by adding two feet right smack in the middle. All I really designed was a new plan for the house. Well, Joe was pleased so he made a deal with my dad and we built the *Barnacle*.

When she was ready to launch I asked, "Joe, would you let me put the name on the *Barnacle?*"

And he said, "Yes, if you want to try it, but I can't pay you."

Well, I did put the gold leaf name on the varnished teak transom of the *Barnacle*. That boat is still in good condition, and is owned by the man who owns or leases the property where the old Seattle Cedar Lumber Company mill used to be.

Launching of J. L. Patton's BARNACLE *from the Blanchard Boat Company, CA. 1931.* (BLANCHARD COLLECTION)

A little later on, and again it was in order to move another engine, Joe and Dad put together the idea that a little $5,000 or $6,000 motor sailer would be a good speculation. They got Ed Monk to design the boat, and I'm sure Joe put up some money, as well as the engine, and that boat became the *Stormy*, which, in the late spring of 1935, was sold to some people in Santa Barbara. My cousin, Curley Blanchard, along with another lad not long out of high school, plus a licensed master who had lost his license because he boozed too much, and I, took the *Stormy* down the coast to Santa Barbara on her own bottom. That trip really cemented my friendship with Joe Patton.

Naturally, part of Joe's job was prowling the waterfront. He sold engines to any boatyard that he possibly could, and he was very well liked. He was a slender man, and always well dressed, but without looking like a millionaire. As time went by, Joe figured his type of business fit more with the Queen

J. L. "Joe" Patton, CA. 1926. (WILEN COLLECTION)

City Yacht Club, and eventually he became commodore of that club. Joe favored the old, air-cooled Franklins for a long time, but finally he started driving Studebakers.

Over the years, by the late 1930s, Kermath and Sterling had become Joe's two best-selling engines. He dealt in some other items, pumps and equipment of that nature, but he didn't get into the electronic stuff at his Seattle Marine Equipment Company.

It was in the summer of 1943, I believe, that it became obvious that the only sensible thing for the old N. J. Blanchard Boat Company, Inc., to do would be to disincorporate. So, as soon as the company made enough profit that my dad could, he bought back the shares of stock from Charlie Seaborn's widow, Ray Cooke, Grandma Blanchard, and Wallace Schoenman. Dad had given me 15 shares as a wedding gift, and at the time he had said, "I don't suppose these are worth the paper they're printed on."

So I sold my 15 shares back to him for just ten dollars, to make it a legal transaction. He didn't actually have that much money yet, and at the time he told me, "Now don't worry, I fully intend to make this right by you."

Just before the war was over Ted Pearson, our former book-keeper, wrote, saying that his job at Douglas Aircraft would soon terminate, and he was still very much interested in the boat business. So it was arranged that my dad would drive down to California that fall, 1945, on a two-week vacation, consult with Ted Pearson, and then come back to Seattle. And the plan was that after Dad had been back a week, to be sure that the work was coming in, I would take off and drive down to California for two weeks to consult with Ted. Dad said that Ted had been very much interested in their talks about forming a new company that would be incorporated, and it was a matter of consulting with lawyers, taking care of the legalities, in order to reach a final agreement.

So, when Wednesday of the next week came, and Dad still hadn't said anything about making good on his word to me, I stopped him in the shop and reminded him of what he had said.

"I know I did," was his reply, so I said, "Well, I can't go down there and talk to Ted Pearson intelligently unless I know what you're going to do."

All he could say was that he'd figure something out. It was perfectly obvious that he was annoyed. And the next day, Thursday, he handed me a check for $2,000. I hadn't talked about a raise all through the war, and I had figured out by that time that if I hadn't been frozen in my job — which was clearly just an excuse, because we were doing very well on the contracts — all he would have had to do was advance me from my title of journeyman to leading man to foreman, and that would have raised my pay level beautifully. But I didn't have any specific figures. I suppose I had relative figures of how well we had done on this contract, compared to the one just previous, but I remember I was terribly disappointed with the $2,000.

Before I went to lunch I went into the office, where Joe Patton was getting ready to clean out his desk and be permanently gone — it had been agreed that he would stay until after the first of the year — and I just laid the check in front of him, and he looked at it and asked, "What's this, Norm?"

So I reminded him of what Dad had told me — Joe knew all about how Dad had had to disincorporate — and he said, "Oh, my God, Norm, you know what kind of arrangement I've had with your dad. With each contract for a new joint agreement, I stepped down five percent and he went up five percent on the division of the profits."

And I said, "Oh, yes, I was aware of that."

"Well," he said, "just this past year," meaning 1944, "I established a fund for my boys of $10,000 each, just so in case I suddenly croaked Uncle Sam wouldn't take such a big bite out of my estate." Well, when I got to thinking about that I felt even worse.

Friday afternoon or Saturday morning Eunice and I started south, and didn't fool around much on the road. Of course there wasn't any Interstate 5 then; it was old Highway 99 all the way. We stayed with Ted Pearson and his wife in Mar Vista, a suburb of Los Angeles.

When I went to the General Delivery window at the post office I found the only letter I ever received from my father, a handwritten letter, and a check for an additional $3,000. I figured out that what I should have made, if I'd been paid on an hourly basis as they would have had to pay anybody else, I would have accumulated $5,000, possibly $7,000. In his letter Dad said that if I elected to go in with the new plan, why he would make up the difference. Well, he almost did, but not quite. I happened to draw for the odd share, 34 shares instead of 33.

Joe Patton continued to be a very good friend of the firm. I think Joe really considered himself retired after World War II. He had some kind of sales job with somebody in Detroit, I believe, but he spent most of his time after that at Doe Bay up on Orcas Island. I attended Joe's funeral, which came shortly thereafter. He died of a heart attack while mowing his lawn or trimming the hedges with shears. A neighbor noticed that he was just lying there on the sidewalk in front of his house on Queen Anne Hill, and called Mrs. Patton, and they found he had died of a heart attack right there on his own property.

TED PEARSON
FROM METER READER TO SECRETARY-TREASURER
OF THE BLANCHARD BOAT COMPANY

DURING THE FIRST part of the Depression, Edward F. Pearson — everyone always called him Ted — was working at the General Insurance Company in the old White-Henry-Stuart Building when he got a call one day from Mr. Auerswald, who was the owner and operator of the business school where Ted had earned a certificate as a bookkeeper. Mr. Auerswald said to him, "The Blanchard Boat Company on Lake Union needs a bookkeeper."

"But Mr. Auerswald, I've only been here a little over six months and they've already given me a raise," Ted answered.

"Listen to me, you whippersnapper," or something to that effect, "the Blanchard Boat Company has a full construction set of books. There's a chance for you to learn something. You flag your ass out there and land that job or I'm going to kick it all the way to Los Angeles." So that's how I first got acquainted with Ted Pearson, and our friendship lasted a lifetime.

Ted was from Victoria, B. C., and had come to Seattle as soon as his youngest brother reached the age of 14, which was the age that Ted was when his father died. Ted's father had been a ship's carpenter on one of the Canadian Pacific Railway boats that served the west coast of Vancouver Island. For some reason or other the ship had lost power, and Ted's father was on the foredeck because it was the ship's carpenter's duty to also man the anchor windlass. The mate was up there with

him, and probably a sailor or two, and they didn't see this wave coming, and Ted's father was washed overboard. Ted's mother went to work as a student nurse, which, of course, paid almost nothing in Victoria in those days, and Ted worked the rest of that school year selling papers to help his mother. He stayed loyal to his mother and tried to help her in every way he could.

Well, as soon as the school year was over Ted was able to go aboard one of those C.P.R. boats as a mess boy in the kitchen, and he soon graduated to the dining room, where the tipping was very good, even in those days.

After coming ashore in Seattle, the only job Ted could get was reading meters for the Seattle Gas Company, which, of course, was very minimal pay, although I'm sure he must have had some savings. After his second month there he got called into the office; the office manager inquired about his background, and finally said, "Well, I wondered if maybe you'd be interested in coming into the office and learning bookkeeping. Your meter readings are so legible and the books always nice and dry," and this guy probably showed Ted one of the other meter reader's books, which were always a mess. So Ted took him up on the offer, and he immediately enrolled in Auerswald's business school.

After finishing his bookkeeping courses Ted was naturally watching the classified ads, and he was able to leave the gas company and go to work for the General Insurance Company, where he stayed until he came to work for the Blanchard Boat Company in 1930. Well, Ted really liked my dad, and considered him a kind of surrogate father, but after less than two years it didn't take a very smart person to see that my dad really couldn't afford a full-time bookkeeper, so in 1931, when he had a chance, Ted went to work for Goodrich-Silvertown, Inc. But he came back to the yard in the afternoons and on Saturdays, and taught my sister, Meda, to keep the books, and he would come in at the end of the month and help her square up for the month. So Ted was really a great friend of the Blanchard Boat Company.

Eventually Ted switched from Goodrich-Silvertown to Firestone and was transferred to Los Angeles. His boss at Firestone really liked him, and one day he said to Ted, "I don't want you to get away, I want to keep my finger on you, and so I'm sending you out to Whittier. Our manager there is a real two-fisted company man, and he will do his best to make life miserable for you, but you'll learn a lot about the company. If you can hack it for 90 days there then there'll be a vacancy over in Phoenix. Would you mind going to Phoenix?"

"Oh, no," Ted answered, "I'd just as soon go to Phoenix."

So on the 90th day Ted returned to the office and said, "I don't give a damn if you kick me out," or something to that effect, "but I certainly won't spend another hour on that job with that guy," meaning the manager in Whittier.

The boss laughed and said, "Well, it was kind of a mean trick, but, like I said, there is this opening in Phoenix, and if you still want to go over there it's available."

Ted was a tall, good-looking, well-built fellow, and he had a perfectly normal interest in girls, and he met this beauty in Phoenix and they got married. Just about one year later he came home at the end of the week and found a Dear John letter; she had left him. He told me, "I really kind of went nuts." He left Phoenix immediately and moved back to a suburb of Los Angeles, and went back to work for his old boss.

Well, about this time Ted's younger brother came down from Victoria and joined him, and they rented an apartment together in Los Angeles. Ted was selling Cadillacs in Santa Monica, and in those days you had to go out to certain neigh-borhoods and knock on doors once a week, and one of the doors he knocked on was Shirley Temple's; he sold her dad a nice Cadillac.

One evening Ted and his brother had some friends in for a party, and one of the lady guests asked, "Ted, what do you and your brother pay for this apartment?"

He said, "Well, we each pay $50 per month."

And so she said, "Well, you've been in my house and you know it's pretty big. There are three bedrooms on the second floor, each with its own private bath, and if you want to, you and your brother can have those two spare rooms for $100 per month, but you will have to do your own housework."

Well, that was too good to pass up in the Depression, and so they moved in with this lady, whose name was Ethel. Come the new year she had to do her income tax, and by this time they'd all gotten pretty well acquainted, so she got Ted to help her with her taxes. He could see that her big problem was eating money. She had plenty of good investments, but they just weren't paying dividends.

After Ted and his brother had been living at Ethel's house for about a year, Ted got a telephone call one Saturday morning from his brother. "Well, guess what? My girl and I just got married and we're on our way to Mexico for a honeymoon."

The next thing Ethel did was to fly off to Victoria and get a monthly room at the Empress Hotel and she proceeded to make Ted's mother's acquaintance. Ted's mother was by then a registered nurse. Ted came up in the summer on his vacation and he and Ethel were married in Victoria.

When they were driving south through Seattle, Ted naturally had to stop by the Blanchard Boat Company to show Ethel where he had his first bookkeeping job. My parents were away at the time, and Eunice was off cruising with the Peier brothers on the *Neoga II*, so I invited them to have dinner with me at the Seattle Yacht Club. Later Ted wrote my dad a letter — I sure wish I still had it, I don't know what became of it — saying what a terrific guy both he and Ethel thought I was. He also wrote that he had been thinking a lot about his future, and he thought one of the opportunities he should look into would be to get back into the boat business. World War II was looming and Dad had already made a business arrangement with J. L. Patton of the Seattle Marine Equipment Company, so he wrote Ted that he couldn't do anything with him at that point.

Shortly after World War II was over, Dad incorporated again and in 1948 Ted Pearson became the secretary-treasurer of the Blanchard Boat Company. Dad, Ted and I drew straws to divide the 100 shares of stock and I happened to get the oddball extra long straw, so I had the swing vote, against Ted or Dad, and we coasted along this way, but of course the company was in excellent shape from our navy contracts during the war.

One day the certified public accountant came to me and said, "You know, your father built this business, and he doesn't like the idea that your vote could go against him in any kind of argument that might come up in the future. He wants to take some of his surplus cash and buy some more stock."

And I said, "Of course." I certainly had no objection to that.

Well, immediately Bill Sheffield came to me the first chance he had, and he said, "You realize your father wants to be in control."

I said, "I realize that, Bill, and I'm not going to oppose him. If that's what he wants to do, well fine." So that's the way it was until Dad died.

At the end of the summer of 1950, after just about two years with the Blanchard Boat Company, Ted came to Dad and me and said he was sorry, but he had to tell us that Ethel had decided she wanted to move back to Southern California so come September 1st of the next year he would be leaving us. Ethel had never lived north of the Mason-Dixon Line — if the Mason-Dixon Line extended through California — and Ted naturally wasn't going to let this issue break up their marriage. So Ted left, and Dad disincorporated, and it was back to the old standard: Dad's business with me working for him.

In his later years, Ted lived in Palm Springs, where we kept in touch by phone now and then until he died in 1998 at the age of 90. We enjoyed a great friendship for almost 70 years, one that I really treasure.

Norm Blanchard, left, and Ted Pearson at a double desk in the office of the Blanchard Boat Company, 1947. Bow of the NAVITA can be seen in the center. (BLANCHARD COLLECTION)

BOB CONDON
THE MAN WHO BUILT HIS BOATS
ON FAUNTLEROY BEACH

ROBERT CONDON WAS the son of Dr. Herbert Condon of the University of Washington. Dean Condon had been almost everything a career man could be at the university except president, and I know he was acting president on several occasions. Condon Hall on the campus is named for him. Bob was Dean Condon's second son, born in 1907. There were four sons and one daughter, but I was not acquainted with Bob's older brother. The Condon home was on 21st Avenue Northeast, just a block plus a house or two from the campus.

Bob's next younger brother, Herb Jr., was my contemporary, and the youngest was Don. All the boys were good looking. Herb and Don went to Roosevelt High School at the time I was there, but neither of them had much time for studies, and they were very, very popular. I didn't know Dean Condon all that well, although my wife was secretary for him all through the years of World War II, but I can see where he might have been a bit disappointed in his two youngest sons because their social life seemed more important to them than their studies.

Bob and I became acquainted when I was in my teens and still racing with Ray Cooke on the *Clarabel*, although I can't recall that we were ever together on the same crew in any races. Bob graduated from the University of Washington, got a job with a big timber firm down in Shelton as plant engineer for their pulp mill, and married Katrina Harley. They had two children, but later were divorced.

Robert Condon. (COURTESY OF SEATTLE YACHT CLUB)

Bob quit his job in Shelton and came back to Seattle, where he became plant engineer for Graystone Concrete Products on the Lake Washington Ship Canal, just across the canal from Fremont. I don't know how much time elapsed, but eventually he had the wonderful good luck to meet Cora Hansen and marry her after a year or two. Bob moved into their house down at Fauntleroy, right on the beach, just a hundred yards or so north of the ferry dock. Cora and her dad had been living there, and Mr. Hansen may have built the house.

Mr. Hansen's career had been as a veterinarian. When he retired he was the state dairy inspector, and he was one of the originators of, and for a long time was active with, the Puyallup Fair, just a delightful old gentleman. Well, sometime before World War II Bob came to me and he said, "Norm, I've decided I want to build one of those 25-footers like you built to Ben Seaborn's design for Mr. Fisken. Do you think I can get away with it?"

I replied, "I don't see why not. I'd certainly be glad to help in any way I can."

We had already built the one for Keith Fisken, and a second for Bill Blethen, so Bob's would be the third boat built to that set of plans. In fact, Keith had enjoyed his 25-footer so much that he had Ben design him a 31-footer, which we built for him the following year. So I told Bob we'd be glad to loan him the patterns and everything, or sell him the patterns. I think we had agreed on the purchase — anything we could do to bring in a few dollars at that time would help.

So Bob bought the plans, and he did a fine job on that boat. He built it at the side of their home on the beach. The road there was above the house, so he had a pretty good shop beneath the garage. I saw the boat two or three times in process. My father went out and looked the boat over less than a month before she was launched, and he told Bob that he had done a better job than we could afford to do for a customer.

The boat was named the *Lively Lady*, and when it came time to paint the name on her transom, Bob said to Cora that he had better hire a sign painter for the job. Cora was not in favor of that idea. She said to Bob, "Now, Bob, you've done every lick of work on that boat yourself so far, and you're perfectly capable of painting the name on her," so he did the job himself

and nobody would have guessed that it had not been done professionally. Bob, Cora and Mr. Hansen did a lot of cruising in her prior to and during World War II.

The Condons bought a piece of waterfront property on a nice little bay on San Juan Island, just south of Friday Harbor, and Eunice and I and the Condons became very close friends, I guess you'd say — that is, we'd have dinner at each other's houses on occasion. When the war was over Bob came to me again and said, "I'm going to sell the 25-footer, and Mr. Hansen has agreed to go in with me financially, and I think what we want is a boat like the *Cavu* that you built for the United Air Lines pilot, Grover Tyler."

Now the *Cavu* had been designed by Ed Monk, and I told Bob, "You'll have no difficulty there, but there's not full headroom for you in that boat."

Bob was about six feet, two inches, and I think he had expected my reaction, because his next comment was, "Well, that was my other question."

I said to him, "What I would suggest that you do is simply raise the freeboard. Don't change the hull shape at all, but I think we ought to have Ed Monk's advice on just how much bow, stern and midships would need to be recalculated."

So that all worked out very well. The boat was redesigned as a 41-foot yawl, and Bob ordered his boat around the first of October 1945. At that time my dad was kind of at sixes and sevens about just what he wanted to do. He was thinking of retiring, and even had a For Sale sign on the place for a short time. Bob's new boat ended up being framed and planked in the shop. Later, Bob laid an Alaska cedar deck over the plywood subdeck that we put on so that she would be reasonably weatherly and raintight for the trip out, and we built him a cradle that he could keep her in, and he took her over to their home at Fauntleroy for finishing. He did all the interior work himself, and I think it took him about a year to finish the boat, and, of course, lots of people will tell you that boats never really get finished. They named their new boat the *Valkyrie*.

The Condons and Mr. Hansen sold the *Lively Lady*. We saw her around; she probably had two, three, maybe even four owners after being sold, and the last owner went sailing in

Cora and Bob Condon at the helm of the VALKYRIE, CA. 1955. (COURTESY OF CORA CONDON)

Lake Washington very late in the season, and the boat sank out from under him. He was alone, it was a very dark night, and I remember we were all very suspicious about it. Whether or not he was able to collect from the insurance company I don't know. She sank in the middle of Lake Washington; no one knows where for sure, but she's probably still down there and could be raised and rehabilitated.

Bob became active in the Seattle Yacht Club. When the club acquired the property on Bainbridge Island in the 1940s for the Port Madison outstation, Bob dug the well over there for them. In 1959 he served as commodore of the yacht club.

In the meantime Bob continued as plant engineer at Graystone, which had been bought by Boise Cascade, although very few positions had changed. Shortly after the

first of the year, sometime in the early 1960s, a convention was held in Miami, Florida, for technicians from concrete-manufacturing plants, and the new boss told Bob, "We want you to plan on taking this in."

When June or July came and it was close to the time for the convention, the boss reminded Bob. Bob said, "Well, I've got three weeks or more of vacation coming. I've never been down that way at all, and I'd like to take a little time to look around."

"Fine, good idea," was the reply.

So Bob and Cora had a three-week vacation, one whole week of which was the convention. When they got back to Sea Tac Airport it was a little before noon so they taxied home and Bob called the office. The boss told him not to bother to come in. "Take it easy, and we'll see you in the morning." And the next morning when he went in they handed him his severance pay.

Bob was 55 years old, and it only took him about two days to come to the conclusion that there was no market for a 55-year-old engineer. However, he certainly didn't feel he could just retire, so they decided to sell their home and move up to San Juan Island. They also sold a half interest in the *Valkyrie* to a couple who had approached them with an offer to buy into the boat.

Well, Bob kept very busy on San Juan Island. He designed a house which, of course, had a lot of concrete block. Actually, it adjoined their cabin, and the new house had a full cement basement.

Sometime in mid-summer a pickup truck turned into the Condons' driveway and skidded to a stop. The driver jumped out and said, "Looking for Robert Condon."

Bob said, "Well, I guess you've found him."

This fellow said, "I understand you're an engineer."

"Oh," Bob said, "I think if I dug deep enough in some of these boxes I might find one of those things that most people frame and put on the wall."

The man introduced himself and said, "I do practically all the surveying in San Juan County, and I've got a job to make a one-foot contour map of Coon Island." We all knew Coon Island; it was Jack Tussler's island, and he had died and the island had been sold.

Bob immediately said, "I can't handle a job like that. That's a three- or four-man job."

This fellow said, "Oh, I've got the crew. I need somebody to run it." So Bob accepted, and they did a one-foot contour map of Coon Island, and then the fellow had more work for Bob, and right after the first of the year Bob and this fellow became partners. So Robert Condon always felt that Boise Cascade had done him a favor by firing him.

The couple who'd bought a half interest in the *Valkyrie* later bought the other half, but it was with the understanding that Bob and Cora would continue to have use of the boat. The next season Eunice and I were on our way home after a cruise on the *Aura* and just happened to drop in at the Condons' bay on San Juan Island. We stayed for dinner, and in the evening Bob told us that, due to their signing over full ownership of their boat, the new owners had just informed them that it wasn't convenient for them to have a cruise that summer on the *Valkyrie*, and they were really disappointed. I looked at Eunice, and she knew what I was going to say, so I asked Bob, "When did you want to go?"

"Well, as a matter of fact, today is the day we had planned to leave," he answered.

I said, "OK, you and Cora take the *Aura*." Well, that worked out just fine. They drove us to the ferry, and they took the *Aura*. We got home all right, and as the ferry pulled out of Friday Harbor there they were, going north in San Juan Channel. And I am *certain* that the *Aura* was never cleaner and tidier in every respect during my ownership than she was when the Condons got back from that cruise.

Later, the Condons had a 36-foot Hunter power cruiser called the *Tahsis* — there's a Tahsis Inlet on the west coast of Vancouver Island. My father always thought that those boats were pretty cheaply built. She was a stock boat, and one of the things that was unique was that the foredeck was perfectly flat, with no crown to it.

And that is the story of Robert Condon, truly a fine yachtsman. He and his wife, Cora, were just wonderful friends. Bob has been gone now for a number of years, but his widow, Cora, continues to live in a retirement home in the north end of Seattle.

A SWIFTSURE AND TRI-ISLAND COMPETITOR
T. HARBINE MONROE

I FIRST MET T. Harbine Monroe during the middle years of the Depression, probably around 1936, and I think we probably struck up a friendship because he was a few years younger than I was and needed some guidance from a friend. The Blanchard Boat Company had taken in the 25-foot sloop that we had built for Keith Fisken and had her sitting on the floor in the shop with a For Sale sign on her. Harbine, I believe, was in his senior year at the University of Washington, majoring in business administration, and he would stop by the shop on his way home to Tacoma, where he still lived with his mother, to look at Keith's boat. After Harbine's third visit my father asked me, "What are you wasting your time with that fat guy for?"

I replied, "He's going to buy that 25-footer." My father merely grunted. And very much to my satisfaction, the fourth time Harbine walked into the shop he handed me a check in full payment for that boat. This was a very gratifying experience in my young life.

T. Harbine Monroe was born in Tacoma in 1915. He got his rather unusual name — and I don't know what the "T" stood for because he always went by Harbine — from his grandfather, Colonel Harbine, who had started one of the first banks in Tacoma. He began attending the College of Puget Sound, but then transferred to the University of Washington. After graduation he returned to Tacoma, and got married there in 1940.

Harbine renamed the 25-footer the *Shutterbug*, because all his life he was an avid photographer. He and his partner, Barney Elliott, operated The Camera Shop on Pacific Avenue in Tacoma, and, as a matter of fact, they were the ones who recorded the collapse of the old Tacoma Narrows Bridge — "Galloping Gertie" — on film in 1940. Barney and Harbine always kept their cameras loaded and ready to roll, and someone called them to say the bridge was dancing and twisting around, so they jumped in their car and raced over there. They hoped to get something on film, and they filmed the whole collapse. Harbine's and Barney's footage of the bridge falling into the Tacoma Narrows was named "outstanding domestic newsreel of the year" by the National Headliner's Club.

Before World War II, the *Dorade*, a 52-foot Sparkman & Stephens yawl, was brought up from San Francisco for Ralph James. Ralph had owned the *Nautilus*, which had been built for Keith Fisken, so Harbine sold the *Shutterbug* and bought the *Nautilus* from Ralph James, and, as I recall, we were not involved as brokers. He kept the *Nautilus* all through World War II. He was either 4-F, or for some other reason was non-draftable, and he got into a partnership with George Lund, operating a machine shop called Puget Corporation, located right on the north side of the harbor in Tacoma. This shop was doing a large amount of marine work directly for the various shipyards around Commencement Bay.

Immediately after hostilities ceased in 1945 we got a commission from Keith Fisken to build a 45-foot sloop from a Ben Seaborn design. Well, Harbine saw this design, consulted with Ben himself, and had a cabin revision made, so in 1946 we ended up building *two* 45-footers, which were sister hulls, and both of them beautiful boats. The one for Keith Fisken, now called *Kate II*, was owned by the late Ned Skinner longer than Keith had her. Harbine named his boat *Nautilus II*.

When it came time for the launch, Harbine, of course, was there and I asked him if there was anyone who might like to ride down the ways in the boat. He said, "I'm glad you brought that up," because it seems he really wanted to do it himself. Now, Harbine was never small by any stretch of the imagination, and I cautioned him how to hold on securely, as the lake level was such that the railway only extended three feet or so into the water, so at the end of the rails the stern would first drop abruptly, followed by the bow. Well, Harbine must have lost his grip, because he went over backwards with his feet straight up in the air and a *Seattle Times* photographer who was there snapped that picture and published it in the

T. Harbine Monroe's NAUTILUS II, *designed by Ben Seaborn.* (COURTESY OF MOHAI)

T. Harbine Monroe flanked by Dr. and Mrs. William E. Merrill on the NAUTILUS II, CA. 1946. (BLANCHARD COLLECTION)

paper. The caption under the photo just said something about a launching that day on Lake Union. It didn't even mention the Blanchard Boat Company, and we were a regular advertiser in that paper!

Harbine joined the Tacoma Yacht Club in the 1940s, and was commodore in 1949. He also joined the Seattle Yacht Club in 1947, served as rear commodore, and later was named a life member.

About the time the Blanchard Boat Company was involved with navy contracts during the Korean conflict, Harbine had us build him a 40-foot Swiftsure Class, also designed by Ben Seaborn. I think he was primarily interested in trying to get that class well established. We actually built three of that class in close succession, the first being displayed in the Seattle Boat

The prototype of the Blanchard-built, 40-foot Swiftsure class, designed by Ben Seaborn, on display at the Seattle Boat Show in the former National Guard Armory (now Seattle Center House), January, 1947. This boat barely fit through the door, and the mast reached to the ceiling. (COURTESY OF MOHAI)

Show in January 1947, in the old National Guard Armory, which, of course, is now the Center House at the Seattle Center. It had been built as a company boat for demonstration purposes. I was racing her, and Harbine saw her in that show, so he bought number two. Of course he called her *Nautilus III*, and we both competed in the Swiftsure race that year.

Because we were racing boats that were exactly alike, we agreed that whatever one boat did, the other boat would more or less do the exact opposite, because an awful lot of luck in racing is involved in where you happen to be at the right time. Well, Harbine had a tremendous lead on us. The race started from Protection Island just west of Discovery Bay, and we were bucking a big flood tide. Harbine got far ahead of us because he headed right out into the strait and caught the wind first. So by evening I said to my crew, "I'm going to turn in early because it's important for me to be up when we get anywhere near the lightship," and my orders were that we

were going to take it kind of easy because it was now blowing 25 knots, or over. We had taken off the genoa jib and were sailing on the working jib and reefed main.

I woke up about first light, around four o'clock in the morning, and the lightship was in view. We were becalmed, and Harbine was still ahead of us. Ken Ollar, the photographer, actually got a good shot from his boat of the lightship, with Harbine heading back into the strait, and our boat in the background. Of course we never did catch up with him, so he managed to win that race hands down.

The Blanchard Boat Company built a fourth one of those Seaborn-designed Swiftsure boats, and that was for Dick Lerner of Lido Island, Newport, California. He lost her in the surf on the beach in lower California, so we weren't blessed with very much luck on those boats.

Later, Harbine commissioned Ben Seaborn to design him another boat, a much more radical, modern design, and that boat became his *Nautilus IV*, and, because the Blanchard Boat Company was still all tied up with the navy, he had it built by Ed Hoppen of Gig Harbor. He had some success racing with that boat, but his interest in racing now seemed to be on the decline. Drinking began to get the better of him, and eventually Harbine and his wife, Marion, were divorced. When, or to whom, he sold the *Nautilus IV* I don't know, but I'm pretty sure that with the sale of that boat his sailing days were finished. Later, Harbine did have a very fast Bertram runabout with just two bunks forward and very little in the way of cruising accommodations. I never was aboard that boat, but I saw it go by several times.

Harbine was just a terrific yachtsman, and over the years he won many trophies, including the Swiftsure and Tri-Island races for the Seattle Yacht Club. Eunice and I were invited to go with him on two cruises, and both times we went into Princess Louisa Inlet. I had, of course, by then been asked to take Jerry Bryant's place on the board of the Princess Louisa International Foundation, a position which I enjoyed immensely until 1992.

Near the end of Harbine's life, after Marion, his former wife, had remarried and been widowed, they got back together. He passed on at the age of 79 in 1995.

A FINE MOTOR SAILER
FOR THE PRESIDENT OF BOEING

IN THE FALL of 1937 my father got a phone call from Mr. C. W. Wiley, the president of Todd Dry Docks, Inc., inquiring if the Blanchard Boat Company had any kind of new boat to build.

My dad replied, "No, it looks like it's going to be another thin fall and winter," or words to that effect, so Mr. Wiley said, "Well, I can tell you this much. I have a very good friend, and he wants a boat very similar to my *Alice*, but a little bigger, and Walter Lynch is already working on the design of it."

Walter Lynch had been a neighbor and friend of my father's during their school days, and he had done a lot of design work for Captain Anderson, who was running the ferries on Lake Washington. I do not think he had any formal education as a naval architect; he was largely self-taught, having studied naval architecture on his own for years. When Lake Washington Ferries was sold to the county, Walter applied for a job at Todd Dry Docks, and he remained there until he retired.

Well, the boat C. W. Wiley was referring to turned out to be a 63-foot motor sailer for Clare Egtvedt, who was then president of the Boeing Company, and, as a matter of fact, he was the first aeronautical engineer graduated from the University of Washington who had a job to go to when he left school. Wiley told my dad, "Don't bother to try to call him. Just wait until you get a telephone call."

Clare Egtvedt was very, very shy about publicity because Boeing was a non-union shop at that time, and he was trying to hold off unionization as long as he could. Can you imagine what any publicity about this project would have stirred up if it had become known that the president of Boeing was having a fine yacht built for himself?

In time Clare Egtvedt did call to arrange a meeting with my dad, and Dad went down to his office at the appointed time. He said that he thought it would be like in the movies, that they would be interrupted half a dozen times during their session together, and he was surprised that nobody disturbed them at all. So a wonderful relationship between my dad and Clare Egtvedt began that day. Mr. Egtvedt wanted to have the same kind of contract that Boeing had with the government: cost plus a fixed fee. My father arrived at what the fixed fee should be, and they drew up the contract. It was stated very plainly in that contract that under no circumstances was the Blanchard Boat Company to permit any photos or answer any inquiries as to whom this job was for.

Mr. Egtvedt conferred regularly with Walter Lynch and the boat company regarding the specifications for all details for the job, and the only question throughout the construction was, is this the best we can do? This was the only boat we ever built that had a complete teak backbone from stemhead to transom; all the keel and backbone came from the same

sailor — to the Seattle Yacht Club, Max Fleischmann's big yacht, the *Haida*, came in. She had been designed by Cox & Stevens and built by Krupp in Germany in 1930. She was 218 feet, diesel powered, but with the clipper bow and look of a steam yacht. I remember that she normally carried a 44-man crew, which was made up of sailors, the black gang, which was the engine-room crew, and the stewards, but when she went to Alaska, the captain always wanted a couple of extra sailors because there was so much rain and moisture up there that they sometimes had to chamois down three times a day. The *Haida* was probably about the largest private yacht cruising on the west coast at that time, and could easily accommodate 12 guests on a stag cruise, but Max Fleischmann always said, "There's not a yacht that's been built yet that's large enough to accommodate more than two couples."

The NAVITA under construction, Blanchard Boat Company, 1937.
(BLANCHARD COLLECTION)

20-inch square of teak that we sawed on our own 42-inch bandsaw. She was also the last boat that we planked with Port Orford cedar.

Regarding the launching, Mr. Egtvedt arranged all the details. He told my dad, "I want you to get the boat ready to launch, and tell me when she's ready, so we can launch her at any time over the next three or four days." By this time all the waterfront was terribly curious about who the Blanchards were building that fine yacht for, but to the best of my knowledge, and I believe I am correct, nobody learned that until we delivered her over to the Seattle Yacht Club. Of course, Clare Egtvedt couldn't obtain a berth for her at the yacht club without their knowing whose yacht it was.

Shortly after we delivered the *Navita* — that being the name Clare Egtvedt chose for his yacht, from the Latin for

The NAVITA ready for launching, Blanchard Boat Company, 1937.
(BLANCHARD COLLECTION)

Well, the story goes that Mr. Fleischmann flew up from California in his private plane and went over to the Seattle Yacht Club to meet up with his yacht for the cruise to Alaska. He spotted the new *Navita* there, and immediately he tossed his trench coat over the rail of the big yacht and went out on the finger pier to examine the *Navita* closely. Eventually, his captain came over and handed him a bunch of messages that had accumulated at the yacht club, but he just shoved them into his pocket and said to his captain something to the effect that he had never seen a finer built yacht than the *Navita*. Considering what *he* was running around in, that seemed like a pretty good compliment.

Later, I heard from one of the lads, whom I arranged for the *Haida*'s captain to take on north to Alaska, that all the sailors in the fo'c's'le on that yacht had either had a dishonorable discharge from the Coast Guard or the navy, or had done time in some kind of a state institution. But, when you stop to think about it, the *Haida* had excellent eats, and made a great place for those guys to hide out.

That first season Clare Egtvedt didn't get a lot of use out of the *Navita*. Mostly he took short trips, and it was either the first or second season that he asked me if I would like to go for a short cruise over a three-day holiday, Memorial Day. We left on the Thursday before. The other guests were all army officers, three of them, plus Clare and myself. Mrs. Egtvedt had prepared all the food at home, and I, being the youngest, did all the serving and washing up and the other chores. We went over to Port Ludlow, and it was a nice trip, but we didn't get in much sailing. After the first season Clare brought the *Navita* into the boat company and had us widen his berth about six or eight inches, and it was done in such a way that even a master boatbuilder would never have guessed that any change had been made.

By the second season that he had the *Navita*, Clare Egtvedt and Ben Seaborn had struck up a nice acquaintance. Mr. Egtvedt noticed Ben during the building of the *Navita,* and was so impresed he hired Ben to work at Boeing. So in the late spring the Egtvedts invited Ben and his wife, Tink, to go cruising on the *Navita*. They headed up the sound, powering all the way, and set their course at Point Wilson for Cattle

An early photo of the NAVITA in Puget Sound. The absence of any sails and the lubberly appearance of the dangling fenders indicate that this was one of Clare Egtvedt's short excursions. (COURTESY OF MARTY LOKEN)

Point on San Juan Island, thinking that they would get into Friday Harbor by 10:30 or 11:00. Halfway across the strait they were enveloped in a thick fog, so they had to slow down. They couldn't find the passage between Cattle Point and Davis Point on Lopez Island, leading into San Juan Channel, but they *did* find Whale Rocks, and on a falling tide.

Well, the boat was hard on the rocks, so they got busy and shut all the seacocks. Under the bulwarks were little vent holes, and they were able to whittle plugs and wrap rags around them and push them into the holes, because they knew the boat was going to go down to port, which she did. They got off in a dinghy because the *Navita* was not equipped with a radio phone — they were very new at that time — and, because it was dark and they couldn't see anything, they didn't try to reach land. They just stayed there with the *Navita* in the dead calm, and as the tide went out she settled very nicely on her port side. With the first light of morning one of the newspapers got a good aerial view of the yacht lying there on her side, heeled over a little more than 45 degrees.

When the flood started coming back, Ben got off on the rocks and checked to make sure everything was all right. At that point it looked as though they were going to get by without any damage to speak of, but the flood runs opposite to the ebb, and was now running against the deck, which was more vertical than horizontal, so there was more resistance to the current. When the tide got high enough to give a little buoyancy, and of course it was still running hard, the *Navita* swung to starboard and dropped over a ledge, about eight or ten inches, maybe a foot, and that broke the rudder, the skeg, and put a hole in her. So she was really sunk.

As soon as they could they got a salvage barge over there — I think it came from Victoria — and somehow they got a patch over the hole in the *Navita*'s hull, and they had her towed down to the Blanchard Boat Company. (I missed this experience because I was in the hospital at the time having a hernia repaired.) Well, she was put right up on our drydock, and the repairs were made, but I don't think Mrs. Egtvedt ever went out again on that boat.

Mr. Egtvedt would take her up to Maple Bay or Genoa Bay with his hired boy, Millard Mattson. Millard's father, Herb, had been foreman on the job when we built the *Navita*, and Millard had that job for Clare Egtvedt every summer as long as he was in school, and as soon as he was finished with school he went right to work for the Boeing Company. He was an awfully nice fellow, always polite, and his dad was a fine man, too, who taught me a heck of a lot about the boatbuilding trade.

Well, to get back to Clare Egtvedt, sometimes he would get someone like Dietrich Schmitz to go out with him; in fact, there's a photograph of the two of them on the stern of the *Navita*. But there just weren't many times when Clare seemed

Clare Egtvedt, left, with Dietrich Schmitz on the NAVITA. (COURTESY OF MOHAI)

to want to take the boat out, or many people he seemed willing to take out with him. So, as far as I know, that was about the extent of his yachting.

As a very young man Clare had been deckhand and fisherman on the halibut boats that worked out of Ballard, where he had grown up, and I guess that's where he got the desire to have a motor sailer — something he could sail when he wanted to, and the *Navita* does sail very nicely.

After Clare Egtvedt's death a man from Portland came up and bought the *Navita* from his estate. This fellow had had some type of boat before, and he worked down there as a demolition contractor. In fact, at that time he was involved in demolition for the I-5 freeway through Portland. This fellow kept the *Navita* in Seattle for a season or two, and then took her to California, where he eventually sold her to a fellow — I think he might have been a psychiatrist — who thought he could have a lot of fun sailing beyond the three-mile limit off San Francisco, curing wealthy kids of drug addiction.

One summer he brought the boat north to British Columbia and spent the summer cruising around in Canadian waters. That fall he headed back toward California, departing from Victoria, and no one knows for sure how far past Cape Flattery the boat got, but the Coast Guard received an SOS signal from them. The Coast Guard contacted the Blanchard Boat Company to see if we could supply them with a photo of the *Navita*, which we did. They began conducting their search with helicopters and airplanes, and, it was the strangest thing, but when they finally found the boat she was at anchor in Neah Bay. It was never determined just where she had been when the SOS signal was sent, or, for that matter, why it had been sent. In fact, it wasn't known if the owner was even on board when the SOS was sent, but apparently the young lads he had brought up from California thought they were in some kind of trouble, and sent the SOS.

Since she didn't seem to be in any crisis when the Coast Guard located her, they didn't immediately go out and arrest or seize the boat, and when they finally got around to doing something about it the *Navita* had already left and was headed back to Victoria. So, the Coast Guard alerted the Canadian authorities, and as soon as she arrived in Victoria she was impounded. When they searched the boat they found a lot of LSD aboard, so they arrested the psychiatrist. The *Navita* was being used by this guy for running drugs, so she was tied up in litigation all through that winter, lying there in the Inner Harbour, and it turned out to be a very severe winter. The hot water tank froze, just about everything on the boat froze, and no one was paying any attention to her.

Finally our federal government got involved and had the boat brought back to the United States. The Canadians took her to the nearest American port, which was Port Angeles, and I had to go up there with a friend to bring her back. She was sold by the U. S. Marshal's Office right on our own front dock,

and Herb Carroll, who owned Carroll's Jewelers on Fourth Avenue in Seattle, bought her. Bill Sheffield, our purchasing agent at the boat company, thought I was crazy not to bid on her, but I had no desire to own the boat. If I had sold the Blanchard Boat Company for about four or five times what I did, well, I might have become interested, because there were two things that are *still* wrong with that boat, which I would have liked to correct.

First, the fo'c's'le is too small for two adult men. The galley is located forward in the old-fashioned, east coast way, immediately aft of the fo'c's'le. The dining saloon has about seven and one-half feet of headroom in it, which makes it awkward to go below from the wheelhouse. I would advise anybody who would like to enjoy the ownership of this boat to take everything out down below forward of the wheelhouse, put the galley right up next to the wheelhouse, and raise the dining saloon sole, because there are Everdur water tanks underneath and the water capacity on the *Navita* is rather limited by today's standards. Then you would have to figure out some kind of stateroom arrangement forward of the galley. Second, the diesel engine should be replaced. It weighs twice as much as whatever you would put in its place, and it's a very out-of-date engine.

Herb Carroll owned the *Navita* for about 35 years. He had her hauled at Vic Franck's yard in the winter of 1994. They pulled the masts out and did considerable repair on them and on the boat, so she was in beautiful shape, but by 1996 when she was sold by Herb's estate she was looking pretty sad again. The *Navita* was a truly beautiful boat when we built her, and she is now in need of a good owner.

HOW THE BLANCHARDS MOVED
TO HUNT'S POINT FOR TEN DOLLARS A MONTH
AND TWO BOTTLES OF WHISKEY

I FIRST BECAME acquainted with Walter Lembke in 1928 when we were both junior members of the Seattle Yacht Club. Walter had spent the first 16 years of his life aboard his father's sailing schooner, carrying lumber to Honolulu. The entire family lived aboard, including Walter's younger brother, Max, who later became very active with the National Maritime Museum in San Francisco and the *Balclutha*, the fine ship they have on display down there.

As an adult, Walter called on the Blanchard Boat Company for the Pacific Marine Supply Company, usually twice a week, or any time we wanted to see him, and he serviced his accounts in a beautiful fashion. He is one salesman we were always glad to see. For example, frequently he would stop by and see that I was busy with a customer, so he would simply leave without saying anything and come back later in the afternoon or the next day. That's the type of thing he did — this guy was really considerate.

In 1938 Eunice and I made a trip to the east coast, and when we got back I mentioned to Walter one day that I had to find a place to live with cheaper rent than we were paying. The reason I needed to reduce our rent was because I had had an acute appendectomy, and we had only been able to pay Dr. Freeman $10, sometimes $15, a month, and it looked like those payments would go on forever.

Walter thought for a second and said, "How about coming over to the point?" He was married by then, and by "point" he meant Hunt's Point, where he and his wife, Druscilla, were then living. They had moved into a brand new house over there on the east shore of the point. In fact, it was unfinished when they moved into it, and Walter worked every evening finishing the interior woodwork, that sort of thing.

So I said, "Walter, I can't add the expense of commuting and save money."

"Well," he said, "you might be surprised."

That evening Walter called us at home and said, "There's a three-room apartment over a three-car garage on the point, facing west, and nobody living in the big house. The owner lives in Spokane. Druscilla and I have looked at it. It could use some paint here and there, which I know you and Eunice are capable of dealing with, and you can have it for ten dollars a month." So, naturally we moved to Hunt's Point, and Walter even talked some Pacific Marine truck drivers into moving us on a Saturday, which was not one of their work days, and that cost us two bottles of whiskey.

During the time we lived on Hunt's Point I was able to pay Dr. Freeman $35 a month, which was a big help, and a sensible thing to do. In fact, during the summer the cost of commuting went down because I could use the company launch, which had no protection from the weather, to get to and from work, and that boat didn't burn even a gallon of gasoline an hour. We enjoyed the Lembkes' company while we were on Hunt's Point. They had a son, Miller, although we didn't get to know him very well because we didn't stay over there long enough, and he was still pretty much of a toddler when we finally came back to the city.

When I first knew Walter he was, of course, still single. His family had a double-ended lifeboat type of boat, wooden, with a sedan cabin, and I think that they had had it built. What makes me think that was because the propeller shaft went right through the stern timber, which was very rarely done unless the boat was built to order. After he was married and living over on Hunt's Point, Walter kept that boat at his home there, in a nice boathouse which was actually bigger than he needed for the boat.

The second boat that he and Druscilla had was a very well-built, trunk cabin cruiser of 38 feet, which they named the *High Seas*. One day Walter came by the yard and showed me some kind of a little device with gold leaf on it, and he said, "I want you to carve me a couple of nice boards for the *High Seas'* transom, with *High* on one side and *Seas* on the other." He didn't specify the design or style, and left that entirely up to me. I went down to the Erlich-Harrison Lumber Company and got a board that I could saw in two in the middle, inch and one-quarter or inch and one-half Honduras mahogany, and I carved those boards so that they looked like a pair of flying ribbons, and gold-leafed the words *High* and *Seas*, one on each piece. Oh, he was sure tickled with that. I don't remember a specific event where we saw each other cruising, but I think it must have happened at least once over the years.

Well, sometime later the Lembkes moved off Hunt's Point and into a duplex on Clyde Hill, where Eunice and I visited them a few times. I've forgotten which one of them passed on first, but the other one didn't last very long at all after that. Walter especially was a good friend, both to Eunice and me, and to the Blanchard Boat Company, for many years, and our friendship with the Lembkes is one that has many happy memories.

GOSTA ERIKSEN
THE SWEDISH DYNAMO

GOSTA ERIKSEN WAS a Swede who traced his ancestry directly back to Leif Ericsson, the great Viking explorer. The Eriksen family had a shipyard on Nagu, one of the Åland Islands in the Baltic Sea. Technically the island is in Finland, but its inhabitants are all Swedish. In fact, the Eriksen family estate included more than just one island. If you look at an aerial view from way up, like a satellite picture, of the Åland Islands you would see that they are probably five times as numerous as our San Juan Islands, but, unlike the San Juans, the Ålands are not rugged. They're relatively flat, more like the islands of the south sound, and they were heavily timbered.

The Swedes continued shipping all through World War I, flying the Swedish flag day and night, and the German U-boats left them alone because they knew that the Swedish ships were often carrying munitions to Germany. The Swedes could order a new ship from an American shipyard, or anywhere for that matter, and probably have it paid for in full after just one voyage. The timber on the Åland Islands was beginning to give out around the time of World War I, and Gosta's father came to the Pacific Northwest to buy lumber for the family shipyard; he wound up settling here.

So Gus, as he was always called, grew up in two cultures, you might say. He was raised largely here, but he spent most summers back in the Ålands with his grandfather. When he

was around 12 or 13 his grandfather had a beautiful little day-sailing sloop built so that the two of them could sail very comfortably, a real miniature yacht, and during the summers that Gus didn't return to Sweden, that boat was not even put in the water. Gus always got along really well with both his parents and grandparents, and probably had what you would call an exceptionally good childhood.

After he finished high school Gus enrolled at the University of Washington. I had not yet become acquainted with him, but Gus turned out for crew at the university and was actually stroke oar on the Husky crew, in spite of the fact that he was just barely six feet tall. He was probably one of the shortest people in that entire crew except for the coxswain, Carlos Flohr, who did happen to be a friend of mine. Gus was a huge physical specimen, though. His forearms were massive in size, and he was always a very active participant in any number of athletic activities.

During the fall of Gus's freshman year at the University of Washington his grandfather back in Sweden died. Now Gus always knew that as soon as his grandfather was gone, his father and the family would have to move back to Sweden and the Åland Islands. I'm not sure how he managed to resolve this, but I do remember him discussing this problem with his sister, and apparently it was decided that he could stay here and complete his education. Well, he had to take two jobs to do this. His first job was washing dishes at Wiseman's Restaurant, which was open 24 hours a day, on University Way where the present University Book Store is, but it was his second job that had more of an impact as a new kind of recreational activity in the Pacific Northwest.

Gus' second job was in the sports equipment department at the old University Book Store, when it was still a very small operation compared to what it is today. The first fall that Gus worked there was the first year that the book store put in a stock of skis, probably mostly just ash skis, manufactured in Wisconsin or someplace like that, but Gus was sharp enough to see that they were selling so few skis that there wouldn't even be a ski department the next year. So he went to the boss, Mr. McRae, and said, "If you'd let me rent these skis," and he had figured out what he thought they should rent for, "I know a lot of people would have a good enough time on their first ski outing that if we let the rent apply to the sales price they would buy them." Well, the boss thought that over and decided to let Gus do it, and sure enough, from then on skiing became a big thing with the University of Washington students.

Gus turned out for crew each year he was at the university and as soon as he finished his course of studies he was hired as assistant crew coach to Al Ulbrickson; I would place this right about the time of, or shortly after, World War II. Eventually he married the daughter of his former boss at the University Book Store.

He bought an old R Class raised-deck sloop that had much more commodious accommodations than the little day-sailing sloop his grandfather had had built in Sweden, although there was no toilet or anything like that at the time Gus bought her. He renamed the boat *Svea*, which is Swedish for swan. She had varnished mahogany planking above the waterline, and had been designed for and come from the Great Lakes region, so she had really been built for heavier weather than in our part of the world. But she also had probably never had as talented a sailor racing her as Gosta Eriksen.

In January of 1945 the Corinthian Yacht Club was established, and after the war Charlie Frisbie served as the first commodore of the new club. Gosta Eriksen was the third commodore. That guy could just spread himself so thin. I remember once when he was either commodore or vice-commodore of the Corinthian Yacht Club they were having their annual presentation of prizes down at the Olympic Hotel. However, it was during ski season and Gus had started and was the coach of the University of Washington ski team and he had work that he had to do for a weekend university ski event.

So on this particular Friday evening, before he could attend the Corinthian Yacht Club event, he loaded up a lot of ski gear, slalom pole markers and other equipment, into two packs in the back of his car, and drove all the way up to the east end of Lake Keechelus, up near the summit of Snoqualmie Pass. He could park there, cross over the railroad tracks and walk back to where the University of Washington had a ski cabin that somebody had given to the school. Well, Gus had to walk west along the tracks for probably a mile and a half, carrying half of this gear, which was probably close to a hundred pounds, and build a fire in the cabin, put the coffee pot on, then go back to the car and get the second load. After making himself some lunch and drinking the coffee, he drove all the way back to Seattle, jumped into his tuxedo, and rushed to the Olympic Hotel in time to present the prizes. And that's not quite all the story.

Gosta Eriksen, CA. 1949. (COURTESY OF CORINTHIAN YACHT CLUB OF SEATTLE)

Gosta Eriksen's SVEA *was the only boat to complete the Tacoma Yacht Club's New Year's Day race in 1949. Gosta in sunglasses and Jean Eriksen in bandana.* (COURTESY OF INGRID HOLMDAHL)

By the time Gus got home it was after midnight. He had made arrangements with one of his crew to take the *Svea* the next morning through the Fremont Bridge and the Ballard Bridge, and he met up with the boat at the locks, got aboard, and they made it in time for the scheduled Saturday race.

Another time, the University of Washington wanted to have a crew race with the University of British Columbia, but there was no money, so Gus agreed that he'd take the shell and oars up on the *Svea* if some of the fellows would go with him, and they went out through the locks with a 60-foot shell on a 40-foot sloop!

Gus was keen for almost any kind of sport, including golf, which was a bit unusual for a sailor. One time while he was still with the University of Washington as assistant crew coach he had to attend some kind of a meeting up in Calgary. He checked into his hotel, which had a golf course right there, so he went down to the pro shop and, yes, they could find him clubs, and he picked out what he wanted. The pro said to him, "A trio of fellows just started. They're just teeing off at the first hole now, and if you hotfoot over there I think they'd like you for a fourth." So Gus went over and said he'd like to play with them, and they said fine, and one of the golfers was a Mr. Crosby, Mr. Bing Crosby, and Gus didn't even know that he was the singer!

Gus and his wife had four children, all girls. They were named Sara, Kristina, Ingrid and Signe, and if you take the first letters of their names, it spells SKIS. Eventually Gus was lured away from the University of Washington to take the head coach's job at Syracuse, New York. I remember that he and his family left Seattle near the end of his term as commodore of the Corinthian Yacht Club, so it must have been around 1949. He immediately became active in racing in the east, although I'm not sure if he had anything that you could consider a yacht while he was back at Syracuse.

At that time Syracuse had a new, beautiful, big, permanent building for the crewhouse, but the upper floor was completely bare and empty. It was named for its donors — the husband was a veteran of the crew at Syracuse — a couple who had left a bequest in their will that this building should be built; it was a big sum of money. Gus thought this empty space in the new building was kind of strange, so he very quietly made some discreet inquiries, and discovered that not very long after the man had died his widow had also died, and the Board of Regents at the university decided they had better use for some of that money elsewhere. Now Gus was the kind who never hesitated to rush right in where angels feared to tread, and while he was at Syracuse he managed to ruffle some feathers. He had a five-year contract, but when the five years were up he knew he was finished.

His father was still living in Sweden, but was not in very good health, so Gus, his wife and the girls, who were high school age by that time, moved back to Sweden. After they did, Gus continued his interest in rowing. The Eriksens decided they liked the area north of Göteborg on the North Sea. There are quite a lot of little fjords in there, and the land is very rocky, but the rocks were rounded off and polished by glaciers. So Gus chartered a float plane and pilot, and they flew all over the area, taking photographs of anything that looked interesting, that had any possibilities. One of the places he photographed was at a little town called Oxevik, near Uddevalla. The town is so tiny that you can't find it on most maps.

The place Gus liked there had been a fish saltery for over a hundred years, and, as with all kinds of businesses in those early days, the floor was just planks with anywhere from one-fourth- to one-half-inch spaces between each one. In the old days, when the workers got through cleaning the fish, they just turned the hose on the mess and it was washed through the cracks between the floor planks and fell on the ground underneath. As a consequence, the place had been for sale for years. No one wanted it because of the terrible smell.

Gus liked this place, and started thinking about what he could do about the smell. He found a chance to buy a truckload of 55-gallon drums of polyester resin that was overage, and consequently not suitable for anything that people would pay money for, such as a boat. Gus bought this resin for about ten cents on the dollar and covered the entire crawl space under the building. He had to cut a few hatches in the floor here and there, but he completely sealed off that smell with polyester resin. Then he converted the waterfront end of the building into his home, and used the upper end and the loft for boat storage.

Now the Swedes love boats, and they've got lots of water to boat in, but they don't have a hell of a lot of money. Gus made a deal with somebody to put in piers and finger piers, supported on ordinary galvanized pipe, in the spring when the ice was gone so that for a fixed rent or maybe a percentage of the cost of the installation, people could have moorage for their boats. But as soon as the boats were all hauled out for the winter, Gus would take in the piers and pull all the pilings because he didn't want the ice to take them out. So that was a pretty good deal all around for everybody.

Gus had another idea. He'd been talking about a boat that would sail well, a small sloop, somewhere in the neighborhood of 15 to 18 feet long, that could accommodate a 15-horse-power outboard to pull water skiers. It had to have sufficient speed for greenhorn water skiers. So Gus worked on this, and eventually he contacted the naval architect, Phil Rhodes, and I don't know if it was Phil's idea or if Gus stumbled onto it himself, but they determined that in order to be fast enough to pull a skier, a boat would have to be pretty flat in the stern. They put twin rudders on the boat so the motor could be right there in the middle, tilted up when they were sailing, but able to pull a skier if the person wasn't too heavy.

Well, Gus never particularly wanted to be in the boat-manufacturing business. The old family place where the big shipyard had been in World War I was still sitting there in the Åland Islands if he'd wanted to go into the manufacturing end of it himself. What he did, instead, was to demonstrate this new design and sign up some orders with the understanding that the owners would not take delivery until maybe April 15th of the next year, and when he got together a sufficient number of orders for boats he would go around to several manufacturers and take bids for construction. In time he actually became pretty good at promoting his product, and eventually he did have to get into the boatbuilding business. He called it Scandia Marine, and he got to where he was turning out 1,200 to 1,500 boats per year. Of course, it helped that they had been designed by Phil Rhodes.

Gus certainly had a many-faceted career over the years. Among other things, he was very much in the forefront of establishing the safety rules and regulations on overnight, open-sea races. In 1970, when I was asked to be on the National Boating Safety Council, they sent me some data on the organization, and there was Gosta Eriksen's name in the literature. I immediately wrote to him and told him that Eunice and I expected to be in Denmark at such-and-such a time, and would be glad to come over to Sweden if he had the time to get together. He telephoned right back, "Delighted to have you come."

Fortunately, I had been forewarned by somebody before I left on the trip that Gus was by then a widower. We made tentative arrangements to meet in Göteborg at a specific time, and I figured that it would just be for lunch. Eunice and I had flown to London and gone on to Copenhagen, where we met up with Eunice's sister, Helen. The three of us went on to Göteborg and arrived at the proper place at one o'clock, but no Gus. I remember that Eunice was a little annoyed when he didn't show up until about 3:30 in the afternoon, so instead of lunch we went out and had an early supper, and then we followed him in our rented car up to his house in Oxevik. That was where Gus had had his boat factory, in a good protected bay, and we had a nice visit.

Later, on another trip to Europe, we ran into Gosta again. As I recall, it was quite by accident, and by this time he was happily remarried. Like so many active and enthusiastic athletes, though, his heart got bad. He survived three heart attacks, but died of cancer in the early 1990s.

Gus was always just a great guy to sail or race with. And that reminds me of one last story about him. *Nobody* ever wanted to anchor too close to him at Port Ludlow or any of the popular places where we might go on a sail, because every morning he rolled out of his bunk, jumped into his swim trunks and dove off the stern of the *Svea*, and as he came up he would let out a hell of a war whoop. It never made any difference how early or late in the season; salt water to Gus was always better than fresh water, any time, any temperature.

THE J. B. HEADLEYS OF ROSWELL, NEW MEXICO,
AND HOW THE BLANCHARDS
ACQUIRED THE *AURA*

ONE MORNING LATE in the summer of 1948 I happened to be standing at the counter in the upstairs office at the boat company when the door opened and in walked a very tall, slender, Professor Piccard-looking sort of man — Professor Piccard was the great balloonist who did early exploration of the stratosphere — and he said to me immediately, "My name is J. B. Headley, I live in Roswell, New Mexico, I've been in Victoria for the month of July, and in the San Juan Islands, mostly Orcas, for the month of August, and I've made it my business to find out that if you want to talk sailboats you talk to the Blanchards in Seattle."

And I said, "Well, I'm Norm Blanchard, Jr., and my dad is here and I'd be glad to get him for you."

"Oh," he said, "I'm sure you'll do very nicely."

So I took him on a tour of the plant and showed him what we were doing at the time, which, as I recall, would have been building the early Swiftsure boats. We didn't have one of our new "33s" at the plant that day, so I took Mr. Headley over to the Seattle Yacht Club where he could see the two "33s" that were over there. By the time I had showed him the advantage of the different ways the "33s" could be outfitted I had pretty much shot the morning, so I asked him, "Would you like to have lunch at the club?"

He replied, "That would be very nice."

So we had lunch there at the club, and I may have even given him an application for membership in the Seattle Yacht Club. During lunch Mr. Headley told me he was a petroleum geologist and had established an office in New Mexico. He also informed me that his health wasn't what it should be, but that the doctors he'd consulted couldn't find any medical explanation for his problems, other than perhaps the dry, hot weather that they suffered through each summer.

After lunch was over he said, "Well, if you can just drop me off anyplace where I can get a streetcar back downtown I'd be very much indebted to you."

So I dropped him off at the corner of Eastlake Avenue and Allison Street, and as I drove the two blocks back to the plant I thought to myself, well, you had a very pleasant morning, and you'll probably never hear from that man again.

I felt better about losing work that morning when, eight or ten days later, I had a very nice handwritten, Emily Post-type of thank you from J. B. Headley. Of course, I had armed him with all of our literature on the Knockabouts, Swiftsures and "33s", so, sure enough, between Christmas and New Year's that year he wrote again to say that he and Mrs. Headley had decided that they wanted to start their yachting on Puget Sound in a Blanchard "33". And there was a check enclosed for $2,500 with a note to let him know if that wasn't enough. That developed into just a wonderful customer relationship.

The next summer, 1949, the Headleys drove their Buick up to Seattle, where they were going to pick up their new "33"

A Bill Garden-designed Blanchard "33" at the Seattle Boat Show in the former National Guard Armory (now Seattle Center House), January, 1947. (COURTESY OF MOHAI)

and then cruise in the San Juan Islands. They had their 11-year-old son, Kenneth, with them. Neither Mrs. Headley nor the boy had been up here before. Mrs. Headley, Johanna, was actually Headley's second wife. She was a Dutch girl from the island of Curacao, and you could tell she had salt water in her veins. She was very attractive, too.

At that time we had a night watchman at the Blanchard Boat Company who was a real character, kind of like a devoted dog, and he did exactly what I told him if I made my point strong enough. This fellow worked days on Saturdays and Sundays, and he lived in the first block south of the plant. I had told him we were expecting Mr. and Mrs. Headley, and that he was supposed to call me if they arrived at the plant. Well, they arrived on a Sunday, and of course the watchman called me as I had told him to do, and when J. B. Headley got on the phone he said to me, "I told that man not to call you, not to disturb you on a Sunday."

He insisted that I not waste any of my time with him on a Sunday, but I did make some suggestions about what they might enjoy in the way of city sightseeing, and maybe they

had their Sunday dinner at the Seattle Yacht Club, because Mr. Headley was a member by that time. They spent a day there at the plant getting things together for their cruise, and as soon as Mrs. Headley was satisfied that she had what she needed they were ready to leave. This was probably the following Tuesday, and I suppose I went out through the locks with them, so that they could see how that operation was handled.

Well, before they left, Mr. Headley made arrangements that on a specific day around mid-July, Eunice and I would drive their Buick up and take the ferry to Orcas Island, and bring any accumulation of mail that he might have received, because he had given our address as his forwarding address for the summer. So on the date we agreed on Eunice and I took the car to Orcas Island, parked it according to Mr. Headley's directions, and then contacted our friend, Rich Exton, who had a little three-seat float plane, and Rich flew us over to Parks Bay on the west side of Shaw Island where we met and had lunch with the Headleys, and I noted that they certainly had settled in nicely. Later Exton flew us back to Orcas, and we caught a plane that flew us to Bellingham, and I think we took the train back to Seattle.

The Headleys had planned to bring their boat, which they had named the *Aira*, back to the Blanchard Boat Company near the end of August and then drive back to Roswell, because the boy had to start school on the Tuesday after Labor Day. They arrived 48 hours ahead of schedule, and I was very much concerned when I saw them tied up at the shop the morning after they had arrived. I think I probably jumped to the conclusion that they had had some kind of a problem. So when I went out to see them, Mr. Headley said to me, "You forget, Norm, it's just as much fun for the Headleys of Roswell to be moored to your float here in Lake Union as it is to be moored to the float in Friday Harbor or any other place where we visited."

He and I walked up to the office, and Louise Sheffield, our bookkeeper, had quite a stack of mail for him. I had things to do, and when I got back to the office Louise said, "Mr. Headley told me that he wants you to come aboard as soon as you can spend half an hour or so."

This was early enough after lunch that I said to Louise, "Well, you tell him that right now the situation is such that I'll have to make that around 4:30, maybe a little before."

So around 4:20 I went aboard the *Aira*, and Mrs. Headley sent the boy on an errand or off somewhere, and when I came below J. B. Headley said, "A situation of this kind calls for a drink," and made three nice drinks for us. I sat across the table from them, and he said, "Now, what Johanna and I have been really racking our brains about is all you've done for the Headleys of Roswell, so I want to ask you a question. If we lived here in Seattle, about when would we be laying the boat up for the winter?"

I said to him, "Around the middle of October, certainly by the middle of November, depending a lot on the weather."

"All right," he said, "and when would it go back in service?"

"Well," I said, "first of March, certainly by the first of April, and, again, the weather makes the difference."

"OK," he said, "that's just what we want to happen to the *Aira*. We want the boat taken care of just like it was your own. I want a good winter cover, just what you think is the best. And we want the boat in the Seattle Yacht Club Opening Day, even though we can't be here. In fact, I want you to treat this boat just as though it was your own boat until we return next season and use it ourselves. Between our trips to Seattle this is to be your boat."

Well, this was totally unexpected! That first winter Mr. Headley wanted us to install a fresh-water cooling system, which I heartily approved of, and, because we were putting fresh-water cooling on, he also wanted us to install a five-gallon hot-water tank that would use waste heat from the engine. He also had us install a cabin heater. It was a car heater really, but for most of those boats we only recommended, and most people stuck with, an alcohol stove or maybe a range with oil burners for heat. So after the Headleys left that season Eunice and I had a nice week's vacation on the *Aira* after Labor Day, and went up to Victoria. From that point on I had pretty regular correspondence with Mr. Headley. He always wrote his letters in longhand, and they weren't too terribly easy to read. The Headleys came back to Seattle the following summer and took the *Aira* north again.

After their second season on the *Aira*, sometime between Thanksgiving and Christmas Mr. Headley went into his office in Roswell and was only there for a very short time when he decided he was just too ill, so he went home and went back to bed, and within an hour or two he had lapsed into a coma. Eventually Johanna got him to the local hospital, and I've never checked the population of Roswell, but I can't imagine it's very big. And of course in that part of the country it was a Catholic hospital, and apparently they just gave him up for lost; they told Johanna that he was soon going to be dead.

Well, Johanna wasn't going to give up so easily. At that time there was just one ambulance plane in the entire United States, and she got that plane to fly from New York City to pick up her husband and herself and take them to Memphis, Tennessee. J. B. Headley's son by his first wife was a doctor or intern in a hospital there where they had a lot of very experienced staff and sophisticated equipment. So they rushed him into surgery as soon as he arrived, and they removed a steel splinter that had been lodged in his brain for seven years.

Evidently, seven years earlier he had been trying to bring in a well and the nitroglycerin bomb was just being lowered into the shaft and went off when it was only down about 30 or 40 feet. The explosion wrecked the rig, seven of the men were killed, and just Mr. Headley and two others survived. I think that was why he had told me, the first day we met, that his health wasn't as good as it should have been. Well, they were successful back there in Memphis, and saved his life.

Later, Rich Exton, the fellow who flew Eunice and me from Orcas to Shaw Island that summer, told me that he had had that same operation for an abscess on the brain as a young man in his mid-20s. According to Exton, J. B. was damned lucky that they found the splinter when they did because nobody had ever survived that operation after they were 30 years of age until J. B. Headley. However, I also learned that the operation leaves the patient with a constant headache of varying intensity that won't go away, and barbiturates won't help, although they told J. B. that the headaches would disappear within four to five years.

We exchanged Christmas cards that year with the Headleys, and our wives corresponded back and forth, and I remember that even though Mr. Headley had almost died shortly before Christmas, young Norm got a gift that year from Kenneth Headley, who had asked his mother, "Can I send my chaps that I've outgrown to Mr. Blanchard's boy for Christmas?" When they arrived Eunice had to turn them up about six inches, but they were real, honest-to-God sheepskin chaps.

It was 18 months or more after J. B.'s operation when the Headleys came back to Seattle, which would have been the summer of 1951. At that time they flew up, although generally he was very opposed to flying. When they arrived he said to me, "Norm, not because of financial pressure, but purely from a mental standpoint I've got to get rid of this boat."

And I said, "Well, Mr. Headley, in the trade that's what we call 'dumping it.' "

"Yes," he said, "I can see that that's a pretty good term for it."

So I said, "Let me talk to my father and I'll see if the company can buy back the *Aira*."

Young Norm wearing the chaps sent to him by Kenneth Headley, Christmas, 1950. (BLANCHARD COLLECTION)

At that time we already had another "33" for sale that belonged to young Norm's godfather, who had had a frightening experience with it. He and his wife had been sailing up around Kenmore at the north end of Lake Washington. They both tended to be kind of "five-by-fiveish," and somehow or other the boat took a knockdown and he ended up in the water up to his waist. When the boat came up in the wind, she didn't have the strength to stay with it, and it was a very frightening experience, so they decided it was too big a boat for them. This fellow worked for the Kroll Map Company and couldn't afford to take a big loss on the boat, but because of the Korean War the second-hand price of all sailboats had really taken a nosedive.

The Blanchard Boat Company was involved again with navy contracts, however, and we were doing well enough that my dad and I decided we could put the *Aira* back in stock. So that year Eunice and I still had the use of her. I did all the rigging, and kept her clean, while we tried to sell her for Mr. Headley.

The first navy contract we had during the Korean War was a 25-boat contract, but ten of them had to be delivered to San Diego, and we shipped ten of them at once on the Coastwise Steamship Line. I was involved with towing the boats to Elliott Bay. They had shipping cradles secured to them and were equipped with their own lifting gear, and we had hired a big floating crane to set them on the deck of the ship. Well, you can't load deckload until you've got all the cargo holds filled and the hatches closed, so it was well after midnight when that job was finished. I went home and got a few hours of sleep, and then probably late the next morning Eunice and I took off to drive south so that I'd be there in San Diego to make the actual delivery.

We had decided that we really wanted to buy the *Aira*, but I was involved with the shipment of navy boats, and we were afraid that my dad would sell her to the one prospect we had, Dr. Byron Ward. In fact, the doctor had bought my Star boat as a Christmas present for his son sometime earlier. But we knew that Dr. Ward was waiting for fall when he could get her for a lower price, so as soon as we got home we remortgaged our house and bought J. B. Headley's boat. Because Mr.

Headley had specified that the name did not go with the boat we changed the "*i*" to a "*u*", and called her the *Aura*.

We cruised in the *Aura* for many years, and when we did finally sell her she went to Bellingham, where she has had several owners in recent years, all of whom, I'm happy to say, were conscientious owners. In fact, in the summer of 1996 I offered to help her current owner return the boat from Lake Union to Bellingham, but we ran into such foul weather by the time we were heading into Saratoga Passage that he decided to delay the rest of the trip.

As I said, Johanna Headley was from the island of Curacao, and due to the poor sanitary conditions there she had contracted undulant fever, maybe even as a child. Sometime after we bought the *Aura*, probably four, maybe five years, Johanna succumbed to her undulant fever. We hadn't heard from J. B. Headley in a long time, but one day, totally unexpected, here came a letter from Roswell, New Mexico. In his letter he explained that he was confined to his bed with a broken hip, and he was living at home alone, although he had a Spanish woman who came in daily around mid-morning to fix him a good breakfast, and then later in the day a second meal.

The Blanchard-built sloop AURA, *formerly the* AIRA, *owned by Norm and Eunice Blanchard for 25 years.* (BLANCHARD COLLECTION)

He listed some items that he wanted me to try to send him, some little blocks and some light line, so that he could make a block and tackle and rig it up to the ceiling above his hospital bed to help him move around more easily. So I filled the order to the best of my ability, and naturally wrote him a nice letter, and I had another letter from him right away. Well, I was still very busy at the boat company with the navy contracts — in fact I was running the biggest crews that I ever ran — so after about the third letter from J. B. Headley I said to Eunice, "Honey, you're going to have to take over the correspondence with Mr. Headley because I simply can't do it." So Eunice started corresponding with him.

At some point a lady who was selling glass cooking containers door to door came in and spent a day with J. B. Headley, and he ended up buying a set of the containers for himself, and he bought two sets for Eunice, one for the *Aura* and one for our home. So before long Bill Sheffield, our purchasing agent, who always had a wonderful sense of humor, started referring to Mr. Headley as Eunice's sugar daddy. Every Christmas, from a different catalog, would come some extravagant fruit basket, things like that, but that's just the kind of wonderful relationship we had.

J. B. Headley lived on alone nearly ten years after he lost Johanna, and he passed on in 1966. I heard that he and his son, Kenneth, were estranged at the time of his death, and I've lost track of Kenneth. But both J. B. and Johanna were very dear friends, and it was unquestionably the most wonderful business relationship that I developed in my whole time at the Blanchard Boat Company.

SOME CANADIAN CHARACTERS
I HAVE KNOWN

HAROLD JONES WAS a Canadian who lived in Vancouver, B.C., where he was in the towboat business. As I recall, he had between seven and 12 tugs in his fleet, all with their uniformly painted stacks, and he was pretty much the Foss of Vancouver. You'd see his tugs pulling logs, helping ships get away from the pier, those sorts of things. He was a damned good fleet operator, and everybody knew his boats.

One of my early trips to Vancouver to visit Harold must have been around 1936, because I recall that I had only been married about a year. Harold had a daughter — his only child — who was around 16 at the time, but thought she was 25, and of course she could do no wrong. Harold was very likeable, and he was always very popular on both sides of the line.

Harold Jones was a prominent member of the Royal Vancouver Yacht Club, and for a long time he owned a boat that my father built, the *Gwendolyn II*, which was previously owned by Fritz Hellenthal. Although I never had an opportunity to sail with him, Harold was a very good competitor until World War II came along, and all racing stopped. Well, shortly after the cessation of hostilities Harold phoned me and said he needed to meet with me — something about Princess Louisa Inlet. I said that that would be OK, but the only time I could go up to Vancouver would be on a Sunday. So we arranged a date, and I drove up to Vancouver.

When I got to Harold's house he was down in his playroom, which happened to be under the corner of the dining room; it had a little octagonal tower on it, which was the breakfast room. I was *highly* surprised to find that in the space of the octagonal foundation in his basement he had built, with his own hands, a lighted diorama of Vancouver from the water, and he had his Lionel model railway running through it.

Harold continued with the *Gwen* for quite a few years, and then around 1947 or '48 he got Ed Monk to design him a new boat, a big sloop, about 65 feet with a nice teak house. He told Ed he wanted to build her skookum, and Ed designed it plenty skookum, and then Harold went and doubled all the dimensions. The frames were steam-bent oak and four inches square — really crazy. The result was that she floated about eight or ten inches below her designed waterline, but that didn't cut down on Harold's pride. He was very decent about how it came out, and always said, "It was my own damned fault."

On his cruises down to Seattle Harold never came alone. He would always come through the locks with a helper. Of course, he could always pull a deckhand off his list to go along with him. The most memorable thing about his coming through the Lake Washington Ship Canal was that he would stand on the foredeck of his boat and play his trumpet. He always had his trumpet with him, and you could hear him coming. If we were planning to have lunch at the Seattle Yacht Club I'd leave the shop as soon as I heard his trumpet. I'd walk out on the dock at the yacht club and here he'd come, with somebody else steering the boat, and Harold still on the foredeck playing his trumpet. You know, in those days very few adult men could play an instrument of any kind unless they were professionals.

Harold Jones was a character, and that reminds me of the five old Canadian gentlemen who owned the *Minerva*. She was still gaff rigged, but she was a big, powerful yawl, about 50 feet long. She belonged to these five old gentlemen, and they always kept a hired "boy" on her — he was only 65!

When the old boys finished their race they would sail right up to their mooring — they'd come in under full sail and pick up their buoy — and there was no sign of a breakwater near the Royal Vancouver Yacht Club like there is now. They always kept their dinghy on the mooring buoy. It was a pretty good dinghy, too, about 11 or 12 feet, because their hired boy would use it to row all of them together into the yacht club float.

These gentlemen always imported their Scotch in the barrel from Scotland, and the barrel sat with a spigot in it between the berths in the after stateroom. As soon as the first one came into the cockpit in his white flannels after a race, the 65-year-old boat boy would show up with a water server, but it was full of Scotch whisky. One by one each of them would show up in the cockpit in his white flannels, and then everybody knew it was open house on the *Minerva*. If you went aboard you were immediately offered a drink, and one of them would start pouring, and if you didn't stop him he'd fill that tumbler right up to the top with Scotch whisky.

Everybody always liked to talk about these guys, and they were a popular topic of conversation. They had an agreement among them that as they died off, the last survivor would own the *Minerva* outright. Of course once they began to die there were only a couple of years before all five of them were gone.

H. ARTHUR AYERS
AN ALL-AROUND YACHTSMAN

WHEN HE DIED in 1998, Arthur Ayers held the longest-standing active membership in the Seattle Yacht Club. His mother was Ethel Ayers, who was an office manager for Captain James Griffiths. Mrs. Ayers and the captain were married when Art was probably about 12 years old. At that time Captain Griffiths was running around in his second *Sueja*, which was an 82-footer, built by my father out at Tregoning's. He soon had both Art and his mother thoroughly acquainted with navigating and running the boat, and in time Art became a real artist at maneuvering that yacht. Of course, it helped that she was twin screw.

Art became a junior member of the Seattle Yacht Club in 1926 when he was 16 years old, which was also the year that Captain Griffiths had the third *Sueja* built, and this was when he and I started to form our good friendship. Art was very faithful about attending meetings at the yacht club, and he was elected junior commodore the year before I was. He sailed quite a bit at that time with Ted Geary on the *Sir Tom*, and, of course, Geary was frequently a guest aboard the *Sueja III* and was always interested in bringing along boys who seemed to have a yen for sailing. Art crewed for various people in their Flatties, including Mary Helen Corbett, but he did not own a Flattie or build any of those boats himself. Being a native Vancouverite, and going with the captain as much as he did up to Canada, Art never got out of touch with Vancouver, and he was really like a citizen of both Vancouver and Seattle.

After Ted Geary moved to Los Angeles in 1930, and Captain Griffiths was still head of the syndicate that owned the *Sir Tom*, she more or less became the property of Art Ayers, and he campaigned her actively in Pacific International Yachting

Art Ayers at the helm of the CIRCE, *with Ray Cooke, CA. 1939.* (COURTESY OF SALLY AYERS)

Association (PIYA) regattas over the next ten years, and actually up until all international competition was interrupted during World War II.

Eunice and I were married in 1935, so I think it was 1936 when Art and Sally Ayers were married. When they were young marrieds Art and Sally bought the *Armida* from Tom Ramsay of the Royal Vancouver Yacht Club, and they cruised in her with their kids for a number of years. The *Armida* was a nice yawl, about 40 feet, if I remember correctly, and she won the Tri-Island Race in 1945. After they sold the *Armida* their next boat was the *Barbara Lee*, a 40-foot power boat that had been built by the Blanchard Boat Company in 1928 for McDonald Smith, and I believe she was Art's and Sally's last boat.

In his early adult years Art worked for his stepfather's enterprises. When the captain died in 1943 his son, Stanley Griffiths, kind of took over operation of the companies, so Art went to work at Todd Dry Docks. For a time he operated a ship service business of his own on the waterfront. He had a few trucks and operated a mobile repair business; they'd do whatever was needed on the ship, and they were always ships, not boats. But he was not very well financed, and when the competition got too tough he closed up and went back to Todd.

During the 1980s Art Ayers was instrumental in compiling information for the publication of the Seattle Yacht Club's centennial book in 1992, and he and I worked very closely together on that project. While his health held he was certainly a very active, all-around yachtsman, both sail and power.

Art and Sally Ayers' beautiful yawl ARMIDA, *built in Vancouver, B.C., in 1935. This photo was once used in a Lucky Strike ad.* (COURTESY OF SALLY AYERS)

SUNNY VYNNE
YACHTSMAN AND SAILOR EXTRAORDINAIRE

EUSTACE VYNNE, JR., was known by *everybody* as Sunny. He was born in Chicago, but the family moved here when Sunny was in his mid-teens, and he graduated from Garfield High School. I think his father did some sailing, probably with Roy Corbett and some of the other people at the Seattle Yacht Club. Everybody liked Mr. Vynne, Sr., but, at six foot four, if I'm not mistaken, and about 75 pounds or so overweight, he was almost too big to get into most of the boats around Seattle at the time. He was just plain *big*.

Sunny joined the Seattle Yacht Club as a junior in 1935, and, at age 14, he was the youngest member of the club. For his birthday that year — I don't know why — the Philco and Transitone radio companies gave him a Moth Class sailboat, called the *Whistle Bug*. Now a Moth was just about as close to a sailing surfboard as a boat could be, and of course this was long before we had ever heard of surfboards. It was an east coast design, and I think they were a one-design class that were mostly amateur built, something like Flatties, and strictly for going sailing and racing. They had very little in the way of a cockpit because the bottom was so close to the deck. And they never did catch on out here.

So Sunny's boat arrived, and I remember it was painted red. Just what the circumstances were I can't recall, but we had to do a little work on it at the Blanchard Boat Company. I imagine it might have been damaged in transit. Sunny started

sailing this little Moth, and there was no competition for it, but he just loved to sail right from the beginning; he was a real natural, and he began winning Seattle Yacht Club races that very first year.

In the late 1930s the Star boat fleet really got going, and that had all started with my Number 908. I don't recall that

Norm Blanchard and Eunice Scholl on the BLUE BOOT, *Star boat #908,* CA. 1932. (BLANCHARD COLLECTION)

Sunny ever had a Flattie, but he became very active with the Star boats. Out near the end of East Madison Street, just north of the old ferry dock, was a garage with a lower floor, where you could rent space for a Star boat for about the same price you'd rent a space for a car. Back then there wasn't much demand for car storage, so that was quite a place for youngsters to build their own Star boats, and Sunny, Bob Lamson and Phil Spaulding teamed up and started building Star boats out there on the lower level of that garage.

Meanwhile, Sunny had become very active in competition with his Star boat. He was a top sailor, winning many races and gathering lots of trophies. Well, one day he was out sailing on Lake Washington — and I imagine it was with his second or third Star boat — and it was a very windy day. Somewhere slightly east of the center of the lake, either just north or south of where the I-520 bridge is now, they got such a knockdown that the boat started to sink by the stern. The headstays came through a fitting on the bow right at the nose, and they had crank turnbuckles so they could bend the mast to flatten the sail in heavy weather. She would have floated if it wasn't for that fitting that led the jib and masthead stay through the deck, because they could hear the air whistling out. It was kind of touch and go for a while, and of course the kids were in the water, but somebody pulled them out. Sunny had enough time before the boat sank to take cross bearings, because he was going to try to get the boat back, although the lake is about 200 feet deep where she went down.

Sunny got together a lot of his friends, Star boat sailors, and they dragged the lake with grappling hooks, but they couldn't locate the boat. I think about six weeks went by, and there was only one group of kids who were still fishing for the boat. They finally did locate it, were able to pull it up and salvage it, and they took it back over to the garage near Madison Beach. They put the boat in a cradle and it sat there for two and a half or three years. All the paint came off it, just because it had soaked up so much water, but eventually somebody rehabilitated it and entered it in competitions again.

Sunny attended the University of Washington, where he rowed on the Husky crew. The day after Pearl Harbor he left the university and enlisted in the Coast Guard, where he

Sunny Vynne in his University of Washington Husky crew sweater, CA. 1941. (COURTESY OF JUNE HELLENTHAL VYNNE)

served in the South Pacific during the war. Sunny returned to Seattle after the Armistice and started his own construction company, and was manager for a construction supplier, very much involved in the construction game, supplying nail guns and all kinds of special post-war, labor-saving devices. His business even took him to Australia for a time, but everywhere he went he was an avid yachtsman.

Sunny and Fritz Hellenthal's daughter, June, had gotten married before the end of the war. June, of course, was a real sailor gal, and she and Sunny had two boys and one daughter. All during this post-war time Sunny remained an active sailor, winning many races, and later becoming involved with the Six Metre Class. In fact, I rather imagine he owned a Six Metre boat at one time or another. Sunny also became a member of, and later was commodore of, the Corinthian Yacht Club, and was very actively involved in the building of their present clubhouse at Shilshole back in 1970. In 1979 he was named Sailor of the Year, and then in 1985 one of the two new Pocock racing shells purchased by the Seattle Yacht Club was named for Sunny Vynne.

About 1970 I got a call from George Schuchart: "Norm, who's the Daddy Warbucks of the Seattle Sailing Foundation?"

I replied, "I don't know, but I know who to ask to find out, and that's Sunny Vynne."

George said, "Well, we need to find out," and he named his two partners.

It seems he had suddenly gotten an opportunity to buy the Twelve Metre *Intrepid*, which had been the America's Cup winner in 1967 and '70. Well, George got in touch with Sunny, and Sunny put together a syndicate that purchased the *Intrepid* for the Seattle Sailing Foundation to challenge for the America's Cup in 1974. And Sunny nearly pulled that off. The *Intrepid* came within one victory, back at Newport, Rhode Island, of getting the right to defend for the America's Cup, so, even with all the trophies he won in his many years of sailing, this one event is what Sunny Vynne is most remembered for in sailing circles.

In 1975 Sunny and June moved up to Friday Harbor on San Juan Island. When he was in his late sixties Sunny had a stroke that was just devastating. Both his and June's lives became very difficult after that stroke, and he finally passed away, I imagine largely from the effects of his stroke, in May of 1996. With Sunny's passing the sport of sailboat racing in the Pacific Northwest lost one of its finest and fiercest competitors.

THE BRITISH WHO SAILED
TO SALTSPRING ISLAND

WHILE CRUISING DURING August of 1954 Eunice and I had stopped at the Royal Victoria Yacht Club so I could call the plant. The Blanchard Boat Company was still very busy with navy work, and my father had died in March. As we were beating into Cadboro Bay I spotted a little boat flying the blue ensign with baggywrinkle on her rigging, and I called Eunice's attention to it. I told her that baggy-wrinkle was for preventing chafing of the gear, and the boat had come in from out at sea and probably from a long way away, maybe Australia. When we got closer we saw she was the *Moonraker* of Foy, and we'd never heard of Foy, so that didn't answer the question of where she'd come from.

We'd been beating in under sail, and when we pulled into the float and had the sails stowed, why it turned out we were moored bow to bow with the *Moonraker*. We were just finishing with tidying up the cockpit on the *Aura* when a lady slid back the hatch, came out of the *Moonraker* and dumped her dishpan of water over the side. She smiled, and we smiled back, and then young Norm — he was nine years old — and I went up to the yacht club to telephone the plant. On the way we stopped and talked with the Jim Greens, who were guests on the *Fishtails*, one of our good customers. After I called the office I spoke again with the Greens on the way back to the boat, and it was agreed that we would come over and have dessert and coffee with them.

Well, when I got back to the *Aura* Eunice informed me, "We have an invitation onboard the *Moonraker*, which is from England, and her skipper is Dr. Peter Pye." So I went over to the *Moonraker* and told the Pyes that there was much more room on the *Fishtails*, and wouldn't they please join us with our friends there.

That evening we learned that Dr. Pye and his wife, Anne, and their deckhand, Christopher Pritchard-Barrett, had sailed out from England just to spend the winter at Musgrave Landing on Saltspring Island with their friends, Miles and Beryl Smeeton. Dr. Pye extracted a promise from Eunice and me that we would stop by the next summer, 1955, to meet the Smeetons.

Dr. Pye had been a general practice physician in London all through the Blitz. He had always planned on retiring from his profession at 60 to do some extensive cruising, but due to the advent of socialized medicine in England he retired at 52. He had already made one previous trans-Atlantic crossing to Florida and back.

The trip to Saltspring Island had come about in a rather odd way. One evening in London, Dr. Pye had been walking home from the *Moonraker*, which was lying on a buoy in a Thames River estuary at a local boathouse. As he was walking along the dike a very tall couple passed by and said, "Good evening." Dr. Pye walked on, but he heard the woman say, "This boat, the agent told me, has a copper sheathing."

And Dr. Pye thought, "That's strange, the only boat along here with copper sheathing is the *Moonraker*," or *Moonie*, as he generally referred to her. So he turned around and went back to the boathouse, and the boathouse keeper introduced him to the couple, Miles and Beryl Smeeton.

The Smeetons were looking for a sailboat, and Dr. Pye helped them find the *Tzu Hang*. They had had little previous experience with a boat, so Dr. Pye taught them how to sail, and then he saw to it that they had everything they needed in the way of books and tables of reference. They taught themselves celestial navigation en route, and then they started from England for their home on Saltspring Island, and apparently got there without incident. The Smeetons used their land for raising sheep, which was really about the only thing it was good for, as it was on a pretty steep side of a mountain.

The Pyes followed with their visit one year later, having spent one winter en route in Tuamotu, where Dr. Pye was able to assist the natives quite a bit. They left Tuamotu the following spring and continued the cruise to Saltspring Island throughout the summer, and had arrived to spend the winter with the Smeetons.

While Eunice and I were there with the Pyes at the Royal Victoria Yacht Club, I was able to persuade Dr. Pye that if he came to Seattle we would drydock him and repair his copper sheathing, because he had, if I remember correctly, kissed rocks two different times in southeastern Alaska, and was quite worried about the damage. Dr. Pye agreed to come, and we went to meet him at Port Townsend, after he had crossed the Strait of Juan de Fuca from Victoria. We kept company as we came down the sound, and then towed him through the locks in Ballard and up to the Blanchard Boat Company on Fairview Avenue. The next day we put the *Moonie* on the drydock and were able not only to do his copper sheathing as needed, but to get all the necessary materials contributed gratis from our various suppliers. The boat was up on the drydock about two full days, maybe three nights, and when we put her back in the water the Pyes took her directly to the Seattle Yacht Club guest moorage.

In the meantime, Eunice and some of our friends had put on a telephone campaign, and we got Dr. Pye to give a lecture at

The MOONRAKER *with Dr. Peter and Anne Pye, being towed by the* AURA, *1954.* (BLANCHARD COLLECTION)

the Seattle Yacht Club about his cruising. He was an excellent speaker, but, being a small man — I don't think he could have weighed more than 105 pounds — he had a small voice, and he insisted on doing the talk without a microphone. Everybody there was very, very quiet, and very, very interested in what he had to say. We made no charge for this lecture, but there was a punchbowl on a table at the entrance, with a card that said, DUE TO BRITISH MONETARY REGULATIONS, *MOONRAKER'S* EXCHEQUER IS LOW. ANY GIFT WOULD BE APPRECIATED. Kitty Chism, whose husband, Mid, was commodore in 1954, (Kitty was absolutely stone deaf) went right up and primed the pot with a $20 bill, which was a lot of money in those days.

The Pyes were very pleased that their visit to Seattle had netted them just a few cents less than $100, as well as many contributions, including two cases of lubricating oil for the engine. I suspect he may have sold one case because he ran the engine so little. Several salesmen for big marine-supply houses were instructed to find out anything the *Moonraker* needed that they could supply. So the Pyes' trip down to Seattle really paid off, and we were very happy about it.

When they sailed north we accompanied them across to Port Madison on Bainbridge Island, and that evening Anne Pye insisted that the crew of the *Moonie* would entertain the entire group with a roast leg of lamb dinner, and there were ten or 12 of us in their tiny cabin, which did not have full headroom even for Anne and Peter. Anne could almost stand up straight if she stood amidships, but Peter would bump his head on the beams. Anne did all the preparation for dinner on her regular Primus stove and her spare Primus, the two stoves doing their work on the cabin floor. The *Moonraker* was 29 feet, and in the forepeak, where Christopher, their deckhand, slept, his bunk was so close to the deckhead that he had to slide out of it in order to have enough room to turn over and sleep on his stomach.

Originally, Christopher had come as far as Victoria with the Pyes, and had found a job on a British ship so that he could work his way home to England and help his dad with the harvest and spring planting. Then he got another sailor's job back to Hudson Bay, and headed west by rail to rejoin the *Moonraker*. Much later I heard from Horace McCurdy that he had met the Pyes at Captain Fred Lewis' house on Coal Island. McCurdy had had a stag party aboard his boat, and after the evening was over one of the men asked, "How much do you suppose Dr. Pye has to pay Christopher to be his deckhand?" And he was informed that, quite to the contrary, Christopher paid Dr. Pye for his share of the grub.

Eunice and I had really been quite charmed by Christopher Pritchard-Barrett, even though we knew very little about him. It turned out that he was really interested in becoming a marine underwriter, and, of course, London is the focal point for marine underwriting for the whole world.

Sometime later Eunice and I flew directly to Paris on the delivery flight of a Boeing 747 for Air France. When we got to London we had dinner with our friends, Beryl and Charles Ables. Later, Eunice and I looked up Christopher's address in London, and much to our surprise, it was a small apartment house just one block from where we were staying near Sloane Square. We knocked, but didn't get any answer. After I had been appointed to the National Boating Safety Council, Eunice and I found ourselves in London again, but we weren't able to contact Christopher on that trip either.

Dr. Peter Pye died tragically. He needed a hernia operation, and he wanted a particular friend of his to do the surgery. This friend had been moved down to the southwest area of the country and was working out of a small hospital. He had had three surgeries that particular morning, and all three patients died. It was later found that the cause was a contaminated oxygen tank they had used. We received this terrible news about Dr. Pye before we left Seattle, but we were able to visit with Anne during that trip. Our brief acquaintance with this wonderful English couple, Dr. Peter Pye and Anne Pye, was one of Eunice's and my most cherished memories.

MOONRAKER being towed from Seattle Yacht Club by the AURA, 1954. Christopher Pritchard-Barrett aloft. (BLANCHARD COLLECTION)

CRUISING IN THE SAN JUANS
ON A SUNDAY AFTERNOON — WITH A
SHELL OIL COMPANY ROAD MAP

JACK TUSSLER WAS a character Eunice and I got acquainted with sometime after World War II; Eunice had known his wife because she was a physical education teacher at the University of Washington when Eunice was there. Jack was originally from somewhere farther south, probably the Bay Area, and he and his wife owned Coon Island in the San Juans. Coon Island is so small that some people don't even know it is there. There were no raccoons on it when Jack had it, but that's how it got its name. There was nothing at all on the island when Jack bought it, and he was kind of an opportunist, so I wouldn't be a bit surprised if he bought it at a tax auction. He built a nice cabin, just a log cabin with a gravel floor, and an outhouse, nothing more, and the Tusslers used it strictly as their summer home.

Jack had a little day sailer, not very big, but it was a keel boat. The boat had a tent that they slipped over the boom, and, as such, it was their cruiser, but mostly their cruising was rather short range. I can't really say that he used an outboard on it, but he may have.

Well, one of their best stories was about the time a boat that was built at Grandy's went by Coon Island. The Tusslers' beach was on the east side of the island, and Jack was there getting their boat provisioned for a cruise when he saw this nice 48-footer; it later belonged to Mrs. Eddie Hubbard, the widow of that great aviator who flew the first air mail contract between Seattle and Victoria. The boat went by well off the island, but awfully close to the reef that's off the east side of Coon, and is covered at high tide. Jack stood there on the beach fully expecting the boat to strike the reef, but they missed it by inches or a few feet, and so he continued stowing the equipment and food aboard his sailboat, using his two-man life raft for a dinghy.

Pretty soon Jack's wife was ready, so they got on the boat and started sailing north. They wanted to go to Sucia Island, and, of course, this was long before Sucia Island became a state park. But they ran out of wind as soon as they got up a little past Jones Island, so they decided to go into the bight on the north side of Jones and drop the hook for the night.

Jack was still standing on the foredeck, after dropping the hook and double-checking that he had it in the ground properly, when he noticed the 48-footer anchored nearby. A man called over to him from the aft cockpit, "Hi, neighbor, wouldn't you like to come over and have a drink?"

Jack said, "That sounds very nice," and Mrs. Tussler approved of accepting the invitation, but she did start her Primus stove and set the pressure cooker on it so supper would be ready in about an hour.

They rowed over to the power cruiser and had a very pleasant hour. When it was about time to row back to their boat, the man said, "Oh, just a minute, please. Tomorrow we want to go to Bellingham, do some shopping, we're getting a little low on this and that. Do we go this way or that way?" pointing each way around Orcas Island.

And Jack said, "Well, as a matter of fact, you can go either way. We're awfully close to the halfway mark right here, but I wouldn't know for sure without measuring it on the chart. Let me show you on a chart."

So the man reached up on the chart table and got out a Shell Oil Company highway map of Washington State. Jack said to him, "Gee, this is awfully small to measure accurately. Don't you have hydrographic charts?"

The guy shook his head; apparently he had never heard of hydrographic charts. Jack, in the meantime, was looking around, and he saw the chart drawers down under the counter to the left of the wheel and he pulled a drawer open and said, "This is what we need. These are hydrographic charts."

"Oh," the guy said, "I can't do anything with *those* things. All those little numbers, they just *confuse* me."

Well, the next morning this couple went on their way, and Jack never heard from them again, nor read of any boating disaster in the newspaper, so he assumed they got to Bellingham all right. That was probably in the early 1950s, and the boat is still around, to the best of my knowledge.

Another story about Jack Tussler — that guy was really a character — he liked to create tableaux for passing boats, on the reef I mentioned earlier. One time he got Dr. George Horton's 16-year-old daughter dressed up like a mermaid, sitting on the reef when it was a little out of the water. She had a mirror with her, and when the ferry from Anacortes came through Wasp Passage she flashed it with her mirror and gave the passengers quite a show. Another time, he set up a real old-fashioned barber chair that he had salvaged off the beach out on the reef, and he and a friend stood out there just like a barber giving a customer a shave. He always wanted to get a horse out there with a guy in a red coat sitting astride it, but he could never convince anyone to go along with putting their horse on that reef.

Jack Tussler was a yachtsman himself, but in a small way. The yachtspeople who knew him liked him, and I never heard a disparaging remark of any kind about Jack Tussler or his wife. And after she lost Jack, Mrs. Tussler married Jack's only brother.

INDEX